ONI

THE OFFICE
OF NAVAL INTELLIGENCE

The Birth of
America's First Intelligence Agency
1865–1918

Jeffery M. Dorwart

NAVAL INSTITUTE PRESS

For
Nel, Catherine, Karl, and Candace

CONTENTS

PREFACE

In 1882 the United States Navy organized the first agency in American history designed specifically for the systematic collection of information about the military affairs of foreign governments. Called the Office of Naval Intelligence (ONI), this tiny organization developed a Washington staff of intelligence officers and a string of naval attachés in major foreign centers. For the next three decades, the Navy's intelligence office remained the U. S. government's most consistent source of information on military developments throughout the world. Gradually, the Office moved away from strictly overt collection of data and toward war planning, espionage, and other secretive activities. By 1918, the intelligence office boasted an elaborate domestic intelligence system and a network of hundreds of agents and informants throughout Europe, Latin America, and East Asia.

Surprisingly, no attempt has been made thoroughly to examine the origin, birth, and development of what might be termed America's first intelligence agency. This oversight is more remarkable because of the continuing concern in the United States for a better understanding of the proper utilization of intelligence resources. The current interest has resulted in a flood of literature on spies and spy organizations, but most of it focuses on the origin, growth, and nature of a post–World War II Central Intelligence Agency and disregards earlier American experiences with organized intelligence. Thus a recent bibliography on *Intelligence, Espionage, Counterespionage, and Covert Operations: A Guide to Information Sources* by Paul W. Blackstock and Frank L. Schaf, Jr. (Detroit: Gale Research Co., 1978) offers barely a dozen pages on pre–World War II U. S. intelligence and not one single entry on ONI.

Students of naval history have been only slightly more successful in discussing the origin of U. S. naval intelligence. The most competent treatment remains "The First Sixty Years of the Office of Naval Intelligence," a master's thesis prepared in 1963 for The American University by James Robert Green. Several official histories and memoirs exist; but all fall short of explaining ONI's significance. Moreover, recent work by Peter Karsten, Ronald Spector, William R. Braisted, and Kenneth J.

Hagan suggests the desirability of further examining naval intelligence's contributions to the rise of a modern U.S. Navy.

It is the purpose of the following study to present the first in-depth analysis of ONI's impact on American history between 1882 and 1918. To what extent did ONI affect naval and national policies during this critical period in the growth of American world power? At the same time, how did the bureaucratic and technological changes, political and public pressures, and periods of war and peace inspire ONI? What relationships did the Office have with other segments of the naval and civilian bureaucracy? More specifically, how did ONI function? What kind of information did it gather, and who consulted it? How did intelligence directors and personnel respond to and influence the development of ONI? Did the Office develop its own character and institutional continuity? And above all, did ONI establish precedents, develop specific tendencies, and raise larger questions about the position of organized intelligence in the United States?

ACKNOWLEDGMENTS

This study is based entirely upon declassified material available in public archives and libraries. A number of people helped locate these records. Richard Heimdahl and Gibson Smith, both formerly of the Old Army and Navy Branch of the National Archives, were especially helpful. Dean Allard and Geraldine Judkins of the Operational Archives of the U. S. Navy Department provided a courteous and efficient environment to study the material in their important collection. Anthony Nicolosi of the Naval War College Manuscript Collection at Newport contributed his knowledge of the sources. William Lundenberg of the Navy History Division of the Smithsonian Institution showed me the T. B. Mason Collection, while Senior Manuscript Librarian James Corsaro of the New York State Library opened the Sigsbee Collection for me. Linda Baggett and Eleanor Stitt of the Rutgers University Library in Camden located dozens of obscure books through inter-library loan.

Though this study has no official connection with either the Office of Naval Intelligence or the Navy Department, several naval officers lent their advice, especially Captain Wyman Packard, USN Retired. Jan Snouck-Hurgronje, Board of Control, and staff of the United States Naval Institute Press added their encouragement and expert advice in the preparation of this book. Professor Rodney P. Carlisle read every draft of the manuscript, contributing pages of scholarly criticism.

The Rutgers University Research Council provided financial assistance during the research phase of the study.

ONI

i

R O O T S   O F   N A V A L   I N T E L L I G E N C E

Never had the condition of the United States Navy been more lamentable than in the years immediately following the Civil War. The great armada collected to subdue the Confederacy lay rotting, a fleet of empty hulks. Officers fresh from heroic exploits against rebel ironclads found themselves competing bitterly for duty on board the few seaworthy ships left on five scattered cruising stations. Seamen from many nations manned U. S. men-of-war, often causing disciplinary and morale problems. At the Navy Department in Washington, the corruption that characterized President U. S. Grant's administrations seeped through bureaus and offices, drawing public criticism. More often, though, Americans simply ignored their naval establishment. The recent conflict left a shattered merchant fleet and disrupted overseas trade, while two vast ocean frontiers continued to provide security against foreign interference. There seemed little reason to look to the seas, and postwar America focused instead on settling a vast western frontier and constructing an industrial empire.

The era between 1865 and 1882 marked a nadir for the Navy in terms of equipment, morale, and operational effectiveness; yet it also helped launch the New Navy. A decrepit fleet, unhappy officers, and public neglect obscured an undercurrent of reformist agitation which swept through the service. Concerned officers demanded improvements in naval equipment, organization, training, and doctrine. This ferment focused on the quest for information to provide direction for postwar naval modernization. The resultant period of professional, scientific, and technical inquiry lay at the root of the establishment of the first permanent agency in American history devoted entirely to intelligence.

Requirements for naval information had accompanied earlier periods of crisis. The tradition of American naval intelligence, however primitive and scattered, probably stretched back into colonial times when various English colonies sought information about the location of hostile Dutch, French, or Spanish fleets. During the Revolutionary War, Americans employed naval secret agents to gather information in Europe and from the West Indies. Naval intelligence also assisted American forces against the British during the War of 1812. The most

3

sensational incident of antebellum operations occurred in 1846 just prior to the outbreak of war between Mexico and the United States, when Navy Surgeon William Maxwell Wood undertook a spy mission deep into Mexican territory.[1]

Routine information collected during peacetime cruises, exploratory expeditions, and scientific surveys also comprised part of the Navy's earliest intelligence heritage. Throughout much of the first half of the nineteenth century, the Navy charted coastlines and explored seas of the world. Such endeavors were not strictly intelligence missions, but information thus gathered could be employed for military purposes. Furthermore, experience in collecting hydrographic and scientific data provided analogous training. Nowhere was this more evident than in the work of Lieutenant Matthew Fontaine Maury, who between 1844 and 1861 headed the U. S. Naval Observatory and Hydrographical Office. When Civil War erupted, the native Virginian left the service, joined Confederate forces, and became one of the South's premier intelligence operatives in Europe.[2]

Scientific investigation lay behind early Union naval intelligence as well. During the summer of 1861 a temporary advisory board called the Commission of Conference collected information to assist Secretary of the Navy Gideon Welles in planning war operations. Professor Alexander Dallas Bache of the Coast Survey and Commander Charles Henry Davis, founder of the Nautical Almanac, provided leadership on the board. For the most part, though, civilian detectives, government secret service agents, and officers on routine reconnaissance performed Union intelligence during the Civil War. The *Lancaster's* wartime experiences exemplified the latter situation. Sailing off Panama in 1863, the Union warship accidently uncovered and stopped a plot by Confederate agents to steal a Pacific Mail Steamer and convert it into a commerce raider.[3]

Culmination of hostilities permitted the Navy to resume hydrographic and exploratory missions. Concurrently the Navy Department separated the Hydrographic Office from the Naval Observatory and equipped vessels with hydrographic outfits. Between 1866 and 1880, the Navy's solitary steamers cruised the oceans and seas gathering data. Many of these expeditions combined scientific investigation with analyses of economic and strategic questions, often reflecting the budding vision of extending U. S. influence into Latin America and eastern Asia. Such was the case with Commander Thomas O. Selfridge, Jr.'s search for an interoceanic canal route through Central America in 1869, Captain Robert W. Shufeldt's circumnavigation of the globe a decade later, and many other peacetime cruises. These under-takings provided valuable details as well as fields for the training of future intelligence officers. Indeed every important naval intelligence agent between 1882 and 1918 served at one time or other on these missions, while four Navy hydrographers became chief intelligence officers. This intimate relationship between scientific endeavor and early naval intelligence accounted partly for the scholarly, research-oriented nature of the first generation of naval intelligence operatives.[4]

Science did not produce the only nursery for naval intelligence. An increase in European military activity and a revolution in overseas weapons technology in the decade following the U. S. Civil War added another arena for the collection of information. Prussia's wars against Austria in 1866 and France in 1870 drew the attention of military experts everywhere, as did improvements in rifled artillery, armor plating, and machine guns. The U. S. Navy shared this interest, and in August 1869 instructed Rear Admiral William Radford, commanding the European Squadron, to obtain information "respecting improve-ments in foreign navies and navy yards." This directive differed from traditional instructions to accumulate news from abroad routinely. It was a comprehensive intelligence document, calling upon officers to investigate specific information. "Officers cannot employ their time in a manner more improving to themselves, or more useful to the Govern-ment," Radford told his staff.[5]

Despite the admiral's apparent enthusiasm for the new order, in fact he resented it. A few months away from retirement, the gruff veteran symbolized the sailing Navy's attitude toward such duties. He com-plained that gathering and collating information interfered with cere-monial visits to foreign ports to show the flag and dine with local officials. Thus when Secretary of the Navy George Robeson ordered him to rush off and witness submarine torpedo experiments at Fiume, Radford indicated that the trip was a waste of time and expensive coal. "Had I not been ordered to Fiume, and not informed that the experi-ments were about to close, I should not have visited Trieste, and would have been saved the necessity of using steam, and of writing this long explanation," he grumbled.[6]

Nevertheless, several officers under Radford zealously pursued the intelligence assignment. Lieutenant Commander J. D. Marvin toured the French naval base at Toulon, visited the "Ironclad Squadron of Evolutions," and sent detailed sketches back to the admiral. "I regret that I have not more data to submit in the shape of drawings, but the secrecy observed by French officials about all matters of real interest is

5

in this respect so great, that even had my time permitted, I fear I should not have accomplished much in this way," he told Radford.[7] Marvin had more success in Essen, Germany, where Friedrich Krupp allowed him to inspect the Cast Steel Works. Concurrently, Commanders Stephen B. Luce and Kidder Randolph Breese reconnoitered the Elbe and Weser rivers and surveyed German naval facilities at Wilhelmshaven and Kiel.[8]

No one adopted intelligence duty more faithfully than Captain Christopher Raymond Perry Rodgers, commanding Radford's flagship the *Franklin*. Robeson instructed Rodgers to visit all major European countries and collect information. "You are expected . . . to take every opportunity to procure information in relation to the enlistment of seamen; equipment of vessels and their methods of discipline; the management and system of conducting Navy Yards; the accountability of Naval and civil officers ashore and afloat, the newest plans of Iron clad vessels and other professional subjects."[9] In compliance Rodgers mobilized a group of young officers to execute these extensive instructions. This pioneering intelligence team included his son Raymond, Ensign Theodorus B. M. Mason, and Midshipmen William H. Driggs, Albert Gleaves Berry, and Giles B. Harber, all subsequently founders of an office of naval intelligence.

European military and technological activity in the 1870s prompted dispatch of several special American intelligence missions to supplement the European Squadron's work. In May 1870, Robeson sent Assistant Naval Constructor Theodore D. Wilson on an excursion to European dockyards. An instructor of naval architecture at the U. S. Naval Academy in Annapolis, Wilson welcomed the opportunity to tour British men-of-war, visit private shipyards along the rivers Thames, Tyne, Clyde, and Mersey, and discuss warship designs with Sir Edward Reed, architect of the revolutionary turreted ironclad.[10] Shortly after Wilson's departure for Britain, Robeson directed Commander Edward Simpson, former head of the Hydrographic Office, to examine European improvements in naval ordnance. Assisted by veteran intelligence officer Marvin and provided with $5,000 for the purchase of blueprints, Simpson visited installations throughout Europe between August 1870 and October 1872.[11]

Chief Engineer James W. King made the most ambitious attempts to gather information, traveling to Europe three times between 1869 and 1876. King's long career spanned the two pre–Civil War decades when steam engines and iron hulls began to replace sail and wooden sides, through the postwar era of rapid technological change. During his service, he personally redesigned the two-stage, steam-powered compound engine used in all U. S. warships. King also led the seemingly endless struggle by engineering and other staff officers to achieve equality with the privileged line officers who commanded and fought the Navy's men-of-war.[12]

On each venture to Europe King found radical changes taking place in the design and construction of ships and machinery. His last journey, in 1876, was the most revealing. Most wooden warships had disappeared from foreign fleets, replaced by new armored turretships such as the 11,407-ton *Inflexible* of the British Navy, the French 9360-ton *Redoutable*, and the 7560-ton *Deutschland* of the fledgling German Navy. At the same time, King observed spacious dry docks constructed to accomodate the nautical behemoths and great iron foundries and arsenals designed to supply these ships with armor and rifled guns. He realized that while recently unified Germany's new maritime force had stimulated expansion at Krupps and other factories, no similar incentives existed in post–Civil War America. United States mills could not roll steel for hulls or provide castings for rudder posts and gun mounts. King knew that in comparison to foreign armorclads which carried breechloading rifles, the largest U. S. Navy warship was a 4,000-ton wooden vessel with full sail rigging and smoothbore, muzzleloading cannon.[13]

After returning to the United States, King compiled a report of his observations, and the first edition of nearly 3,000 copies sold out within a few months in 1878. This popular volume contributed to an informational ferment in the U. S. Navy, which matured rapidly during the seventies. The book helped convince some line officers that increasingly technical characteristics of naval information required engineering expertise. At least line officers doing intelligence work readily learned and borrowed from King's model report. He showed them how to combine personal observations, conversations with foreign experts, visits to private shipbuilders, and surveys of naval literature in preparation of intelligence reports. He emphasized the importance of scanning technical journals such as *Engineering, The Engineer*, and *L'Annee Maritime* to gain an overview of naval progress. Furthermore, King stressed the importance of attaching naval officers to overseas diplomatic missions. "In London may be found naval attachés of nearly every important nation," he wrote, "watching and studying with ceaseless vigilance the principles and science of naval architecture and engineering, especially the newer and later inventions, the experiments in artillery practice, and the progress made every year in the science of warfare, offensive and defensive."[14]

Chief Engineer King's report was the last flourish of intelligence activity under the Robeson secretaryship, an administration more remembered for its tinge of corruption than reformist impulses. New Secretary of the Navy Richard W. Thompson continued to promote such work between 1877 and 1880. Although ignorant of naval affairs, Thompson complemented the administration of President Rutherford B. Hayes and Secretary of State William M. Evarts in their tentative probings for greater American commercial, diplomatic, and naval contact with the rest of the world. The Hayes government expressed concern over European control of a proposed canal through Central America, and Thompson advocated establishment of a naval base in the area as well as an increase in the U. S. fleet. The secretary also accelerated the department's search for information. He dispatched Shufeldt on a world cruise, ordered naval officers to the Paris Electrical Exhibition of 1878, and endorsed Chief of the Bureau of Ordnance William Nicholson Jeffers's efforts to learn about foreign weapons. Like Robeson, Thompson encouraged intelligence missions to Europe, sending Professor James Russell Soley of the Naval Academy and Lieutenant Commander French Ensor Chadwick to collect data on overseas naval questions.[15]

Intelligence gathering proliferated under both Secretaries Robeson and Thompson, but many of the data were wasted. The department had no coordinating office to collate and distribute information and no central planning board to organize scattered news and apply it to larger policies. A key report might disappear into the files of one of the eight jealous and autonomous departmental bureaus, never receiving the circulation it deserved. Thus, the informational ferment existed in many divergent voices.

Lacking a formal departmental organization to centralize new ideas and information, a group of forward-looking naval officers founded a semiofficial United States Naval Institute at Annapolis in 1873 to discuss professional and scientific data. The Institute held seminars and published scholarly papers in its *Proceedings*. Views exchanged by members helped crystallize thinking on naval problems and forced definition of areas in need of reform. It taught naval officers to collect and publish information on technical progress, foreign affairs, naval organization, and commercial relations. The Naval Institute provided a forum and clearinghouse for theories behind a "New Navy," which developed

8

during the last two decades of the nineteenth century. It served as well as a prototype office of naval intelligence. This intimate relationship was explained in 1879 by Naval Institute Secretary, and later first Chief Intelligence Officer, Lieutenant Theodorus B. M. Mason. "We must constitute ourselves a sort of mutual learning company; all must help," Mason told fellow officers; "officers on foreign stations, where they have, or might have if they chose, such excellent opportunities to study out foreign inventions and novelties; officers doing scientific duty, . . . make the Naval Institute the bureau of information of the navy."[16]

As Mason hoped, the Naval Institute gave direction to the burgeoning information reaching the department from surveys, expeditions, and special intelligence sorties. However, it lacked official status in the Navy, existing as little more than a vocal but private study society. Early members were the first to admit this, and like Mason advocated a formal departmental office of information. Still, the department found no urgent reason to create such an organization, remaining satisfied to continue uncoordinated intelligence errands to Europe. Then in 1879 naval developments closer to the United States gradually changed departmental opinion. The War of the Pacific pitting Chile against Peru and Bolivia broke out, providing a catalyst and final impetus for the foundation of a naval intelligence office.

As in 1870, C. R. P. Rodgers became a central figure in the process of developing a naval intelligence system, for on the eve of the Pacific war, Rodgers had assumed command of U. S. naval forces on the Pacific Station. At age fifty-nine, he was a veteran of forty-five years in the service. He had fought the Seminoles in 1841, the Mexicans in 1847, and most recently the Confederates. But his major contributions had come from peacetime service on the European Station and as superintendent of the Naval Academy. During the latter duty, between 1874 and 1878, Rodgers expressed growing concern for the Navy's future and its reluctance to adjust to technological, strategic, and organizational modernization. The senior officer chaired meetings of the Naval Institute, encouraging critical discussion of the service. He brought dynamic assistants to the Academy to teach and exchange novel ideas. When he left for command of the Pacific Squadron, he took many of these officers with him, including Commander Edward Terry, Passed Assistant Engineer Charles Whitesides Rae, Lieutenants John Forsyth Meigs, Royal R. Ingersoll, Duncan Kennedy, T. B. M. Mason, and his son Raymond Perry Rodgers.[17]

The South American conflict presented a unique opportunity for the elder Rodgers and his eager staff to pubilicize the operation of newer warships in actual combat, since both sides possessed European-built ironclads; and the warring parties soon gave his neophyte intelligence agents ample material to examine. In June 1879 the Peruvian iron-hulled vessels the *Independencia* and the *Huascar* engaged several Chilean men-of-war. Four months later, the powerful Chilean ironclad frigates the *Almirante Cochrane* and the *Blanco Enclada* captured the *Huascar* after a bitter sea fight. Rodgers assembled a board to examine the engagement. "Should free access be given us to the ironclad *Huascar*, you will visit that ship upon her arrival here (Chile); and will make a careful examination of the injuries she has sustained, and the effect produced upon her armor and hull by the Chilian projectiles."[18]

Chilean officials permitted inspection of the captured enemy man-of-war, and an intelligence team composed of Captain Breese, Chief Engineer Edward Dunham Robie, and Lieutenants Ingersoll, Kennedy, and Mason poured over the 196-foot turreted ram. The Americans marveled at how the tiny warship had withstood the pounding of huge Palliser armor-piercing projectiles. Though nearly obsolete in comparison to European ironclads now coming out of foreign shipyards, the *Huascar* nevertheless impressed Breese and his colleagues with her obvious superiority over any wooden U. S. Navy steamer.[19]

Admiral Rodgers was more careful in his estimation of the *Huascar*. He understood that while the Latin American craft was exciting for his people to study, it was only an outdated version of bigger European models. Further, a few Chilean warships, no matter how powerful, posed little threat to the United States. Instead Rodgers worried about the interest taken in the fighting by Europeans. He wondered if the U. S. Navy could defend the principles of the Monroe Doctrine, which proscribed foreign interference in the affairs of the Western Hemisphere. To this end, he wrote Secretary Thompson in November 1879 about how he had observed from the deck of his wooden flagship a parade of mighty British, French, and German armored warships as they steamed into the Peruvian harbor at Callao. "All these ships are full-powered steamships very fast, and armed with modern guns," Rodgers advised. "There is not a smoothbore gun upon any ship-of-war on this station, except the ships of the United States."[20]

Secretary Thompson resigned a month after Rodgers had dispatched his message and probably never read the warning. But already the admiral had instilled such concerns in a new generation of officers who would carry his forebodings to succeeding secretaries of the Navy. Moreover, he had prepared a cadre of future intelligence officers to collect and articulate naval information for use by those who wished to reform and modernize the service. For one, Mason continued to compile intelligence reports on the Pacific Station after Rodgers's departure, and the new commander-in-chief forwarded them to incoming Secretary William H. Hunt.[21]

It would be Hunt and his successors who after 1881 would found and develop a New Navy of steel warships and expansionist doctrine. Yet Robeson and Thompson had stimulated conditions that helped launch this naval revival. They were more than hack politicians and incompetents, as they were often seen by critics. Both confronted corruption, inefficiency, and indifference and still initiated intelligence missions that they knew revealed inadequacies in their own Navy Department. Furthermore Robeson and Thompson encouraged officers to collect data for naval modernization, thus providing an environment conducive to the creation of an organized office of naval intelligence.

AN INTELLIGENCE OFFICE

Secretary of the Navy Hunt issued General Order No. 292 on 23 March 1882 creating an Office of Intelligence attached to the Bureau of Navigation. This executive act passed almost unnoticed amid the flurry of activity within the department caused by President Chester A. Arthur's decision to support naval modernization. Catapulted to the presidency by the assassination of James A. Garfield, Arthur voiced immediate concern for the Navy's recent decline. "I cannot too strongly urge upon you my conviction that every consideration of national safety, economy and honor imperatively demands a thorough rehabilitation of our Navy," the corpulent chief executive proclaimed in 1881.[1]

In the months before Arthur replaced him, Hunt urged Congress to fund a "new navy." The secretary convened a Naval Advisory Board in June 1881 to help him define the basic requirements for this naval rejuvenation and to resolve differences over what type of warship should be added to the fleet. Though the fifteen-member advisory body reached no consensus, it recommended construction of steel steamers of war, armed with rifled ordnance. In December, Hunt asked for money to build such ships.[2]

As Congress debated Hunt's proposals in 1882, the U.S. Navy carried on its own discussion concerning the nature and mission of the proposed new navy. No common school of thought emerged, nor was there a clear division between older and younger officers, or insurgents and conservatives. Participants ranged from senior Admiral David Dixon Porter down to Master Carlos G. Calkins. Some officers favored cruisers and monitors for coastal defense and commerce raiding, while others preferred deep-water ironclads to expand American naval power. Some advocated combinations of sail and steam power; others called for elimination of all rudiments of the Old Navy. Most insisted that no matter what type of warship or strategy might be adopted in the future, naval expansion had to be tied to improvement of the American merchant marine.

Out of the seemingly incoherent debate a small group of naval officers articulated a more precise train of thought, mostly in the pages of the U.S. Naval Institute *Proceedings*. Proponents of complete and thorough modernization of ships, training, organization, stations, and doctrine included Stephen B. Luce, French Chadwick, J. D. J. Kelley, Richard Wainwright, Edward W. Very, Carlos Calkins, Seaton Schroeder, William H. Beehler, W. W. Kimball, and Charles Custis Rogers. These were the most vocal of the 481 members of the Naval Institute, hoping through constant revelations of superior foreign naval developments to influence Congress, the public, and fellow officers to support rehabilitation of the Navy. They expected Hunt's order of March 1882 to provide an agency to collect and disseminate such news, and many soon joined the staff of the Office of Intelligence.

Three months after formation of the intelligence bureau, the department selected thirty-four-year-old Lieutenant Theodorus Bailey Myers Mason as its first chief intelligence officer. Mason had long exhibited particular skill in pursuing intelligence duty, first on the European Station and then during the War of the Pacific. Always encouraged by C. R. P. Rodgers, Mason traveled throughout Europe, collecting ideas about naval intelligence. The French Ministry of Marine's policies most impressed him. "Officers showing great proficiency are detailed as a sort of intelligence bureau, furnishing material for general improvement," Mason noted.[3] At first, he expected the Naval Institute to provide similar impetus in the United States and threw himself into its organization by contributing timely lectures and essays on topics of naval modernization. It soon became obvious that the group provided a poor substitute for a formal intelligence agency. Despite the Institute's best efforts, Mason lamented: "There is no possible way for an officer to keep himself informed as to what improvements are going on, what appliances he may be expected to manipulate, . . . in fact, a thousand and one points of useful information which can only come, to be of any value, from official sources."[4]

Still, in the months before the department founded an intelligence office, Mason assumed that the U. S. Naval Institute was the most that could be expected in the direction of a bureau for naval information. But if Washington was considering the formation of an intelligence organization, no one bothered to consult Mason, even though he continued to agitate for such a reform. Upon his return from his tour off the Chilean coast in 1881, the department unceremoniously dispatched him to Annapolis for another tour as gunnery instructor. While at the Academy, the restless officer brooded, and released some of his frustrations by publishing critical essays in Lewis B. Hamersly's new journal *The United Service*, founded by the ex–naval officer to promote military reform, and in Hamersly's monumental *Naval Encyclopaedia*.[5]

But Mason had politically influential friends in Washington, including Rodgers, Luce, and the new chief of the Bureau of Navigation, Commodore John Grimes Walker. Undoubtedly they convinced Secretary of the Navy William H. Chandler to invite Mason to his office in the late spring of 1882. Several days after this meeting, the department revoked Mason's orders for duty on board the trainingship *Constellation* and ordered him to Washington for special duty.

Mason reported to bureau chief Walker during the second week of June. At first appearance the two officers seemed to have little in common. Almost twenty years older, Commodore Walker had already become a Civil War hero while Mason struggled to pass his examinations at the Naval Academy in wartime exile at Newport, Rhode Island. Furthermore, the two differed substantially in social background. Son of prosperous New York City utilities magnate Colonel T. Bailey Myers and namesake of street railroad entrepreneur and maternal grandfather Sidney Mason, young Mason enjoyed his boyhood wintering in Europe with his mother, attending elite private academies, and receiving the proper upbringing for a New York society gentleman. On the other hand, Walker had been raised by a family so impoverished that they had sent him from New Hampshire to live with relatives in the Midwest.[6]

Differences in age and background presented no obstacles to intimate friendship and immediate collaboration between the two men most responsible for the birth of ONI. Both shared a deep concern for and frustration with their Navy's current state of ineffectiveness. Perhaps influenced by the competitive spirit of Social Darwinism which dominated their era, Walker and Mason believed that they must combat indifference from public and government and lethargy within the service in order to promote naval progress; and the aggressive officers' crusade to inform and convert opinion in favor of naval modernization and expansion focused on development of an intelligence office.

Fortunately for the fledgling intelligence agency, Walker and Mason received encouragement from Secretary Chandler, the wily New England politician selected by Arthur to replace Hunt. Although Hunt had created the intelligence office, he had failed to complete its organization. Chandler immediately finished the work by calling Mason to Washington and issuing a directive on 25 July 1882 that outlined policy and procedure for the Office of Naval Intelligence. In his memorandum, Chandler instructed ONI to collect, compile, record, and correct information on fourteen categories of naval intelligence, ranging from descriptions of foreign warships to data on coastal defenses. He urged the Office to share this material with the Naval Institute so that it might become available to every officer. His July directive also specified requirements for the selection of intelligence personnel. "The younger officers of the service will be encouraged in collecting and reporting intelligence and in writing original articles on naval subjects." Officers displaying such abilities would be chosen for intelligence duty either at the intelligence office in Washington or as part of a "corps of correspondents, in the persons of Naval Attachés to our foreign legations (and of) special aids to our commanding officer abroad," the first ONI instruction concluded.[7]

Mason's ideas dominated Chandler. Whether or not the intelligence chief actually wrote the original ONI document mattered less than the memorandum's articulation of Mason's philosophy of intelligence work. Above all, ONI had to be employed to stir interest in naval modernization, and Chandler's emphasis on the distribution of information to the Naval Institute provided one important outlet. The appeal for younger officers also revealed Mason's guidance. Though satisfied with the Navy's system of seniority, Mason believed that the service needed to offer incentives to junior officers who might become discouraged by lack of ships, few creative assignments, and slow promotion.[8] Walker helped by appointing promising Academy graduates to duty with the Smithsonian Institution and other scientific agencies, but Mason considered ONI an even more attractive alternative, since its work led directly to improvement of the Navy itself.[9]

Surprisingly, the first officers selected to assist Mason were neither young nor promising. It was a competent if not otherwise distinguished collection of officers, including several who soon resigned on account of poor health. The original recruit, Lieutenant Albert G. Berry, simply moved his desk down the hall from the Hydrographic Office in June 1882. The following month Lieutenant Miers Fisher Wright, an uninspiring fellow with twelve years' service, joined the Office. Others with more talent passed through. Ensign Templin Morris Potts drew warship sketches, Lieutenant William Hale Driggs collected data on ordnance and prepared plans for his own domestically produced rapid-fire gun, Lieutenant William Henry Beehler translated articles from European technical journals, and Passed Assistant Engineer James Peyton Stuart Lawrance used his mechanical engineering degree from Lehigh University to help construct papers on naval machinery.[10]

Only one of the more than a dozen officers who served with the first chief intelligence officer fit Mason's ideal of youthful exuberance and potential leadership in the field of naval intelligence. He was one of Mason's former gunnery students at the Academy, Ensign Charles

15

Custis Rogers. Arriving in ONI in September 1882, the native Virginian eagerly tackled his new duties, writing a monograph on recent British naval operations in Egypt and collecting material on foreign natural resources and harbor and coastal defenses. However, Mason found even more important work for his zealous disciple; unhappy with the apathetic response to his office, he encouraged Rogers to publish a paper on naval intelligence with the Naval Institute. Rogers's essay, which appeared in early 1883, outlined the entire rationale behind formation of a naval intelligence agency. Far more than a publicity document, this article supplied the strategic underpinning missing from Chandler's instruction of July 1882. Rogers explained how an intelligence office served the peacetime Navy by collecting vital information to prepare it for future war. "The necessity for readiness becomes every day more absolute, while the means for obtaining the latest information increases with the growth of national armaments and with those helps to swift action—steamers, railways and telegraphs," Rogers insisted.[11]

Rogers argued that only a naval general staff could adequately prepare the peacetime force for war, a view that was not entirely original. Mason and others on the European Station in 1870 had noted the importance of the Prussian general staff in planning military campaigns against Austria and France. Stephen Luce had visited a number of German officers in 1870, and he later attended the U.S. Army Gunnery School at Fort Monroe, Virginia, where he discussed ideas for a general staff school with foremost American military theorist Major-General Emory Upton. Luce drew upon the Prussian example and Upton's theories in his agitation for a naval war college. But while these men and others received credit for stimulating the concept of a general staff in American military circles, no one explained the role of a central military organization in readying a nation for war more meticulously than C. C. Rogers in 1883. For this soft-spoken Southern officer, ONI was the critical first stage in the creation of a formal naval general staff and provided the basis for operational planning.[12]

Rogers concluded his discussion of naval intelligence for the Institute with a definition of what he termed general naval principles and their relationship to an intelligence bureau. Applying theories on the art of war then circulating among more progressive American officers, Rogers explained how the U.S. Navy needed to coordinate fleet operations with carefully integrated tactical and strategic plans if it expected to defend American interests. "The broad issues of our great national defence questions will therefore depend in their solutions upon a full knowledge of the resources of all those nations with whom we may become involved in war," he argued. Dangers to American security came not only from established powers such as Britain and France but also from newer potential enemies such as Germany and Italy. Drawing inspiration from a previous Naval Institute paper on future war, prepared by his commanding officer in 1879, Rogers predicted that unless the American service studied every aspect of a potential enemy's resources and capabilities, the U. S. Navy might one day suffer humiliation at the hands of a second-rate naval power. The Italian Navy with its new battleship *Dandolo*, he postulated, had the strength to lie off Coney Island unopposed and shell New York City with its long-range, 100-ton rifles.[13]

While Rogers worried about imminent conflicts and dabbled in higher strategy, Mason's other people pursued the tedious and monotonous routine of compiling information cards. Using a cataloguing system borrowed from the State Department, Berry organized and filed general information, while Wright prepared studies on French naval action in Tunis, which ONI offered as one of its first volumes in what would become a twenty-year series of monographs. Since theirs was the initial attempt to organize information in a central repository, the first intelligence officers confronted a great mass of material. Mason's staff prepared an index for the Navy Department Library thrown in with the intelligence office, studied literature from journals and newspapers, and hand-copied relevant articles on file cards. When Mason could pry reports from the jealous bureaus, he had his people transcribe them. In 1883 consular intelligence on ports of the world, trade, and merchant vessels began to trickle into the Office from the Department of State. When Mason's team seemed about to catch up with its work, Lieutenant Commander Chadwick, recently appointed the Navy's first permanent naval attaché, forwarded bags stuffed with intelligence reports and printed matter from his London post.[14]

New information arrived from shipboard intelligence officers. In June 1882 Walker had directed each commanding officer to appoint such an agent and had forwarded packages of blank intelligence forms to the scattered warships. Though many complained that watch and other duties prevented investigations for ONI, most commanding officers completed intelligence reports in 1882–83. Officers from the *Richmond, Ashuelot, Essex, Monocacy,* and *Palos* forwarded information about China, Japan, and the Pacific Ocean. In Latin American waters, Lieutenants Raymond Rodgers, Nathan Eric Niles, and George A. Bicknell and Ensign Washington Irving Chambers sent thorough reports. Their observations covered the progress of Ferdinand de Lesseps's company on a Panama Canal, Chilean railroad construction, and purchase by the Argentine government of a new torpedoboat. Most early intelligence forms merely recited facts with a minimum of strategic analysis. One exception came from the *Enterprise* off the coast of South Africa in 1883, where Commander Albert S. Barker's intelligence staff studied the military and economic importance of Capetown and Port Natal.[15]

Gradually the new intelligence office filled its heavy wooden cabinets and bookcases with data. Information on the specifications, speed, and armaments of the world's warships lay on index cards. Other files recorded new construction and proposed foreign naval budgets. Intelligence on naval personnel, training schools, organizations, officer corps, dockyards, and reserve forces soon became available to any U. S. naval officer or bureau wishing the latest on these topics. ONI accumulated data on ordnance, armor trials, torpedoes, boilers, engines, propellors, military masts, electric searchlights, hydraulic gears, and dynamos. Natural resources, commerce, topography, munitions factories, and political conditions received attention. Indeed, anything relating to naval affairs might be found in the growing files of information.

Mason was not satisfied, however. He knew that for his agency to have an impact on naval modernization, those responsible for erecting a new Navy must use his information. Yet bureau chiefs and senior officers seemed reluctant to consult ONI. Few dared openly defy Walker's support, but indifference could paralyze intelligence just as surely as announced opposition. Besides, a power struggle between Walker and Chandler might soon settle matters by removing ONI's firmest advocate. "Chandler who I think likes me personally well enough has evidently made up his mind to take from me one duty after another until he forces me to resign as Chief of a Bureau," Walker wrote his brother-in-law Senator William B. Allison of Iowa. Walker blamed opposition to ONI and other innovations for the secretary's precipitate actions. "The old fogy element rebels," he explained to Allison, "and their ranks are swelled by all the deadbeats and the staff as a body."[16]

Walker fought back. He used political pressure, threats, and persuasion to convince Chandler of his indispensability. The bureau chief succeeded, emerging from the tussle of 1883 more powerful than before and in a position to promote reform and help shape the direction of the New Navy. He urged officers to put their ships through steam evolutions, hounded derelict and drunken officers, and found choice assignments for the most capable. At the same time, Walker advocated an increased naval presence in Asia, Latin America, and the Pacific Ocean and the constuction of a battle fleet. Above all, he defended and promoted ONI as a symbol of progress in the Navy. When he heard suspicious inquiries about Chadwick's unusually lengthy stay in London, Walker responded curtly: "He is in England, an attaché of the Legation, is doing first rate work and will undoubtedly be kept there for the present." [17]

Other influential officers rallied to ONI in its first years. There was always Rear Admiral Rodgers, but he stood close to mandatory retirement age. More important were modernist officers reaching the prime of their careers. Commodore Luce expected the intelligence office to promote his dreams for a naval war college. "I hope you will help push the matter thru so that we may make a start of some kind this winter," he wrote Mason in November 1883. [18] Respected naval scientist Commander Charles D. Sigsbee lent encouragement from his post at the Naval Academy. "Everything seems smooth here at present," he advised Mason, "and there is evidence on my table and in the air that the Office of Intelligence is a success for which I offer hearty congratulations." [19]

Still, most established officers disregarded Mason's office, and only the most junior members of the U. S. Naval Institute expressed genuine enthusiasm for ONI. The Institute's annual prize essayists acknowledged their indebtedness to the intelligence office for providing data with which to prepare articles. Later, ten of the fifteen first prize winners between 1882 and 1900 worked for ONI, including Carlos Calkins, Albert Parker Niblack, Seaton Schroeder, Richard Wainwright, and Roy C. Smith. Their essays for the *Proceedings* stressed modernization of naval organization, education, tactics, doctrine, and equipment. ONI advice helped most on papers concerning naval technology. Such was the case in a *Proceedings* article on the Navy's first steel cruisers, compiled in 1883 by Assistant Naval Constructor Francis T. Bowles. "Through the courtesy of the Office of Naval Intelligence," Bowles concluded, "I am enabled to append to this paper a list of war vessels building at the present day, which shows that by far the larger part of the money employed in shipbuilding for war purposes is devoted to the construction of ironclads." [20]

ONI contributed more than publicity for the new steel men-of-war. Between 1883 and 1885, the Office collected data on recent techniques of hull design, ordnance, electricity, boilers, and engines for the Navy's constructors. At the same time, through Chadwick in London, naval intelligence ordered blueprints, armor plate, castings, guns, and ammunition for the ships of the New Navy. Direct help from the intelligence office figured in every one of the first steel warships.

When Mason left ONI in April 1885, the U. S. Navy had embarked at last on a modernization program. The ferment of the preceding decade led to an era of naval expansion. Mason could be certain that no matter how tenuous the initial steps, naval intelligence had shared in formulation of a more positive naval policy. Furthermore he had firmly grounded the intelligence agency and instilled in it his own philosophy. But inexplicably the intelligence post marked the apex of his career, and gradually Mason slipped into obscurity. He remained close to Walker and other influential officers, but never secured another attractive or important assignment in the U. S. Navy. Perhaps a lingering illness contracted on one of his earlier cruises to Latin America impaired his effectiveness. In any case the department passed over Mason for promotion until 1894, when after twenty-two years at the rank of lieutenant he finally became a lieutenant commander. By that time, however, his health had deteriorated, forcing him to resign from the service. Mason died five years later at the age of fifty-one.[21]

THE NEW NAVY

Lieutenant Raymond Perry Rodgers replaced Mason as intelligence chief on 2 April 1885. A perfect selection to continue the pioneering intelligence work, Rodgers had served with Mason both on the European Station and again in Chilean waters during the War of the Pacific. When Mason drew the ONI billet, Rodgers became a successful intelligence officer on the *Tennessee* in the North Atlantic Squadron. Not as articulate or dynamic as his predecessor, Rodgers earned the respect of fellow officers by his sincerity. "He is one of the best all around men I know," Lieutenant William S. Sims once observed.[1] He attracted new personnel easily and encouraged those more talented to prepare essays on naval topics, seeing to it that their material found proper channels to influence naval modernization. Thus between 1885 and 1889 Rodgers collected one of the most remarkable staffs ever to sit behind the desks of the fourth floor offices of naval intelligence in the State, War, and Navy Department Building next to the White House in Washington.

Rodgers's first recruits included Lieutenants John Charles Colwell, Benjamin H. Buckingham, and Seaton Schroeder. Brooding and brilliant, Colwell was the most irreverent, too radical indeed for his boss. Rodgers desired naval modernization but held no ambition to upset the established order with precipitate changes. Nevertheless, the intelligence chief harnessed Colwell's energies by directing him to write criticisms of the Navy's failure to adopt a naval reserve force similar to those of other navies. Buckingham appeared more manageable but still highly disparaging of the current condition of his service. Schroeder stood closest to Rodgers. Their life-long friendship extended back to boyhood days around Washington and continued through four years at the Naval Academy between 1864 and 1868. But unlike classmate Rodgers, Schroeder developed an unusual literary talent, composing essays on a variety of economic, political, and technical subjects.[2]

While Rodgers supplied administrative leadership, Schroeder assumed charge of publicity. In order to promote the importance of naval intelligence among fellow officers, Schroeder selected as the topic of his first ONI essay a most crucial question then confronting the Navy, how to prevent the corrosion of the new steel warships' hulls. Hoping to attract the attention of bureau chiefs, naval constructors, and concerned officers throughout the Navy, Schroeder prepared a careful study, synthesizing all known methods of preserving ship bottoms against rust, including chemical treatment, paints, and different types of sheathings. Without a worldwide system of drydocks, Schroeder concluded, the U. S. Navy ought to rely on sheathing hulls rather than on paints, which required frequent scraping and refinishing. Undoubtedly, this early ONI study contributed to the department's decision to sheathe some warships with copper.[3]

Despite Schroeder's literary accomplishments and contributions, he was neither the most prolific author nor scholarly officer on Rodgers's intelligence staff. These distinctions went to a pair of juniors, Ensigns Washington I. Chambers and John Baptiste Bernadou. Both captured the enthusiasm among younger personnel for the stirrings within the service during the late 1880s for a modern fleet with larger strategic commitments. They displayed an unusual grasp of the relationship between sea power and national economic expansion and expressed the sentiments of those who welcomed a more vigorous foreign and naval policy. Moreover, they understood rapid technological change, mastering details of new ship design, machinery, explosives, and ordnance. Modernization could not occur rapidly enough, and they kept pace with the transformation while many fellow officers fell back.

Chambers's early career in ONI exemplified the problems of the postwar Navy and opportunities of the New Navy. He graduated in the middle of the class of 1876, his only academic strength lying in drawing. Unless Chambers could adapt this skill to the needs of the New Navy, there would be little opportunity for good assignment, promotion, and reward in the hard times of the mid-1880s. Two developments provided the openings, creation of the Naval Advisory Board in 1881 and of the Office of Intelligence the following year. When the board solicited designs for new ships in 1881, Chambers forwarded his sketches for a 6,000-ton "advanced ironclad monitor." Though the board filed his drawings, Chambers's efforts resulted in publication of the proposal by the Naval Institute.[4] Encouraged by the acceptance of his article, he submitted an essay "The Best Method for the Reconstruction and Increase of the Navy" to the Institute's prize essay contest the following year, winning first place. Such recognition recommended him for a special ONI mission to accompany the Nicaraguan Canal surveying team in 1884 and permanent attachment to Rodgers's staff in 1885.[5]

Fellow intelligence officer Bernadou proved equally successful in composing articles on international law, foreign policy, or chemical composition of smokeless powders. Before joining the intelligence team, Berandou had been one of eighteen naval officers serving with the Smithsonian Institution. In this capacity he had journeyed to Korea, recently pried open to foreign contact, investigating the peninsula's economic and strategic potential. While in the Asian kingdom, Bernadou developed definite ideas about the importance of the area for American foreign policies and as a site for future naval operations and advanced bases.[6]

Rodgers welcomed Bernadou to his staff shortly after the latter's return from East Asia. Naturally, the intelligence chief assigned him to the study of international economic conditions, particularly the world's supply of nickel ore. This task became more important as the U. S. Navy turned to new process steels, using nickel for its warships. Bernadou also collected material on foreign seaports, helping Rodgers prepare a monograph on international ports and coaling stations. The talented ensign contributed one other dimension to naval intelligence. He translated articles from French, German, Russian, Swedish, Spanish, and several other languages for ONI, an accomplishment never equaled by any other intelligence officer.[7]

Rodgers's accomplished crew provided a stark contrast to the timid intelligence staff who had served with Mason. They were better trained, more articulate, and more aggressive than the original staff. However, they inherited an office already in working order and merely expanded established methods of gathering, organizing, and circulating information. Furthermore, they faced a naval and political environment far more conducive to intelligence work than the one confronted five years earlier by Mason's team. President Grover Cleveland and Secretary of the Navy William C. Whitney supported naval expansion and construction of first-class warships capable of holding the seas against the bigger men-of-war of other powers. The president even favored increased intelligence operations, specifically mentioning the topic in an address to Congress. The legislature, itself, contained more vocal, influential, and successful pro-Navy factions than before, advancing programs of increased naval expenditures.[8]

Given this favorable environment, Rodgers and his officers found attentive, eager readers of intelligence propaganda. Whitney was the most receptive. Reputedly an opponent of graft and waste, the new secretary of the Navy sought to eradicate corruption in the department. Early denunciation of Secretary Chandler's intimacy with John Roach, successful bidder on all four of the Navy's first steel ships, reflected this crusade to cleanse the service of the taint of past misdeeds. At the same time, the incoming department head promised to free the Navy from old ideas and equipment. Whitney's streak of reformism and modernist assumptions endeared him to the officers in ONI. In return, the secretary relied on naval intelligence to assist him in construction of the New Navy.[9]

Whitney ordered ONI to collect data on the latest foreign warship designs as a guide for his own program. He purchased blueprints for torpedoboats, cruisers, and armoured warships from leading European firms through ONI agents. But the secretary's interest in naval intelligence went deeper than acquisition of drawings; he followed minute details of ONI work, expecting Walker to leave intelligence documents regularly on his desk. The bureau chief hesitated to allow naval intelligence to make any move without Whitney's personal approval, including routine publication of warship pictures in its information series. "I should give the order to go ahead with the work myself," Walker informed the vacationing secretary, "but Rodgers tells me that you wish to know about the matter and personally give directions."[10]

Whitney coordinated ONI with State Department intelligence resources. Earlier Mason had underscored the importance of such contact, and bits of consular news had drifted into this office. The current Office received an enlarged volume. Using friendship with Secretary of State Thomas F. Bayard to advantage, Whitney assured a steady flow of diplomatic data into ONI, particularly consular reports from British shipbuilding centers along the Tyne River. However, such material varied in importance and reliability. While one State Department agent sent superb drawings of Armstrong's new triple expansion steam engine, others simply forwarded newspaper clippings of launchings. The consul at Cadiz, meanwhile, revealed Spanish experiments with the secret submarine torpedoboat *Peral* fully two months after Commander Bowman H. McCalla cruising off the Iberian coast had learned about the trial runs.[11]

On its part, the State Department showed a surprising willingness to consult the Navy's fledgling intelligence agency. Perhaps Bayard's intimacy with Whitney or his search for allies in pursuing a foreign policy, which had recently come under partisan attack, motivated closer cooperation. More likely, State and Navy Departments found a great number of mutual interests in promoting involvement in Panama, Samoa, and Hawaii. Walker and other expansionist officers were most vocal in their defense of Bayard's active concern for these strategic areas. Whatever the motives, the secretary of state solicited ONI views on international developments.[12]

24

Naval intelligence established smooth working relations with other officials. A master of political influence, Walker urged closer and more amicable contacts with individual congressmen to promote the New Navy. "We must 'lubb and bear away' a little in order to steer clear of the many snags in Congress," he told a fellow officer in 1886.[13] Consequently, Rodgers developed regular lines of communication with Chairman of the House Committee on Naval Affairs Hilary Abner Herbert. The intelligence chief bombarded Herbert with comprehensive memoranda on foreign naval construction, organizations, and equipment. He provided the Democrat legislator with damaging evidence of Republican mismanagement of the Navy. Gradually the handsome young naval officer and the former Confederate general became warm companions, and Rodgers succeeded in infusing modernist naval philosophy in the mind of the future Secretary of the Navy Herbert. It was not unusual for the intelligence chief to rush over to Herbert's hotel room in the evening to help the Alabama lawmaker thrash out some problem of naval legislation.[14]

Rodgers engendered similar enthusiasm for intelligence material among fellow officers. He prepared everything from a table of dimensions on gunboats for the Board on Additional Vessels to a file on electric lights for the newly created Office of the Naval Inspector of Electric Lighting. He sent Ordnance the latest on gun development overseas to aid in its designs for new American naval rifles. Rodgers forwarded cruiser blueprints purchased from the British to the Bureau of Construction and details of cork packing for hulls to the Bureau of Equipment. Specifics on foreign dockyards went to the desks of the Bureau of Yards and Docks.[15]

Bureau chiefs and other officers appeared anxious to receive this technical assistance and employed it to build the earliest steel warships. However, many of these same officers displayed less enthusiasm for ONI's promotion of the Naval War College, founded at Newport in 1884 to study war problems, higher strategy, and naval history. From the beginning, the postgraduate school confronted opposition from officers and civilian administrators who considered Newport anything from a duplicate Naval Academy to an expensive summer resort. Ordnance chief Montgomery Sicard's refusal to help the college exemplified the early service opinion. When he was asked to send ammunition for gunnery practice to be carried out in conjunction with classroom exercises, "the bare proposition nearly frightened him to death," Walker recalled. "As I did not want to kill the old fellow I let him alone. . . ."[16]

Walker, Rodgers, and ONI were among the minority to view the Naval War College as an important adjunct of the New Navy. The intelligence chief assisted the college between April 1886 and November 1888, carrying on a vigorous correspondence with college presidents Luce and Alfred T. Mahan. ONI fed the founding officers maps, charts, and data for course work and strategic studies. The intelligence officer may also have been responsible for purchase overseas and introduction of the *Kriegspiel*, a naval war game that became a favorite college tool to plot out tactical solutions on a huge war board. Moreover, Rodgers lent staff intelligence officers Lieutenants Calkins and Sidney A. Staunton to the instructor-starved school to present lectures on naval reserve forces, coastal defenses, and training systems. After the close of the 1888 session, Mahan thanked Rodgers "for the kindness and readiness shown by you, throughout my connection with the College, in forwarding all matters in which I have asked you to help."[17]

In order to provide fresh data to college, bureau, and congressman, Rodgers's office constantly improved methods for the gathering of information. In May 1885 Assistant Engineer D. C. Humphreys urged the chief to employ cameras as an ONI resource. Rodgers adopted this innovation at once. By late 1887, Luce informed him that the gunboat *Dolphin* had a complete "photographic outfit" and the new cruiser *Atlanta* had three "photographists." Early photographic intelligence included twenty-nine pictures of the Armstrong coast defense guns in Valparaiso harbor taken by Lieutenant Charles Vreeland and forty-three shots of the disputed Canadian boundary zone mailed to ONI by Lieutenant Commander Charles M. Thomas. Work with primitive cameras was not always successful. Lieutenant Thomas Snowden apologized in 1888 for the defective plates sent Rodgers on the forts in Halifax harbor.[18]

ONI also helped develop a new Navy Code between 1885 and 1889 after Rodgers complained that confidential information sent to the Navy Department from Panama by commercial cable had leaked to undesirable sources. The intelligence chief understood that the Navy needed a reliable secret code if it was to expand and refine intelligence service in the age of telegraphic communications. Work on such a code progressed slowly, and by May 1887 Walker admitted to Chadwick in London that ONI needed professional assistance, importing from Europe to help the department an expert named Hawke. Walker warned his attaché to remain silent, "because if it gets out it will at once be published in the newspapers and used as a means of attack upon the Navy Department which would spoil the whole business."[19]

Five months later, seven men in two empty rooms were still working on the code, probably without assistance from the mysterious Mr. Hawke.

Finally in September 1888, after nearly another year of labor, Walker proudly announced completion of the Navy Secret Code. "I want you to give a practical trial in actual service," he advised Captain Francis Ramsay, about to depart on the new steel cruiser *Boston*, "and will be glad to have you use it during your present trip when convenient." [20]

Code making was not the only test of ONI capabilities. Along with information on useful inventions, the Office received a flood of infernal-machine letters, promising for a few dollars to reveal the world's most awful secrets of destruction. Whitney forwarded the plans of a North Carolina inventor for an "invisible turret," which "will withstand the rough usage of actual warfare." The bargain price stood at $500. Meanwhile, an Ohio manufacturer offered to test his "chisel shot" exclusively for Rodgers. The trial must be held in secret, he told the intelligence chief, since public tests "would expose it to the world." The note concluded, "Lieut. —this sounds cranky but I mean it." [21]

Naval intelligence experienced other growing pains in the late 1880s. Many shipboard intelligence officers approached their new duties with slight enthusiasm. Others refused to do the work at all. One on board the *Marion* ignored orders to collect data on Singapore because a previous officer had visited the area years before; another reported the loss of all intelligence forms when his Chinese servant threw them overboard with the garbage. At the same time, the commanding officer of the *Adams* claimed every single intelligence document had disappeared from his ship. [22]

Never a patient man, Walker grew tired of the excuses. He lashed out at Rear Admiral Samuel R. Franklin, the somewhat relaxed commander of the European Station. "The Department desires to call attention to the unsatisfactory character of the Intelligence Reports which have been received from the European Station." The *Quinnebaug* lay anchored a few miles from the huge gun factories and shipyards of Sir William Armstrong & Company, yet not one officer bothered to visit the plant. Walker lectured Franklin on the purpose of naval intelligence:

The Office of Naval Intelligence was established in order that the Navy Department might be supplied with the most accurate information as to the progress of naval science, and the condition and resources of foreign navies. As the Maritime Nations of Europe afford the best field from which to obtain this information; it is desirable that the officers on the European Station selected for this duty should be given every practicable opportunity and be encouraged to carry out the wishes of the Department. [23]

Despite limitations, naval intelligence showed signs of maturing during the late eighties. The naval attaché system branched out to reflect European power alignments, and by 1889 included all major continental capitals in addition to London. Meanwhile, Office publications during Rodgers's tenure ranked with the best to come out of naval intelligence. The compilation of information on coaling, docking, and port facilities became a standard work, going through five editions by 1909. ONI's General Information Series for 1888–89 presented a series of essays by different staff intelligence officers and outside naval experts on specific subjects such as ordnance, naval reserves, natural resources, submarine boats, and electricity. Taken together, these disparate writings documented the various threads of thought pulsing through ONI between 1882 and 1889 and presented a synthesis of modernist naval doctrine in the early years of the New Navy. The basic assumption underlying these compositions stressed that rapid changes in naval technology rendered future operations too complex for traditional limited tactics and planning, and in the future the Navy must be guided by "grand strategic principles of national attack and defense."[24]

Operational planning was more than an intellectual exercise, however. Twice naval intelligence initiated tentative war plans in the late 1880s, once for Panama and the other time for Canada. Walker coordinated both projects. Between 1885 and 1887 he dispatched agents to Panama, including Bowman McCalla, C. C. Rogers, and William Wirt Kimball, to collect data on strategic questions. These trips departed from traditional reconnaissance missions, stressing instead evaluation of information for planning military operations. Thought was given to how the U. S. Navy might hold the Isthmus of Panama against some unnamed enemy, and Walker ordered McCalla to examine local islands in the Bay of Panama as possible sites for an advanced base. His secret directive of 6 April 1885 read:

> Give them a careful examination and report what you think about them, how completely they would control the Bay of Panama if we were to occupy them with a permanent force, whether good fresh water can be had on them, or whether it would be necessary to collect cistern water; the depth of water and how near heavy ships can approach—in fact give everything necessary to a thorough understanding of the value of those islands to us should we desire to occupy and hold them with an armed force.[25]

Walker turned next to Canada, which in 1886 disputed with the United States over coastal fishing rights. Stirred by Irish-Americans and partisan politics, the Cleveland administration found itself making bellicose statements over Canadian treatment of American fishermen who violated territorial waters. Soon relations degenerated into a war scare. Walker went into action at once, writing Lighthouse Inspector Commander Charles V. Gridley on the Great Lakes to request information about the best places to attack Canada. He also asked for data on the fortifications at Kingston, Toronto, and other strategic locations. "I have been thinking somewhat of sending one or two officers from the Office of Naval Intelligence to obtain all the information possible, and have thought a little of going with them myself," he informed Gridley. "I suppose if we could have a few days in your tender for passing through the Welland Canal and for visiting a few points on Lake Ontario it would assist us much and would enable us to see a good deal without attracting any attention to ourselves." [26]

Apparently Walker made an intelligence trip to Canada during the summer of 1887, since he submitted an expense account in September for travel to Buffalo, Cape Vincent, Quebec, and Montreal. No such account indicated which ONI operatives accompanied him, nor was it clear how far war planning went against Canada or its protector Great Britain. In any case, by early 1889 a new treaty and cooling tempers prevented further preparations. The following year, though, Mahan probably borrowed Walker's intelligence material to compile a contingency plan for operations against Great Britain. [27]

The early efforts at war planning marked an appropriate culmination of Rodgers's years in ONI. During those months, the intelligence chief shared in the excitement and stirring that punctuated the early stages of the New Navy. He worked intimately with Walker, Whitney, and Herbert. He assisted Luce and Mahan. Moreover, his intelligence officers contributed ideas to naval thought and policy during this formative period. Their theories were transitory, institutionalized later by others, but their synthesis of expansive naval doctrine was far more advanced than any previous effort. In some ways they reflected the probings of the first Cleveland administration itself, which gradually committed the Democrats to the same diplomatic and naval expansion that their Republican predecessors had supported. During his term as chief intelligence officer between 1885 and 1889, Rodgers experienced the movement and progress in the Navy, adding to this spirit and benefiting from it as well.

iv

THE FIRST ATTACHES

The success ONI enjoyed in contributing to the birth of the New Navy resulted to a large extent from information and material supplied by its overseas representatives, the naval attachés. Between 1882 and 1889 the U. S. Navy attached its first permanent naval representatives to foreign diplomatic missions. These earliest attachés were consistently competent and perceptive observers of overseas naval progress, and became ONI's primary source of fresh intelligence.

At first, the seasoned military and naval attachés of the world's great powers looked somewhat patronizingly at the inclusion of North American officers in their smoking rooms and exclusive clubs; but the first U. S. naval attachés soon earned their respect. The attachés moved easily among their military colleagues and through the aristocratic salons, banquet halls, and court circles. They made valuable contacts with naval, government, and business officials and established close relations with shipbuilders and arms makers. The prospect that the U. S. Navy might buy lavishly abroad in order to modernize its decrepit fleet opened numerous doors. It helped also for them to be representatives of a navy that posed no threat to any of the host countries. The United States might be an annoying economic rival but was hardly a factor in the world balance of power. The unassuming American officers seemed pleasant additions to the social whirl of dances, fox hunts, and dinner parties.

Attachment of service officers to diplomatic staffs in order to report on foreign military activities probably originated in the eighteenth century when the French employed such agents. Napoleon Bonaparte accelerated the attaché network to provide specific military information from various European capitals in the early nineteenth century. France also detailed the first naval attaché to London, in 1860. European naval attachés came to the United States during the American Civil War, to observe the momentous developments in naval architecture, ordnance, and operations. During the Franco-Prussian War of 1870 and four subsequent decades of imperial, naval, and military rivalries, the employment of attachés expanded, so that by the time the first U. S. naval attachés journeyed to Europe, every capital contained a goodly number.[1]

The Franco-Prussian War also influenced the development of a U.S. naval attaché system. Naval officers had traditionally dabbled in diplomatic relations, and at times even served as diplomatic representatives, but not until 1870 did they operate as roving attachés in Europe. Though an informal arrangement, Simpson, Marvin, and Rodgers's team reported officially to American diplomatic representatives in countries visited, and worked from legation offices. The first officer referred to by the Navy Department as an attaché was undoubtedly Commander Francis M. Ramsay, who followed Simpson to Europe in 1872 to continue investigations for the Bureau of Ordnance. A decade later, the department attached Captain Shufeldt to the U.S. legation in Peking as a temporary expedient for the State Department.[2]

The Navy's first formal attaché under the auspices of ONI was Lieutenant Commander French Ensor Chadwick, a brusque West Virginian noted for his uncanny ability to recollect facts and details. Chadwick's attachment to U.S. Minister James Russell Lowell in London in 1882 resulted from his prior success in gathering information overseas for the Bureau of Equipment. During an earlier visit to Europe, Chadwick had compiled a study of naval training systems so informative that the U.S. Congress published it as a Senate document. More important, he had contacted influential naval officers and officials, laying the foundation for permanent assignment to Europe in 1882.[3]

Initially Chadwick operated without formal attachment to any American legation and without an official designation as naval attaché. Secretary Chandler's instructions in July merely ordered him to gather information on a variety of topics. Chandler solicited data on foreign life-saving, coast guard, and hospital services, as well as on systems for inspection of steam vessels. The next month, the department ordered him to buy books, periodicals, and drawings and to travel to the European continent in search of information. Finally, on 28 October, fully three months after his arrival, Chadwick became a naval attaché. "You will regard the Minister of the United States as your superior officer," Walker instructed, "and will at all times comply with such instructions as he may give you." However, Walker made it clear that Chadwick's mission was to serve the Navy. "You are authorized to visit such portions of Great Britain and the continent of Europe as you may consider essential to the performance of your duties."[4]

For three years Chadwick served alone in Europe, shuttling back and forth between Britain and the Continent. He had sweeping duties and assignments. In addition to finishing compilation of information required by Chandler's original directive of July, he filled requests for materiel and data from the Gun Foundry and other boards being convened to help launch the New Navy. In 1884 he was attached temporarily to the U. S. legation in Berlin in order to visit German Army maneuvers and steam trials of new gunboats on the River Weser. Back in Britain, Chadwick inspected armor plates being rolled for the U. S. monitor *Miantonomah* at Sheffield. At the same time, the American attaché directed the first batch of U. S. Navy cadet engineers to study at the British naval schools in Greenwich and Glasgow.[5]

Perhaps Chadwick's most rewarding task came in purchasing the *Thetis* and the *Alert*, vessels specially designed to sail in Arctic waters. The U. S. Navy urgently required these craft for a search and relief mission to locate a lost exploration team. "Your announcement by cable of this date of the departure of the steamer *Alert* for New York, so soon after her reception from the British government," the department cabled in March 1884, "is additional evidence of the ability, energy and zeal which you have displayed in preparing and despatching the two vessels obtained in Great Britain for the Greely relief expedition of 1884."[6]

Chadwick presented other evidence of the indispensability of a permanent naval attaché. Almost from the day he landed in Britain, he unleashed an endless flow of informative dispatches, covering everything from the Board of Trade to Le Creusot's ironworks, and from the design of German torpedoboats to the naval policies of European powers. In the latter connection, Chadwick sent a report to Whitney that discussed the British practice of subsidizing lines of merchant vessels, not only to promote trade but also as sources of potential auxiliary warships. A new line in the Pacific Northwest, he warned, "will go far toward lessening American influence in the Asiatic seas." To gather such information, Chadwick developed key contacts at the Woolwich Arsenal, Kew Observatory, and among the shipbuilders at East Cowes. Surprisingly, British Admiralty officials proved cooperative, quietly turning over specifications of new British warships. Chadwick also joined certain select organizations, including the Institute of Engineers and Shipbuilders of the Clyde.[7]

While Chadwick rushed to keep pace with the many demands of attaché work in Europe, another U. S. naval officer became an attaché on the other side of the globe. On 13 November 1883, the department ordered Lieutenant j.g. George Clayton Foulk as naval attaché to the newly opened U. S. legation in Seoul, "Kingdom of Corea." Foulk's title as naval attaché was something of a mystery. ONI never listed him as one, and all later histories failed to include him with Chadwick and his European successors. Yet Chandler expected Foulk to work through the intelligence office. "You will acquaint yourself with the forms of the Office of Naval Intelligence," the secretary advised, "and as information therein called for shall be obtained the reports will be forwarded together with additional reports of the progress of your work and of information of special importance and immediate value to the Department." [8]

Perhaps a clue to neglect of Foulk in ONI records lies in the nature of his appointment. Though he received instructions through proper naval channels, his assignment came personally from President Arthur and Secretary of State Frederick Frelinghuysen. Moreover, while they recognized Foulk's obligation to supply information to the Navy, they expected the officer to operate primarily as a diplomatic agent. Secretary Frelinghuysen gave him private directions. "Your reports . . . to this Department will be acceptable, and whatever suggestions you may be enabled to make from personal observation respecting an increase of our commercial relations with that government (Korea) will be received with satisfaction." Several years later when the properly accredited minister to Seoul left, the State Department formalized Foulk's position by naming him chargé d'affaires. [9]

Whatever Foulk's status in ONI, the Office recognized Lieutenant B. H. Buckingham as its second naval attaché. Ironically, Foulk and Buckingham had drawn departmental recognition as potential attachés together, when in company with Ensign Walter McLean they had traveled from Korea, across Siberia, and through Russia, compiling an extraordinarily detailed intelligence report, which ONI published in 1883. Several years later Buckingham joined the intelligence bureau, and Rodgers rushed him to New Orleans to visit the Industrial and Cotton Centennial Exposition. "The foreign sections are not much more than bazaars for the sale of cheap trash," he cabled his chief. This ability to distinguish between useless gadgets and important technological advances was essential for his next assignment, in November 1885, as the first permanent attaché to continental Europe. [10]

After meeting Chadwick and touring British shipyards with the senior officer, Buckingham crossed the channel and reported to Minister Robert McLane in Paris. Later he presented credentials as naval attaché to St. Petersburg and Berlin, since he represented the department in all three capitals. Even though Chadwick's path-breaking work had smoothed the way for Buckingham, the new attaché found it necessary to assemble additional sources of information in France, Germany, and Russia. When Lieutenant Aaron Ward relieved him later, Buckingham claimed: "I may say that his start will be much easier than mine was as

I was able to introduce him to many that took me some time to get acquainted with, and he starts as high in that respect as I was after being here two years." [11]

European officials welcomed the jovial, seemingly bucolic American attaché. Naturally exuberant and friendly, Buckingham became more bouyant as he pursued his search for information, buying after-dinner cigars for fellow foreign officers and exchanging humorous stories. At dinner parties, official residences, private clubs, and in shipyards he met important people. Everywhere he went, Buckingham discussed professional matters, learning all he could on the spot. In addition, he told industrialists that the U. S. Navy wanted to buy materiel and that he needed to examine their latest weapons, ships, and blueprints before making a decision to purchase. He traveled widely, one day visiting French naval yards, pausing long enough to catch his bearings, and then heading for Holland, Denmark, and Sweden to inspect their naval resources. No sooner had Buckingham returned from this tour, than off he went to the Black Sea to study Russian ironclads at Sevastopol. [12]

German naval progress amazed Buckingham. He marveled at how government subsidies stimulated shipbuilding and steel production, praising German efficiency, organization, and planning. The Vulcan shipyard at Stettin particularly impressed the American observer. Government work on torpedoboats and cruisers filled the orderly plant to capacity. "Start a subscription among your rich friends," Buckingham needled his comrade McCalla, so that the Navy could purchase one of these sleek foreign vessels. [13] He longed to get inside the sprawling steel works of Friedrich Krupp in Essen, but no promise of contracts or cajoling could pry open the secrets of the world's most successful arms maker. In frustration, Buckingham fired a protest at the cannon king, telling Krupp that the U. S. Navy would turn to Hotchkiss and other manufacturers for ordnance. Despite the setback at Essen, Buckingham preferred the German environment to other areas of Europe. "I had a most interesting time at Kiel and Wilhelmshaven," he wrote Chadwick from Paris, "the German officers were very cordial, something that these damn Frenchmen never are and they showed me many things I had never been allowed to see before." [14]

A third attaché joined Buckingham and Chadwick in 1888. In November Whitney delegated Lieutenant Nathan Sargent as the Navy's agent in Rome and Vienna. Up to this appointment, Sargent's major contribution had been revision of the *Gunnery Question Book* and publication of scholarly essays, his overhaul of the gunnery volume having drawn praise from modernist officers. "Your work presents in a compact and handy form, the pith of the more cumbrous Ordnance Instructions," Luce wrote in July 1881, "and is exactly the book needed in this branch of the service both for the instruction of the boys and their advancement from class to class." Luce ordered 100 copies for his training squadron. Other writings soon followed, including essays for *The United Service* and the Naval Institute *Proceedings.* In 1884 Sargent penned a brilliant article on squadrons of evolutions, war planning, and strategic studies. This paper presented ideas far in advance of those current in the service, and it forecast by a decade concepts that were later expanded and synthesized by others. Such modern theories drew Walker's attention and provided the impetus for the intelligence assignment in Italy and Austria-Hungary.[15]

Sargent found Italian and Austrian officials anxious to please. "In beginning my duties here and at Vienna," he reported from Rome, "I spoke plainly to the naval authorities, told them that of course they had no jealousy of America such as they felt for adjoining continental countries, and assured them that they need feel no hesitation in giving me information. . . ."[16] Whether his candid approach impressed foreign naval officials or not, Sargent believed they provided more information to him than to attachés of other nations. Indeed, he gained almost unrestricted access to navy yards at Taranto and Pola, the steel works at Terni, and the torpedo factory at Fiume.

Easy access to data aided the department in its quest for accurate specifications and drawings to build its steel fleet. "The work done by the Attachés during the next six months will be very important to the Department," Rodgers informed Sargent in April 1889, "and, if exact and complete, will be highly to their credit and that of the intelligence system."[17] The chief intelligence officer desired explanations of how foreign naval architects distributed armor on warships and protected guns. "This seems to be a most important question in design today and it is very important that the Navy Department should have every bit of information on the subject attainable," he told the attaché.[18] At the same time, Ordnance Chief Sicard wanted news of the windage of European guns, head of the electrical bureau Royal B. Bradford requested details of electric lighting on Italian warships, and the Bureau of Construction required exact weights of machinery, engines, boilers, and condensers.[19]

Between 1882 and 1889, then, Chadwick, Buckingham, and Sargent forwarded hundreds of reports on new equipment, ideas, and doctrine to Washington. Many of these documents provided vital information for completion of new warships. They also purchased blueprints, drawings, and materiel for the New Navy. Gradually many doubting officers began to find some value in ONI labors. The department singled Chadwick out for special commendation. As Buckingham observed wryly in a letter to Chadwick: "I have not yet impressed Dept. with a due regard for my infallibility, which you have succeeded in doing—by years of usefulness."[20] The department soon recognized Buckingham as well. "I cannot imagine a better model for any one to copy in forwarding information to the Department." Rodgers observed in 1888. "His reports are always concise and precise, well illustrated by sketches, and of positive technical value."[21] At the same moment, stuffy chief of the Bureau of Navigation Francis Ramsay, noted for dogmatic enforcement of three years' sea duty after three on shore, extended Sargent's attachéship for a fourth year.[22]

Despite success as collectors of naval information, U. S. naval attachés operated at a disadvantage compared to some of their more prosperous colleagues. Many European officers received substantial stipends and employed private fortunes to collect data. The American attachés complained perpetually about inadequate salaries and an allowance of $100 per month for all expenses. Funds for extraordinary purchases such as blueprints or equipment existed, but day-to-day operations and more creative enterprises suffered from lack of money. Despite popular impressions, the U. S. attachés never lived in foreign splendor.

The quest to maintain a proper social footing stimulated interest on the part of some attachés in seeking lucrative commissions from munitions makers for promoting their products. Buckingham discussed the question with Commander Francis M. Barber, who had taken leave to represent Le Creusot in the United States. The attaché refused to use information to benefit any individual, he told Barber, because "if it was known that any agent had access to such in America, it would work against my getting additional—so I wrote to Rodgers to be careful about it."[23] Apparently he never succumbed to temptation, since Buckingham complained for three years about his terrible financial condition. He grumbled when the Treasury Department disallowed application for hotel costs which he considered part of the duty in traveling back and forth among three distant European capitals. "I had congratulated myself that I had been extremely light on travelling expenses," he wrote McCalla, "and Chadwick who is careful told me he didn't see how I could get along on so little."[24]

The question of money influenced the American attachés' participation in the European social swirl. The officer served both diplomatic and military functions, accompanying ministers to public affairs, and representing the legation at smaller gatherings. Teas, dinners, court receptions, balls, and military reviews took up weeks of valuable time and became increasingly expensive. During the day the attaché circulated among proper residences and government buildings to leave his visiting cards. It was tiring, monotonous duty with little reward in terms of concrete information or even personal contacts but a necessary adjunct of the attachéship. Not all officers found the life pleasant. "The military attachés here are great swells, and are invited everywhere," Buckingham wrote, "so that a social light should he have the other requisites could succeed far better than one who will not go out—of course it is not necessary to give ones self up to society, but one has to put on an appearance, get presented to everyone." [25]

The first U. S. naval attachés found a world of glamour and excitement in late-nineteenth-century Europe, but also long hours of touring sooty shipyards and factories. For every lavish banquet, the attaché spent months hand-copying over reports and reading foreign naval journals. These officers had not received elaborate training in intelligence, international law, or war planning; their reports were simple, straightforward accounts of observations and information. Although few spoke any foreign language except French, members of European diplomatic and military circles spoke little else. Social life and education at the U. S. Naval Academy had prepared them for most aspects of this duty, and they moved effortlessly into their attachéships, becoming major suppliers of intelligence for ONI.

V

AN UNDESIRABLE BILLET

The New Navy grew with frustrating deliberateness. Design problems, shortages in materiel, and contract squabbles delayed launchings of the first steel warships for several years. Not until 1889 did the fleet contain enough modern vessels for an experimental squadron to test tactical steam evolutions. Commanded by Commodore Walker, this Squadron of Evolution included the Navy's first four steel steamers, the *Chicago, Atlanta, Boston,* and *Yorktown.* These were ships of transition, combining sail and steam. They were tiny, unarmored men-of-war, and as Walker observed, "not as good as we could wish, but when we consider that their plans were made five years ago I think we should be pretty well satisfied with them."[1]

Despite limitations, the white-hulled craft were the Navy's first modern ships-of-war and carried breech-loading rifles and electricity. Moreover, regardless of their size and strength compared to current European armored warships, the formation of a tactical squadron marked a step toward overall naval modernization. Furthermore, it reflected the larger policies of the new Secretary of the Navy Benjamin Franklin Tracy and President Benjamin Harrison. This dynamic Republican administration pushed the United States toward active participation in world affairs. Their vigorous policies required a naval force more formidable than the current defensive array of cruisers, forecasting instead reliance on larger, armored warships. In 1890, a naval advisory board recommended construction of ninety-two ships, but the more realistic Tracy asked Congress for three 10,000-ton men-of-war, the first modern battleships in the U. S. Navy.[2]

Passage of the Naval Act of 1890 delighted ONI. During the past few years, the Office had come to expect intimate participation in each departmental step toward naval rejuvenation. With the three battleships, naval intelligence assumed that Tracy would turn often to ONI for advice and assistance. As Lieutenant George W. Mentz observed in 1890, the civilian secretary "can not possibly have all the professional and technical knowledge required for these duties, and the problem has been 'how to give the best professional advice and assistance under the most responsible conditions.'"[3]

The incoming chief intelligence officer, Commander Charles H. Davis, Jr., agreed, and anticipated an increase in his own authority. Son of Admiral Charles Henry Davis, one of the most influential officers of the old sailing navy, young Davis wished to exert his own sway over the New Navy as leader of naval intelligence. He would establish the same intimacy with the secretary experienced by his father with Gideon Welles years before. Development of this relationship accelerated when Tracy revived Welles's Office of the Assistant Secretary of the Navy, dormant since Civil War days, and transferred ONI to it from the Bureau of Navigation. Now Davis had immediate and daily access to the secretary. Moreover, there were other signs to encourage the chief intelligence officer. His brother-in-law Henry Cabot Lodge currently sat on the important House Committee on Naval Affairs, and Davis imagined that he would become more important than his predecessor in cooperating with Congress. If Rodgers and Herbert had formed a partnership, then Davis and Lodge promised to establish an irresistible combination to promote the New Navy.[4]

Fulfillment of Davis's prophecies started on schedule. Tracy turned at once to his Office for advice, asking ONI to investigate progress by foreign manufacturers on the production of nickel steel to harden armor plate. When naval intelligence learned that the British Admiralty had successfully tested steel plate at Portsmouth, the secretary ordered ONI to secure complete descriptions of the trials and arrange for similar tests in the United States. The resulting competitive trial of armor plates held at the Naval Ordnance Proving Grounds in Annapolis removed all doubts about the superiority of nickel steel over compound armor (iron plates with steel welded in front) and all-steel plate. Tracy ordered adoption of the new product for future American warships and negotiated with several U.S. steel firms in order to establish a domestic supply.[5]

Demands for information did not stop with nickel steel. Proposed construction of the Navy's first true battleships required all kinds of data and specifications from abroad. In January 1890 ONI supplied memoranda on military masts, heating jackets for rapid-fire guns, and copper sheathing for ship hulls. Several months later, naval intelligence provided information on shell detonators, butts and seam fittings, and caulking for armor plating. Next came intelligence on gun mounts, smokeless powder, and boiler steel. The Navy sought information on foreign steam trials, given all new warships to measure the capacity and speed capabilities of engines and boilers. Data gathered by Sargent on

Italian practice were employed by the U. S. Navy in April 1890 to lay a course off the New Hampshire coast to test engines on the new cruiser *Philadelphia*.[6]

Not everyone approved of the technical competence of naval intelligence during those early months of Davis's leadership. As applications for news from overseas increased, so too did requirements for technical precision and expertise. For example, in foreign armor tests, ONI ordered its agents to supply exact specifications on powder density, muzzle pressure and velocity, striking energy of projectiles, and extent of recoil, as well as routine target distances, sizes, and structures. The Bureau of Ordnance expressed particular dissatisfaction with ONI performance. "Ordnance get more from this office than any other Bureau, but is the most unsatisfactory to deal with," intelligence officer Lieutenant Frederic Singer complained. He told one attaché not to worry about such grumbling because bureau chiefs did not understand the difficulty in securing exact data. Moreover, when ONI asked them to define their requirements, these same officers replied simply "that they want to know everything."[7]

Despite minor controversy with some bureaus, ONI weathered the transition from Democrat Whitney to Republican Tracy and from Rodgers to Davis with a minimum of difficulty. The enthusiasm for intelligence work and the growing sense of belonging to a select team which had developed earlier carried over to the new administration. Young modernist, almost insurgent, officers still flocked to the Office, including Lieutenants William Henry Hudson Southerland and Charles Eben Fox and Ensign John M. Ellicott. Southerland contributed essays on smokeless powders, rapid-fire guns, and range-finders, undoubtedly influencing departmental adoption of the first two innovations. The momentum provided by naval modernization forecast new opportunities for ONI, including possible duty as a board to plan building programs and strategic operations. "I have no doubt that before very long it will be an Intelligence Office in the principle of the German General Staff instead of what it has been heretofore, an 'Office for Filing Information' which would eventually get the dry-rot," Singer wrote enthusiastically.[8]

Singer's prediction that ONI might become an informal naval general staff moved closer to reality in late 1891 when tension between the United States and Chile threatened to lead to war. Relations with Chile had been troubled for some time, growing acute during the Chilean revolution against the government of Jose Manuel Balmaceda. The United States maintained a troubled neutrality, alienating insurgent forces by providing sanctuary for Balmacedistas, and seizing a rebel arms steamer, the *Itata*. Throughout the insurrection, U. S. warships prowled menacingly close to Chile's coast, protecting American interests and according to the revolutionary forces lending aid to Balmaceda. When the insurgents defeated Balmaceda in August, most U. S. warships withdrew except for the unarmored cruiser *Baltimore,* which remained in Valparaiso harbor. Anti-American feelings still permeated the area when, on 16 October, Commander Winfield Scott Schley gave shore leave to his crew. Not unexpectedly, trouble occurred at a nearby saloon, leading to the death of two American sailors and injury to seventeen others.[9]

Harrison and Tracy reacted strongly to news of the sailors' deaths. This was the most severe crisis confronted by the active administration. There had been tensions earlier with Great Britain and Germany over the Samoan Islands, and a minor war scare with Italy over the lynching of some Italians in New Orleans, but nothing as critical as the Chilean affair. Moreover, in previous disputes Secretary of State James G. Blaine had remained a moderating influence, but he had fallen ill in the late summer of 1891 and had left the humid Washington climate to recuperate. President Harrison turned to Tracy, his only real friend in the cabinet. Secretary of the Navy Tracy proved far more bellicose than the absent Blaine and resolutely pushed preparations for war against Chile.[10]

The possibility of conflict had occurred to Tracy before the *Baltimore* tragedy. Several months earlier he had ordered Captain George C. Remey of the cruiser *Charleston* to seize the *Itata*, even if interdiction meant collision with the big Chilean warship *Esmeralda*, sent to escort the munitions steamer. Fortunately the two men-of-war missed each other. Nevertheless Tracy had continued war planning, including dispatch of Captain Mahan to Washington in late 1891 to join a secret (though informal) strategy team composed of Assistant Secretary of the Navy James Russell Soley, Commodore William M. Folger, and possibly Chief Intelligence Officer Davis. Apparently the group's first action was to request intelligence about Chile, since on 1 September the department asked the commander-in-chief of the Pacific Squadron to obtain authentic information on conditions in the area.[11]

After the *Baltimore* incident, Tracy's war preparations became more frantic. He assumed complete charge of operations, though probably with guidance from the intelligence office, which recommended purchase overseas of armor-piercing shells and other commodities of war. Meanwhile, the secretary established personal contacts with the

Holmes Steamship Company and other shipowners for use of their vessels as auxiliaries in the event of war. He leased four colliers to carry coal to Commodore Walker's squadron of cruisers, then taking on supplies at Montevideo in passage around Cape Horn to Chilean waters. And finally, Tracy rushed five coast defense and harbor mining experts to the Pacific coast to make arrangements for security.[12]

At least once during the crisis Tracy panicked. Piecing together bits of information, he concluded that a mighty Chilean battle fleet had assembled secretly to intercept Walker's ships. He cabled Commander Robley D. Evans in Valparaiso for his opinion, and the officer agreed that Chile might attempt to stop Walker. The secretary's rising fears resulted from inadequate intelligence. ONI admitted that it had little idea where Chile's warships were cruising or even what was occurring in Chile. Davis's office had some information on Valparaiso's defenses but little else.[13]

Intelligence reports about Chilean activities in Europe proved more useful. ONI supported three attachés in European capitals in late 1891. Sargent represented the Navy in Berlin, Vienna, and Rome; Lieutenant Commander William H. Emory manned the London post; and Aaron Ward served in Paris and St. Petersburg. Britain, with substantial commercial ties to Chile and an abundance of shipyards and arsenals, was the most important station, and Emory traced rumors of foreign purchases. He pursued a number of leads, visiting shipyards along the River Tyne. The attaché cooperated with consular agents, hired civilian detectives, and interrogated a friend of naval architect Sir Edward Reed. Nothing turned up. Meanwhile, Sargent found similar conditions in Italy. After spending money in appropriate places, he uncovered one tiny warship under construction for a foreign power. Further expenditure revealed that the craft was for the sultan of Morocco, not the Republic of Chile.[14]

Only Ward in France unearthed potential danger. There, Chile had ordered a giant warship, the *Capitan Prat*. The armored man-of-war worried Davis, and he asked his staff in December 1891 to evaluate Ward's reports, estimating when the *Capitan Prat* would be ready to join the Chilean Navy. Lieutenants Mentz and George W. Peters and Ensign Edward Simpson studied the problem, concluding that the battleship would be in fighting condition by February. Davis passed the information on to the strategy planners, unsettling Mahan as much as ONI. Tracy and the others seemed unconcerned, however. "It is astounding that our government should allow matters to drag so, when there is a question of so formidable a vessel as the *Prat* thus getting trim to escape," Mahan wrote Luce in January. "We are so confident in our bigness and so little realize the great extra load entailed by the distance of Chili, in case of war." [15]

As intelligence accumulated, ONI was able to send a packet of information on Chile to Walker in Montevideo. The intelligence office prepared an early version of the War Portfolio, later an integral part of the Navy's war planning process. Davis's portfolio evaluated Chile's economic and military resources and proposed areas of naval operations. ONI observed that while Chile's steel fleet looked formidable to casual observers, it was in poor condition with boilers run down and condenser tubes broken. Naval intelligence estimated that the U. S. Navy could easily cripple Chile. "Arica, Pisaqua, Iquique, Antofagasta, Caldera, and Coquimbo can readily be taken possession of by a force of four or more modern ships, and all commercial traffic stopped thereby cutting off the customs revenue and consequently injuring the credit of Chile in a financial sense." [16]

By February 1892, tensions had eased and war danger passed. Davis appeared content with his Office's performance during the recent crisis. "I think myself, that the office met a pretty good test in the preparation for war with Chile," he wrote in March. He tempered his satisfaction, however, recognizing that in reality ONI had performed minor duty. Tracy consulted it rarely and even then casually. Davis admitted that ONI's influence had declined during the war scare. "It is not a desirable billet for a commander," he concluded. [17]

The Chilean incident brought out Davis's long-festering uneasiness with the intelligence post. Part of his cynicism with ONI duty stemmed from his own personality. Irritable and sensitive, he did not always get along with subordinates. He disliked the affable Buckingham and so tormented one promising officer that Walker had to step in and save the young man. Moreover, Davis lacked the patience, sense of fellowship, and administrative acumen of either Mason or Rodgers. Though articulate and exceptionally well-read in history and science, he chafed under the day-to-day routine of intelligence assignments. Furthermore, he lapsed into moody reflections on superiority of life in his father's sailing navy. "The service has forgotten its past, or at the best remembers it only as a subject for curiosity, bearing a very trifling relation to the present," he philosophized. "Tradition and the trace of continuity are lost." [18]

Davis exhibited annoyance at bothersome details. He complained about inkspots on attaché reports and imprecise drawings. He worried that someone would steal intelligence reports or a copy of the cumbersome three-volume Navy Secret Code. Above all he lashed out at the U. S. Army's new intelligence service. "This office is a good deal of a nuisance to us as it is continually pestering us for assistance and information," he wrote Sargent. When Davis discovered an Army intelligence officer borrowing a report from his files, he expressed more anger. "Such an incident as this served to make me doubly cautious, especially in dealings with these army people, who in matters of tact or discretion seem to me to be a lower order of intellect than the mule." [19]

Domination by Assistant Secretary of the Navy James Russell Soley added to Davis's irritability. Contrary to expectations, the reorganization of ONI under the assistant secretary's office never led to closer relations between Davis and Tracy. Not only did Soley act as a buffer to restrict access to the secretary, but he also seized leadership of intelligence work from Davis. The assistant secretary thoroughly enjoyed coordinating intelligence. An aggressive, Harvard-educated former instructor at the Naval Academy, Soley had tasted such duty in 1878 when he had collected information on European naval schools and practice ships for C. R. P. Rodgers. He had also joined Luce and Mahan in the late eighties in establishing the Naval War College, lecturing there on international law. A friend of Mahan and future law partner of Tracy, Soley held the complete confidence of the inner circle of department leadership, while Davis hovered at the edges. [20]

If Davis entertained visions of serving as his father had done during the Civil War as coordinator of naval intelligence, Soley put an end to those ideas. All correspondence with ONI crossed the civilian administrator's desk before it reached Davis, and Soley reminded attachés that all letters must first go through the assistant secretary's office. Not content to oversee ONI, Soley dabbled in its daily business, sending his own instructions and advice to intelligence personnel in the field. Commenting on his years with the two men, intelligence staffer Singer concluded simply that Soley patronized Davis. [21]

Davis's demoralization and waning influence affected the entire intelligence organization. Under Rodgers, ONI had been filled with enthusiastic officers and had developed a sense of unity and esprit approaching that of a select corps. Increasingly influential with civilian administrators and legislators, Rodgers's elite team had become more critical of those who opposed naval modernization. All this changed with Davis. Secretary Tracy firmly established strict civilian control over ONI, while Davis lost interest in his office because of its subordinate role. Soon Rodgers's people left Davis for other assignments, and replacements lacked equal dynamism or insurgency. The ONI staff grew somnolent, not from overwork but from frustration. "Time and patience will straighten this out no doubt but it is discouraging and I for one am looking for another billet," Singer observed.[22]

Already notorious for avoiding intelligence duty, officers on board ship often simply stopped sending information altogether. When Lieutenant William Sims became intelligence officer on the *Charleston*, he observed that in his first three months he had filled more pages of intelligence material than his predecessors had in years. Naval attachés shared this despair, and Sargent's diary entry for 16 December 1891 spoke of "the indifference shown lately to the work that Ward & I have done."[23]

Davis cleared his desk and left ONI on 31 August 1892. He held no recriminations or self-pity for the decline of the Office during his tenure, blaming only the Navy's system of organization for ONI's imperfections. "It is pretty hard work sometimes maintaining a proper stand when it comes to a question between this office and a legally constituted bureau which has its own appropriations to spend and whose chief is responsible for all his actions," Davis concluded.[24] Moreover, the remaining intelligence staffers predicted a reinvigoration of their billet by the incoming intelligence chief, Commander French E. Chadwick. One officer believed Chadwick's appointment assured ONI's future success: "Chadwick may be able to set the poor old office on its feet again."[25]

vi

THE WIDENING INTELLIGENCE FIELD

No other officer in the Navy was better suited than Chadwick to undertake rehabilitation of the undesirable intelligence billet. As pioneer naval attaché he had legitimatized the system, and his reports between 1882 and 1888 had become standards for all future overseas naval representatives. His interest in improving seamen's training won Luce's recognition, and advocacy of a naval war college earned Mahan's commendation. Indeed Mahan expected Chadwick to replace him as college president. Both Tracy and Soley admired the meticulous officer as well, and his appointment to the intelligence bureau indicated their concern for its demoralized state.

Chadwick's training and endearment to top naval leadership had an immediate impact on ONI. In November 1892 the department asked naval intelligence to participate in policy planning and problem solving. Several months later, Tracy instructed Chadwick's staff to prepare a paper demonstrating how the Harrison administration had constructed a Navy that could compete with those of Germany, Italy, and Britain. The intelligence chief and his ship expert, Lieutenant Edward J. Dorn, compiled tables of comparison and presented evidence to show, as one staffer chided, how on paper the U. S. Navy could knock the stuffings out of foreign navies.[1]

An assignment of more consequence arrived in early 1893 when President Harrison directed naval intelligence to prove the strategic value of the Hawaiian Islands for American military and commercial security. After a recent revolution on those islands, the new leaders had asked for annexation to the United States. Harrison viewed acquisition of Hawaii as a fitting climax to his energetic administration, concluded a hasty pact with the revolutionary clique, and rushed the annexation treaty to the Senate on 15 February. The president needed ONI evidence to bolster his case in Congress and hence instructed Chadwick's team to draft such a document. Obligingly, the intelligence chief prepared an elaborate chart for the president, illustrating how the Hawaiian Islands stood in a vital location in relation to a proposed Central American canal and the markets of the Far East.[2]

A sense of movement had returned to intelligence work. Chadwick took every measure to bolster spirit, and broke office monotony by sending staffers out to observe steam trials, ship launchings, and gunnery tests. In the spring of 1893, ONI completed details for the long-awaited International Naval Rendezvous and Review, held to celebrate the Columbian Exposition. The intelligence office communicated assignments for anchorages and harbor rules to visiting naval contingents. Chadwick, Peters, and Dorn assumed charge of the *Monmouth,* a rented steamer carrying congressional, judicial, and political personages. Meantime, Mentz commanded the coast survey vessel *George S. Blake,* borrowed to shuttle diplomatic visitors around New York harbor to see the rows of foreign warships. And finally, Singer served as the Navy Department's official representative to the Review.[3]

Despite the promising beginning, however, Chadwick's brief tenure never produced the expected rejuvenation of ONI. Exceptional officers failed to flock to his side. The most competent remained Singer and Peters, holdovers from the Davis years. Peters was a brilliant officer, but experienced recurring illness and could not always devote full energies to his duties. Of the new additions, Lieutenant Edward Francis Qualtrough carried the best credentials, though an affinity for liquor impaired his effectiveness. Lieutenant John W. Stewart was a tired officer who resigned shortly after his tour with Chadwick. Several others drifted through, including Lieutenant James Hamilton Sears, son of Secretary Tracy's oldest friend Charles Sears. Soon, Chadwick removed him, because as Singer observed, Sears "got an attack of enlargement of the 'cabesa' after he lectured at the war college and the Chief Intelligence Officer told Soley that he could be spared although the office was short-handed."[4]

Nor did the attaché system flourish under Chadwick. Election year economy forced cutbacks in funds for overseas intelligence work, and in order to curb expenses Chadwick suggested that Rodgers, now naval attaché in Paris and St. Petersburg, cancel a routine trip to present his credentials to the Russian government. Angrily, Rodgers replied that if Chadwick didn't want him to go to Russia, he should not have assigned him to St. Petersburg in the first place. In another letter, he informed the current intelligence chief that when he had been chief intelligence officer, he had always secured reasonable pay allowances and extraordinary expenses for intelligence trips.[5]

Rodgers overreacted by blaming Chadwick for the inadequacies of attaché duty. Conditions had changed in Europe since Rodgers had directed the first batch of naval attachés. Overt collection of information

47

confronted new obstacles. Accelerating international political and naval rivalries had intensified, adding to more emphasis on secrecy in military matters. Britain, long dominant on the seas, had begun to feel pressure from German, French, and Russian naval construction and the contest for overseas markets and colonies. Earlier casual attitudes toward release of official information on naval architecture and equipment had faded, and new laws hindered the release of data. "The Naval Attaché in England since the passage of the 'Secrets Act,' to be of any use to his government beyond that which he can effect by mere clerical labor," Commander William H. Emory wrote in 1892, "must in London and in the provinces cultivate and form his friendships among the shipbuilders and manufacturers to the exclusion of the so-called other classes." [6]

The American intelligence service, itself, contributed to the difficulties. In the summer of 1892, U. S. military attaché Captain Henry D. Borup had purchased secrets of Toulon's fortifications from a traitor in the French Ministry of Marine. When the Frenchman was caught, Borup boasted about his complicity. The U. S. Army recalled Borup, but French suspicion toward all foreign attachés continued. Naval attaché Rodgers denied that the case affected his work, however. "Whatever may be the position of the French government in regard to the Borup incident it seems that its feeling of resentment has been in no way directed toward our naval attaché." Nevertheless Rodgers admitted that he confronted growing obstacles in securing information. [7]

Even private munitions firms grew cool toward American attachés who bought little and demanded much. "I gather generally that all the manufacturers, shipbuilders &c. regard us as people who wish to get much and give no order or return of any kind," Rodgers informed Chadwick in 1892. [8] The attaché requested some blueprints and drawings of new U. S. warships to exchange for information from foreign officials. He wanted hull specifications and machinery dimensions for the battleship *Iowa* and the armored cruiser *Brooklyn*. "In regard to *Brooklyn*'s plans about which we are secretive or mysterious, I may be trusted to use them discreetly and perhaps to advantage—one must occasionally give *something* in order to receive *much*." [9]

Rodgers alienated others by promoting American manufacturers to compete with Europeans. He provided introductions for American steel company representatives, writing Sargent about the arrival of one in Italy. "Any assistance that you can give him will I am sure promote our American interests." Rodgers distributed the addresses of Cramps Shipbuilding Company of Philadelphia, the Winchester Arms Company, and other firms to potential overseas buyers. "I think the Cramps could build you as fine and well equipped a vessel as you could procure anywhere," he informed one foreign naval representative.[10]

Given time, Chadwick promised to iron out some of the problems in both ONI and the attaché system. Unfortunately, he had no opportunity to apply his talents and experience to adjust naval intelligence to changing needs. In June 1893 the department transferred him to head the Bureau of Equipment, appointing in his place Lieutenant Frederic Singer. Singer's selection as chief intelligence officer indicated a departmental demotion of the intelligence organization, since for the past six years a commander had headed the Office. More positively, it also marked the Navy's recognition of Singer's own important contributions to ONI. "You have done so much excellent work in the office," Rodgers wrote in July, "that it is but justice that you should have succeeded Chadwick."[11]

German-born Singer entertained few illusions about restoring ONI to the position of influence it had occupied under Rodgers. A twenty-four-year veteran, he knew the Office relied on sporadic financial handouts from the department to run its daily business and support overseas attachés. Singer was not even surprised when in 1895 Congress voted to cut back on funds for ONI information publications. He believed the growing influence of the Naval War College meant a commensurate decline in war planning and other functions by the intelligence bureau. A loyal officer and efficient bureaucrat, who had seen ONI pass through periods of purpose and reformism and through utter dismay, Singer made the best of his nomination by directing collection of information and keeping ONI ready in the event the department wished to employ its talent in other directions.

The election of the second Cleveland administration added to the bleak picture. The new government provided a stark contrast to the bouyant Harrison years. Cleveland and his secretary of state, Walter Quintin Gresham, pledged to reverse the expansionist policies of their Republican predecessors, and early rejection of the Hawaiian annexation treaty confirmed this promise. Moreover, high tariffs, political radicalism, inflation, labor unrest, and economic dislocation plagued the United States; and concern for the domestic difficulties and anti-imperialist proclamations threatened continued naval construction and modernization. The president's first annual message in December 1893 pointed in that direction. "While I am distinctly in favor of consistently pursuing the policy we have inaugurated of building up a thorough and efficient Navy, I can not refrain from the suggestion that the Congress should carefully take into account the number of unfinished vessels on our hands and the depleted condition of our Treasury in considering the propriety of an appropriation at this time to begin new work." [12]

ONI found one friend in the new administration, however—old ally Hilary Herbert became Cleveland's secretary of the Navy. Herbert renewed his close association with intelligence personnel, traveling to Paris to help Rodgers check on alleged price fixing by an international steel consortium. Trying to play secret agents, the two companions donned disguises and traveled under assumed identities—all to no avail when armor industry detectives saw through their cover and blunted the mission. Back in Washington, Herbert borrowed ideas and information regularly from ONI to aid in his shipbuilding program, which after a hesitant start expanded to approximate that of Secretary Tracy's. Information provided by naval intelligence had a direct bearing on designs for torpdeoboats, electric turrets, rapid-fire guns, and elimination of woodwork on new ships. Herbert's decision to sheath hulls of several gunboats with copper to prevent corrosion undoubtedly received impetus from ONI as well, while Naval Attaché William S. Cowles in London convinced the secretary to adopt the Obry gyroscopic mechanism to keep torpedoes on true course. [13]

Herbert's cultivation of intelligence resources encouraged Singer. So too did addition of promising intelligence officers to his staff. Lieutenants William Wirt Kimball and Edward Buttevant Barry held prior intelligence experience and an interest in applying data to war problems and strategy. Lieutenant Philip V. Lansdale and Ensign Sumner Ely Wetmore Kittelle showed promise. Singer also attached the first Marine Corps officer to ONI, Lieutenant Lincoln Karmany, a small-arms expert. [14]

Slowly, Singer brought the Office back to respectability. His staff rushed technical reports to the receptive Herbert, while the department expected fresh information on rapidly changing naval conditions in the world of the mid-1890s. Indeed, the international environment favored expansion of intelligence operations. European, Asian, and Latin American nations feverishly ordered new warships. Colonial and economic rivalries intensified, forecasting eventual world conflict. Diplomatic relations grew uncertain, and nations cast about for new allies. Navies big and small threatened each other or at times revolted against their own governments.

Everywhere Singer's people looked fresh fields for investigation opened. Between 1893 and 1896 ONI accumulated data on a Brazilian naval revolt, the Sino-Japanese War, and European naval demonstrations in the Caribbean. During the Brazilian insurrection of 1893–94, the U. S. Navy dispatched four new cruisers to Rio de Janeiro harbor, purportedly to protect U. S. shipping. Intelligence officers from the warships poured over the Latin American roadstead, examining anchorages, foreign warships, and coastal fortifications. Naval Cadet Yates Stirling sketched the entire defensive arrangement of the embattled Brazilian capital, while Lieutenant Albert Weston Grant prepared dossiers on local conditions. ONI pioneer C. C. Rogers wrote a monograph for the intelligence office about his observations as intelligence officer on the *Detroit* in Rio de Janeiro harbor during the naval revolt, explaining how one large rebel armorclad kept the mutiny alive for six months against the combined forces of the Brazilian government. His conclusions reinforced themes recently popularized by Mahan that a nation required large warships to maintain control of the seas.[15]

No sooner had ONI completed work on Brazil than conditions in the Far East drew the attention of naval intelligence. On 1 August 1894 Japan and China declared war. The conflict lasted less than nine months and became a lopsided affair as highly disciplined, well-equipped Japanese units smashed poorly armed Chinese and Manchu resistance. However, the war featured several interesting naval encounters, including a sharp exchange off the Yalu River in September between two fleets of modern, European-built, steel warships. The Chinese force contained two battleships, each displacing 1,000 tons more than the biggest U. S. Navy warship, the *Maine*, then undergoing final steam trials. Ultimately, the four-hour battle off the Korean coast ended in mutual withdrawal, although the Chinese fleet suffered serious losses.[16]

The Yalu encounter created a sensation in naval circles, since it was the first battle between fleets of modern warships. The U. S. Navy found it of especial interest both because of the remarkably similar stages of development between Japanese and American fleets and because of the current U. S. government interest in the development of larger battleships. Herbert urged the commander-in-chief of American naval forces in East Asia to gather as much information as possible about Yalu. He instructed intelligence officers to examine battle damage, visit Asian warships, and tour repair yards. "Afford every facility for intelligence officers of our fleet to obtain information which forward as soon as practicable," Herbert cabled.[17]

The U. S. Navy initiated its most comprehensive intelligence exercise in the nineteenth century during the Sino-Japanese War. Lieutenant Commander William M. Folger, Lieutenant Daniel Preston Menefee, and Ensign Chester M. Knepper from the gunboat *Yorktown* examined Port Arthur, the former Chinese naval base now in Japanese hands, and visited numerous Japanese warships. An intelligence team from the *Charleston*, consisting of Commander George W. Coffin and Lieutenants William Porter White, Alexander Sharp, and William S. Sims, gathered volumes of data on Yalu and later about the naval action at Weihaiwei. Sims compiled over 400 pages of notes, sketches, and maps, suffering cramps in the hand so severe that they required medical attention. The pain was worth it, Sims assured his family. "Remember that this is the first time real sure enough modern guns have been in action and the first time modern ships have been under fire, and the effect one would have on the other was a matter of conjecture." [18] At the same instant, former naval attaché Emory took his tiny gunboat *Petrel* to Newchwang where he studied troop movements and prepared charts of Manchuria for naval intelligence. [19]

The Asian war tested the U. S. attaché network as well. The Navy's representatives in Europe watched responses to the war, noting preparations to send naval forces to the Far East. William S. Cowles in London recorded British sympathy for China, and as Japan humbled Britain's lucrative commercial partner, reported ominous rumors of military intervention to save China from collapse. Meanwhile, Rodgers warned the department about Russian ship movements, predicting intervention in the war. In fact, Russia joined France and Germany in diplomatic and naval pressures to force Japanese moderation at peace talks ending the war in April 1895. [20]

The Sino-Japanese War led to the assignment of ONI's first permanent naval attaché to a non-European country. Both Commodore Shufeldt and Ensign Foulk had assumed the title attaché as a temporary expedient and for diplomatic purposes. In January 1895 naval intelligence dispatched Commander Francis Morgan Barber as naval attaché to Tokyo and Peking. A torpedo expert and sometime arms salesman, Barber expected to combine both talents at his new post. However, the Japanese took slight interest in him, refusing to show the attaché anything except a few obsolete boats. Undaunted, the officer told Washington about the immense opportunities in East Asia for American shipbuilders, steel makers, and manufacturers. Neither Japan nor the Navy Department encouraged him to pursue the Asian market, and by December Barber complained about his health and asked to be retired. No replacement would be sent for three years. [21]

Intelligence duty in Singer's office seemed anticlimactic after the Sino-Japanese War terminated in April 1895. This letdown was remarkable in light of sensitive American relations with Spain over Cuba and with Britain in Venezuela. Sporadic reports about Spanish military preparations, troop movements, and deployment of warships in the Caribbean trickled into ONI. One document even alluded to a possible secret Anglo-Spanish combination against the United States. Despite such news, the Spanish question caused only minor concern in ONI in 1895–96.[22]

More important, ONI provided almost no fresh news about the Anglo-Venezuelan border dispute, which threatened to involve U. S. naval forces. Goaded by anti-British propaganda, the Cleveland government entangled itself in the boundary dispute, calling for enforced arbitration to delineate the long-contested territory between British Guiana and Venezuela. By January 1896, heated discussions between the United States and Britain led to a full-blown war scare. The British Admiralty organized a flying squadron of armored cruisers for possible operations in the Caribbean and made other preparations. Apparently ONI knew nothing about British activities, and Naval Attaché Cowles in London consistently assured Washington of Britain's good will, relating how British officers toasted President Cleveland's health at dinner parties.[23]

Despite ONI's seeming unconcern and ignorance of the British threat in 1895–96, others in the Navy were not indifferent to the need for war planning. President of the Naval War College Henry Clay Taylor directed departmental measures. "The secretary is now using me and the college as a general staff," Taylor wrote Luce in January 1896.[24] Indeed, Taylor's people at Newport prepared studies on naval conditions on the Great Lakes, fleet operations near the Florida Keys, defenses on the Atlantic coast, and plans for an attack against Halifax and adjacent Canadian territory. At the same time, the intelligence office served as a mere depository for Taylor's operation. "I have examined with a great deal of pleasure the war chart and defense plan sent to the Intelligence Office," Herbert informed Taylor.[25]

During these early war-planning exercises, neither Taylor nor Herbert employed ONI resources. Both corresponded directly with Commander Gridley on the Great Lakes, whom they ordered to accumulate details for an operation against Canada in the event of an Anglo-American confrontation. Meanwhile, Herbert personally selected intelligence officers Lieutenant Commanders Eugene H. C. Leutze and Uriel Sebree and Ensign William Carey Cole to reconnoiter the Canadian border. None was attached to the intelligence office, and the secretary told them to keep their assignments secret, including presumably from the Navy's own agency. "The political situation might be seriously disturbed should these preliminary preparations become public," he warned.[26]

Neglect of ONI pointed to the larger question of the Office's proper mission in the expanding intelligence environment. Although it had never served as a central planning agency, ONI staffers often suggested that this was one of the Office's functions. While the Naval War College remained weak and threatened in the late eighties and early nineties, it appeared that ONI would become the nucleus for a general staff or office of naval operations. But after Tracy and Herbert secured the college firmly, and Taylor became president, rivalry between ONI and the Newport school developed. Taylor emphasized this growing division in a letter to Luce in December 1895. He sought information from the Japanese naval attaché in Washington, without consulting ONI. "I would write to him myself, but the Intelligence Office is very particular—especially at this time—about anything done by the College that seems to infringe upon its prerogatives, and a letter written through the Intelligence Office might be subject to long delay."[27]

Several years later, Captain Francis William Dickins recommended consolidation of war college and intelligence bureau. He wanted the college brought to Washington and placed under ONI. Defenders of war college autonomy rushed to the institution's defense. Current president Caspar F. Goodrich made an impassioned plea to retain the Naval War College's independence, educational integrity, and location at Newport. Dickins quietly shelved his proposal, but the incident underscored the continuing tensions.[28]

Whatever the evolving definition of ONI's responsibilities, Herbert had provided enough tasks of a clearly defined informational nature. Investigation of steel makers, new ship construction, technological innovations, and foreign conflicts kept the staff fully occupied. In some ways, the anti-imperialist Cleveland administration expanded the intelligence field more abruptly than had the bellicose Harrison regime. Gone were the days when scholarly and scientific experience might be the only training needed for intelligence work. Fading too was the missionary zeal of an intelligence office intent upon promoting and publicizing the needs for naval modernization. What the Navy required now were technicians and strategists of modern naval warfare not essayists. As weapons became more sophisticated and international relations more complex, intelligence officers had to redefine their functions. They needed to apply information to internal questions of preparedness, organization, and tactics, providing data for others to plan overall strategies and policies.

vii

PLANNING FOR WAR

Lieutenant Commander Richard Wainwright inherited the task of molding ONI into an intelligence agency that could adjust to the changing intelligence requirements and needs of a modern navy. However, the erudite officer's experience lay more in the scholarly past than the strategic present. In fact, Wainwright's career paralleled that of the first chief intelligence officers nearly fifteen years before. He had graduated from the Naval Academy in 1868 with ONI pioneers Mason and Rodgers, and had shared the traditional hydrographic, surveying, and informational duties. Like Mason, Wainwright had served a term as secretary of the U. S Naval Institute.[1]

Thus trained in the methods and perceptions of late-nineteenth-century naval intelligence, Wainwright stepped into an office in April 1896 that was grappling with problems of a new era. He found former shipmate W. W. Kimball the senior intelligence officer present and ONI holdovers Barry, Witzel, and Ensign William K. Harrison. By January 1897 the new chief's intelligence team numbered eight, the smallest naval contingent to man the bureau since 1882. Moreover, with the exception of Kimball, the professional staff was not particularly gifted. Few capable officers flocked to Wainwright.[2]

Nevertheless ONI under Wainwright's tutelage became a vital and integral part of the Navy's operational planning group, mainly through the intelligence chief's intimate relationship with Theodore Roosevelt. "While I was Assistant Secretary of the Navy and President, I leaned a little more on you than on anyone else," TR later wrote Wainwright.[3] Roosevelt's greatest interest lay in the sweeping forces of international power, imperial rivalries, and historical processes, and Mahan's application of such forces to the study of sea power particularly fascinated him. Fortunately, Wainwright shared the larger strategic notions and spoke Roosevelt's language. The naval officer expressed his world view in an essay for the Naval Institute. "We must strengthen our trade with Japan, we must seek for a market in all portions of the globe; but above all we must develop our commerce with Mexico, Central and South America," Wainwright wrote.[4]

The chief intelligence officer and the assistant secretary complemented each other and assured growing ONI influence with the most dynamic navalist in the incoming administration of William McKinley. The enthusiastic TR bombarded naval intelligence with requests for information, asking for data on everything from a comparison of monitors and battleships to proposed sites for naval stations. He read intelligence reports by Sims on latest naval gunnery experiments, range finding, and target practice, using the information to promote gunnery reform in the U. S. Navy. Roosevelt funneled ONI reports to Secretary of the Navy John D. Long. In a typical flurry of activity the assistant secretary sent a memorandum to Long that included intelligence on the Dry Tortugas as a desirable naval base site, a complete ONI file on torpedoes, and a naval attaché report on the condition of Spanish warships. [5]

Roosevelt encouraged the intelligence office to compile war plans. War planning was not entirely alien to ONI, but earlier participation had been peripheral. However, Wainwright directed the most comprehensive efforts to sythesize data, suggest operations, and cooperate with the Naval War College made by the Office before creation of a Navy General Board in 1900. Wainwright's office focused most carefully in the months prior to war with Spain on two potential enemies, Japan and Spain.

Warnings about Japanese intentions in Korea, Hawaii, and the Pacific Ocean had reached ONI at least as early as 1893, and during the Sino-Japanese War the following year, American naval observers had commented on Japan's growing power. Complications in Hawaii increased awareness of Japan's naval potential and competitive interest in the islands. In 1897 the War College studied the problem of Japanese demands on the Hawaiian Islands and U. S. efforts to counter them. Since the problem required adequate intelligence, the department dispatched ONI veteran Lieutenant John M. Ellicott on a reconnaissance of Hawaii. Secretary Long ordered the survey of strategic points for use in naval operations. Wainwright employed this and other intelligence material to buttress his article on "Our Naval Power" for the Naval Institute, stressing the vital strategic significance of the Hawaiian Islands for U. S. sea power in the Pacific Ocean. [6]

Wainwright's principal planning effort was directed at possible conflict with Spain. Soon after he entered the Office, the intelligence chief ordered Kimball to cooperate with the Naval War College on a strategic study of a Spanish-American collision. In June, Kimball finished a paper entitled "War with Spain, 1896, General Considerations of the War, the Results desired, and the Consequent Kind of Operations To Be Under-

taken." The Kimball Plan called for a bold U. S. thrust to cripple
Spanish naval and economic resources in the Philippine Islands and at
the same moment obtain control over the Caribbean Sea with superior
naval forces in order to blockade Spanish Cuba. Wainwright distributed
the documents to the chiefs of the Bureaus of Ordnance and Navigation,
the president of the Naval War College, and the commander of the
North Atlantic Squadron. Together they constituted a sort of war board,
reporting directly to Long but probably working more closely with
Roosevelt, who expressed early support for "a cabinet or board of
admiralty."[7]

The two officers most instrumental in giving birth to a mature war
plan against Spain, Wainwright and Kimball, remained with naval
intelligence only a short time after formation of a top-level strategy
board to discuss their proposals. In November 1897 the department
transferred Wainwright to the armored cruiser *Maine,* an ironic assignment since the sinking of that warship several months later mobilized
the Wainwright-Kimball war plan. Kimball left ONI in 1897 to command a flotilla of torpedoboats. TR later recalled his work: "During my
year of service in the department, Kimball was one of the men with
whom I was thrown into intimate contact. He did invaluable work, not
merely with the torpedoboat squadron but in formulating and preparing
plans of action for the war with Spain."[8]

Wainwright made an impact on naval intelligence during his brief
period of leadership. He improved the filing system, consulted freely
with the Naval War College, and issued more frequent pamphlets on
naval information from abroad than any of his predecessors. Yet he
served less than two years and operated with the smallest and least
distinguished staff of any previous chief. Why the Department reduced
the complement from twelve to eight at this critical time remained a
mystery. The neglect was remarkable because Roosevelt showed more
interest in ONI than any other immediate supervisor had shown since
Walker. TR consulted daily with intelligence and forwarded data to the
secretary, interested congressmen, and probably even the press.

Wainwright's close personal collaboration with Roosevelt accounted
for his contribution as an architect of naval intelligence rather than
minor office reform. The two men viewed ONI as part of a grandiose
scheme of naval power and international politics, whereas earlier chiefs
had considered war planning in a cursory fashion, mostly studying
strategies and tactics of foreign navies and wars. It was fitting that
Wainwright should fill the American intelligence bureau with ideas for
military planning on the eve of a U. S. war. After two decades of

watching other people fight, American intelligence officers would finally be tested by their own war.

When Commander Richardson Clover replaced Wainwright in November 1897, however, war still seemed a distant possibility as diplomats on both sides attempted to find some common ground to settle differences. A previous Spanish-American war scare in 1873 had ended in compromise, and the two nations might once again reach reconciliaton short of hostilities. Moreover, the new chief intelligence officer and his staff of five officers worried about Germany not Spain. They examined reports from Naval Attaché Lieutenant Niblack in Berlin which insisted that Germany was the most probable enemy in the near future. Niblack warned of how German imperialists greedily watched unrest in Latin America such as the Cuban revolt in the hope of advancing their aspirations in the Western Hemisphere. "Germany resents the Monroe Doctrine," Niblack concluded.[9] The attaché followed Reichstag debates over fleet laws, and after passage of each appropriation for increase of the German Navy, noted how funds were planned for offensive battleships rather than coast-defense vessels. Clover's staff echoed this view. "The extensive program for the increase of Germany's naval strength is one of the most important steps taken by any of the European countries to augment sea power," veteran staffer William H. Driggs commented in January 1898.[10]

While ONI pondered the possibility of conflict with Germany, President McKinley dispatched the armored warship *Maine* to Havana harbor to protect American interests during disorders in Cuba. Though the U. S. government called it a friendly visit, Captain Charles D. Sigsbee and executive officer Wainwright considered Havana a hostile port and took appropriate precautions. They wished to avoid Schley's blunder in Valparaiso during Chilean tensions of 1891 and refused to grant the crew leave on shore. Despite safeguards, on 15 February a huge explosion rocked the ship, and the *Maine* settled in the harbor mud, taking 260 American lives. Everyone suspected Spanish treachery rather than accidental ignition of the powder magazine. The tragic incident provided a catalyst for the "Yellow Journalism" of William Randolph Hearst and Joseph Pulitzer, unified many Americans behind more belligerent congressional opinion, and gradually pushed the McKinley government into war.[11]

The *Maine* disaster mobilized naval intelligence. Between the sinking in February and declarations of war in April, ONI undertook extensive and secret measures for war preparation against Spain. Once again Roosevelt coordinated activity. In late February he asked naval attachés to evaluate supplies of coal and war materiel available in Europe for U. S. purchase. TR cabled current London attaché John C. Colwell to discover the names of colliers that might be for sale. Several days later, the assistant secretary sent more comprehensive instructions. "What men-of-war and torpedoboats, deep sea class, can be purchased in Europe? Please give a rough estimate of cost and report condition of." Roosevelt asked Colwell to buy fifty Whitehead torpedoes and collect competitive bids from Thornycroft, Yarrow, Thomson, and Laird for construction costs of the powerful new *Albatross*-class torpedoboat destroyers. All transactions must be made through another party, TR warned, so that sales would remain secret.[12]

Initially, Colwell kept pace with the flood of requests. He found several available warships, including two previously ordered by the Brazilian government. He discovered shipowners anxious to unload colliers and merchantmen at a profit to hard-pressed Americans. Top-quality Welsh coal stood ready. "I can send sufficient coal; any quantity any locality," he cabled Roosevelt confidently on 2 March.[13] U. S. Ambassador Henry White praised Colwell. "I am much impressed with Colwell's knowledge of details and capacity for work," White wrote TR. "He seems to have the faculty of attracting information and of being able to discriminate between that which is more or less worthy of credence and that which is not."[14]

Colwell's enthusiasm soon faded when the Admiralty blocked efforts to buy destroyers and private shipyards withdrew offers of foreign warships then in their building ways. Speculators and munitions firms tried to gouge the U. S. attaché, while agents for arms makers blocked his attempts to gain fair prices or demanded exorbitant commissions. Even the Navy Department's own overseas shipbrokers, Charles R. Flint & Company of New York, apparently skimmed illegal profits and lied to Washington about prices. The final demoralization occurred when Secretary Long sent special ship purchasing agent Commander Willard H. Brownson to London. Colwell "is I fear rather hurt at being practically superseded by him," White informed Roosevelt.[15]

Acerbic Colwell's communications became strained. He demanded more money to defeat speculators and authority to hire special agents to negotiate for ships. Alluding to Brownson's mission, Colwell asked to be recalled, since he felt the department had lost confidence in his ability. At this moment, the U. S. embassy in London reported that Colwell had collapsed from nervous exhaustion. Consequently, Long ordered him to Paris for rest and recovery. To fill in temporarily, the department selected the naval attaché in France, Lieutenant William S. Sims.[16]

Brash and enthusiastic, Sims relished the opportunity to prepare the Navy for war. He possessed none of the eccentricities or moralistic reservations of his colleague about dealing with speculators and arms merchants. The Navy needed ships—Sims would buy them. He avoided illegal transactions. When Macora Brothers of Glasgow offered a bribe for him to take their steamships, Sims refused. "I bought seven steamers in England, and lots of other things and could have gotten a commission of $10,000 on each steamer," he boasted.[17] In addition to ships, Sims secured chronometers, torpedo tubes, and rapid-fire guns. He cabled Colwell in Paris for authority to spend more funds, but the senior officer lectured Sims instead about the evils of munitions agents, refusing to extend credit for new acquisitions. Sims rushed a cablegram to friend Roosevelt, complaining of Colwell's "highly discourteous language" and greatly excited state of mind. "He was just as well as I am, and has behaved very badly being just a plain pig," Sims wrote about Colwell in another letter to his family.[18]

At the height of the Colwell-Sims feud, Spain and the United States declared war. Colwell rushed back to Britain, and Sims resumed his duties in France. Crisis tempered the controversy, and though Colwell continued tirades against corrupt speculators, he settled down to buy weapons. The department assigned Lieutenant Arthur Bainbridge Hoff to Colwell's office as an assistant attaché, and this efficient officer monitored the vast amount of paperwork and detail engendered by contracts with suppliers. Together the two Americans purchased hundreds of armor-piercing shells and thousands of rounds of smaller ammunition. Colwell informed Secretary Long that he had accumulated a great store of materiel for the United States at Antwerp, Belgium, including 55 tons purchased from Vickers, Son & Maxim and 235 tons from Armstrong's. Since the British government now restricted sale of most war goods under their Neutrality Proclamation of 23 April, Colwell resolved to ship the câche under the neutral Belgian flag. He used other deceptions as well. One huge crate filled with Hotchkiss guns left Britain for New York as machinery labeled "Marine Espagnol."[19]

In Germany, meanwhile, Niblack procured equipment in the days immediately preceding declarations of war. Using the Emergency Fund passed by Congress, he bought a torpedoboat at Schichau. Designated the *Somers,* the tiny craft sprang a bow leak during passage to Britain for transhipment to the United States and remained in a British port until after the end of Spanish-American hostilities. But the attaché had better success with shipment of Schwartzkopf torpedo compressors, sending them to New York as agricultural pumps.[20]

While overseas ONI agents busily stocked the Navy's arsenal with foreign equipment, in Washington intelligence officers joined Roosevelt to discuss strategic deployment of U. S. forces against Spain. TR required naval intelligence to provide papers on the handling, cruising range, coal endurance, and fire power of all U. S. warships. He wished for comparisons of the sea-keeping qualities of monitors versus armored cruisers and battleships such as the *Oregon*.[21] These preliminary exercises led to more formal integration of ONI into strategy sessions when, on 15 March, Roosevelt asked Clover to join a board "to formulate a plan of campaign." The group included Navigation Chief Arent Schuyler Crowninshield and Chief of the Bureau of Ordnance Charles O'Neil. The first formal meeting occurred sometime in late March, possibly the 23rd, since on that day O'Neil placed an unusually large order for weapons with Clover's office.[22]

The department convened a formal Office of the Naval War Board the first week of April. Clover, Crowninshield, and Captain Albert S. Barker, recently detached from command of the battleship *Oregon* and now on special duty, comprised the original board. The three officers met with the president and his cabinet, pressing for a surprise attack on Spanish forces. Clover also gathered with Army and Navy War Board members, a Cuban revolutionary leader, and Senator Henry Cabot Lodge at TR's Washington residence to talk about acquisition of a naval base in Cuba. After this meeting, members of the Naval War Board visited the White House several more times to discuss war preparations with McKinley.[23]

What information could naval intelligence offer the president and his advisors during the weeks before actual war? Attachés had been watching Spanish activities for some time, and TR made certain the administration learned about every suspicious movement. The assistant secretary told Long about Niblack's report that Italy had sold two armored warships to Spain, both more powerful than the best U. S. cruiser, the *New York*. Meantime, Lieutenant Commander George Leland Dyer, dispatched as the department's first attaché to Madrid in late 1897, forwarded rumors of growing war talk in Spain. "There is much confidence expressed that if the squadrons meet the Spaniards will win the first few fights and that they will destroy our commerce and devastate our coast," Dyer wrote.[24]

Dyer, Sims, and other ONI sources became more agitated. Dyer revealed Spain's "extraordinary precautions" to mask ship movements and acquisition of twenty-one auxiliary cruisers for duty in the Atlantic. The Madrid attaché warned that, contrary to earlier reports, Spanish warships carried enough ammunition to fight a prolonged naval battle. Sims sent concurrent information about Spanish cruiser flotillas headed for the Western Hemisphere to intercept the *Oregon* on its way around Latin America from the Pacific coast. He passed on additional intelligence about Spanish plans to disable U.S. armored warships with secret magnetized automobile torpedoes. Such ominous intelligence, later revealed as an overestimation of Spanish preparations and capabilities, reached the Naval War Board and the president at a most critical phase in deliberations.[25] Undoubtedly, it stirred the perplexed McKinley cabinet to pursue a tougher policy toward Spain. Finally, after increasingly hostile proclamations by president and Congress, Spain declared war on the United States on 24 April. The following day the United States took identical action, going to war for the first time in three decades.

··· VIII

WAR WITH SPAIN

The Spanish-American War gave the U. S. Navy an opportunity to put months of planning into operation. Commodore George Dewey rushed toward Manila with his cruisers, while Rear Admiral William T. Sampson's North Atlantic Squadron moved cautiously toward Cuban waters. The indefatigable Mahan joined oldtimers Crowninshield and Sicard on Secretary Long's Naval War Board. Younger officers coveted sea duty, with applications for reassignment on board ship draining the entire ONI staff. To replace Clover and his team, the department selected retired Captain John Russell Bartlett, most noted for his command of the *Atlanta* during recent scandals over the cruiser's terrible state of disrepair.

Bartlett confronted an awesome task. Cables poured into his cipher room at a maddening pace. Some came from naval attachés and presented information on Spanish movements; others arrived from State Department agents, private sources, and commanding officers. The intelligence chief estimated that during the war he handled 300 cables from attachés and 800 from other sources. At the same time, the Naval War Board hounded ONI for fresh information from abroad and demanded daily intelligence summaries. As Bartlett scrambled to keep pace with critical intelligence communications, the department saddled him with new tasks by placing the Coast Signal Service and Auxiliary Naval Force under ONI supervision.[1]

For all the increased work, Bartlett directed only one other naval officer during the first weeks of war, Retired Ensign Edward E. Hayden. Lieutenant Humes Houston Whittlesey manned the cipher room and decoded messages, but he served as Crowninshield's personal aide and spent more time with the Naval War Board than in assisting the hard-pressed intelligence bureau. In addition, Bartlett borrowed six copyists and a draftsman from Hydrographic and Nautical Almanac Offices.[2] They were not enough. Mahan, Crowninshield, and Sicard agonized about unconfirmed rumors of a Spanish cruiser squadron sent to intercept the *Oregon* off the Brazilian coast and another enemy force under Admiral Manuel de la Camara expected to surprise Dewey in the Philippines. "What we appear to suffer from most," Sicard warned

Long, "seems to be an absence of correct information from abroad."[3]

Partly to remedy lack of intelligence about Spanish intentions, the Naval War Board dispatched two secret agents to Europe. Ensign William H. Buck boarded the yacht *Juno* on 26 April and, posing as a wealthy civilian traveler, cruised the coast of Europe in search of data on the strength, location, and condition of Spanish warships. Belatedly, he located and tailed Camara's squadron through the Mediterranean Sea and the Suez Canal, cabling Washington about the Spaniard's progress. Concurrently, Ensign Henry Heber Ward spied on the Spanish West Indian fleet, fitting out in Cadiz harbor. Ward had been on the ill-fated *Maine* and then assigned as a decoder in the cipher room along with Whittlesey. He longed to avenge the deaths of his shipmates, and as an aide on the war board he learned at once about the poverty of concrete information and volunteered for the dangerous secret mission. Ward's adventures took him to Spain, St. Thomas, and the Madieras. In June he visited Puerto Rico disguised as an English gentleman, only to be seized by Spanish authorities. In collaboration with local British officials, Ward convinced the Spaniards that he was not an American spy, and they released him.[4]

Despite the sensational endeavors of Buck and Ward, naval attachés remained the first line of information. Bartlett communicated the war board's frantic quest for enlightenment to them. The intelligence chief begged his attachés to buy information, insisting that money was of no concern. "The Board thinks that the Attachés at London, Paris, Berlin and in Italy, should be made to understand that there is a considerable sum to the credit of the information department, which can be drawn upon judiciously, say fifty thousand dollars."[5]

Drawing from this "Secret Service Emergency Fund," the naval attachés hired spies and bought information. In France, Sims employed a retired military officer and an impoverished nobleman with intimate contacts in the Spanish government. Niblack's replacement in Berlin, Retired Captain Barber, recruited a former naval officer as his agent in Cairo to watch the Suez Canal and an American fencing champion then in Germany for a dangerous spy mission to Spain. Colwell's British-based web of intrigue was the most extensive. He planted an agent in Madrid on 25 April, paying the operative $2,500 per month. Agents "E" and "F" soon followed, each drawing salaries of $1,500 a month. Agent "G" skulked around the London waterfront for $10 per month to watch the embarkation of cargoes to Spain. At the same time, Agent "K" worked in the Spanish Embassy in London, spying for the U. S. Navy for $200 monthly remuneration. Agent "L" operated in Egypt at a stipend of $1,000, "G" roamed Paris (possibly to keep an eye on Sims) for $1,500, and an Antwerp spy intercepted cables and reported on shipments to Spain from that neutral haven. Though he probably destroyed their records, Colwell undoubtedly employed others, since his wartime expenditures on spies amounted to over $27,000.[6]

What information did these secret agents purchase for the United States? Much was gleaned from newspaper clippings, rumors, and casual conversations. Several operatives apparently provided nothing, charging the department for imaginary spy trips. But since Dyer had left Madrid because of the war, even scraps from Spain proved of some value in studying Spanish internal conditions. The only American to penetrate Spanish territory during the war, Edward Breck, promised to provide better news. Posing as a German doctor on vacation in Spain, this former Heidelberg student and part-time journalist treated his mission as a Victorian adventure, complete with false mustaches, elaborate disguises, and hidden pistols. However, Breck learned little of value for the Navy, and found it impossible to transmit what he did have out of the country. Indeed, in spite of clever cloaks and heavy expenditures, American espionage overseas during the Spanish-American War lacked professionalism. By July, Sicard still considered available intelligence inadequate and told ONI to cable its agents for more details.[7]

If U. S. naval intelligence displayed imperfections, Spain's appeared worse. There was an attempt to form a Spanish spy ring in Canada under former Spanish naval attaché to Washington Lieutenant Ramon de Carranza, and rumors reached the Navy about Spanish agents penetrating departmental offices. The U. S. Secret Service expressed uneasiness at possible espionage operations from just across the border in Montreal and instituted measures of surveillance and detention against a few suspects. ONI took no part in counterespionage activities within the United States, but practiced a form of counterintelligence by leaking false information to Spain. Naval intelligence planted misleading dates among Spanish informers concerning an American invasion of Cuba, and circulated rumors about an armored cruiser force on its way to raid the Spanish coast. This latter deception agitated Madrid and forced recall of Camara's ships from Suez. Later, Mahan assumed credit for initiating these clever ruses, but the entire war board and naval intelligence service participated in the stratagem.[8]

Once bits of news reached ONI, it cabled relevant data to Key West, Florida, whereupon dispatch boats rushed information to Sampson's flagship. Thus the commander-in-chief of American forces in Cuban waters knew about the slow speed of foul-hulled Spanish warships, faulty gunnery on the big cruiser *Pelayo*, the strength of Spanish harbor defenses, locations of cable lines, and any number of other vital details. Bartlett prepared a "Memorandum of Information" for squadron officers, updating data regularly. Though ONI lacked modern radio communications and sophisticated methods, it provided enough information to Sampson and his commanders to indicate the vast superiority of American forces over those of Spain. The U. S. Navy's extreme caution in prolonging the Cuban blockade and delaying an engagement with Spanish warships cannot be explained by lack of intelligence material.[9]

Throughout the fighting, ONI monitored foreign naval opinion. In Britain, Colwell found officials correct in their attitudes toward both belligerents but sensed widespread sympathy for the United States. The Mahan vogue brought on by the recent popularity of his book on sea power still embraced many, while the rhetoric of kinship and cultural affinity permeated naval quarters. British sympathizers slipped the American attaché several useful reports of Spanish activity in the Canary Islands and elsewhere. But the Spanish-American conflict itself made an insignificant impression on British naval doctrine. "As far as I am able to judge, the late war has been without influence of any kind upon the responsible Admiralty officials or upon Commanders-in-Chief," Colwell reported.[10]

The war excited much more interest in Germany. Indeed German Vice-Admiral Otto von Diedrich's meddlesome interference with Dewey's operations in Manila Bay caused friction. Consequently, the Navy Department asked Barber, in Berlin, to ascertain whether the German fleet was readying for war. Though the American attaché discovered no unusual preparations, he warned that Germany coveted a coaling station in the Philippines, territory in the Caroline Islands, and other compensation in return for continued good will toward the United States. Moreover, Barber learned that Teutonic war planners had borrowed the only available map of the Philippines from a local archive. Such intelligence agitated the ever-nervous Naval War Board, which recommended reinforcing Dewey with big-gun monitors and fortifying American positions around Manila.[11]

Fortunately for the outgunned U. S. Navy in Manila, sudden and resounding victory over Spain precluded foreign complications or collision. Termination of fighting also allowed the Navy to discontinue its patchwork spy system. Several agents continued to provide information on Spanish peace plans until late September, but then the department severed connections with all special hirelings. Nevertheless, former spies plagued ONI for several months. Sims's agent in

Spain demanded more money, while a contact in the Canaries tried to blackmail the American officer. Unable to pry money from Sims, the operative challenged him to fight a duel. Sims ignored the offer. Meantime, Colwell's spies haunted him, one demanding thousands of dollars for alleged assistance in uncovering a plot to blow up U.S. warships with magnetic mines. Even Breck caused trouble. The American described his adventures in two lead articles for *Cosmopolitan Magazine*. "I had no idea that so discreet a spy could be so indiscreet afterward as a sensation writer," Barber wrote the department in December 1898.[12]

These melodramas played themselves out in the months after the United States and Spain signed a peace treaty. The aftereffects of America's war with Spain posed other difficult questions for naval intelligence, however. The decision to hold on to the newly acquired empire placed additional burdens on ONI resources. The department requested intelligence on and surveys of the islands of Guam and the Philippines. Military occupation of the latter precipitated almost three years of guerrilla warfare against Filipino nationalist Emilio Aquinaldo and his followers. During this fight, the U.S. Navy pressed coastal, riverine, and landing operations and surveyed sites for proposed naval bases. All required extensive reconnaissance. Former attaché Niblack contributed a study of the island of Luzon, while Lieutenant Charles Hermann Fischer landed on Cebu, dressed in a disguise, to report on local conditions. ONI veteran Lieutenant Ellicott earned a position on the Naval War College staff by collecting information on Manila and Cavite bays as possible sites for a naval base.[13]

The Philippine War tested naval attachés as well. Colwell purchased supplies for American forces, including the Australian refrigeratorship *Culgoa*. More important, U.S. naval agents watched arms shipments from European ports that might be headed for Aquinaldo's forces. This proved a complicated duty, since a number of potential markets for weapons existed, including the Boers in South Africa and Boxers in China. Barber's replacement in Berlin, early ONI staff officer Lieutenant William H. Beehler uncovered a number of clandestine cargoes of guns and ammunition leaving German ports for unknown destinations. For one, the steamer *Emma Luychen* headed from Hamburg to Hong Kong with 30,000 Mausers and a million rounds of ammunition. Beehler cabled his fear that this shipment was destined for Filipino insurgents.[14]

Beehler's cables caused concern in Washington, and the State Department ordered its consuls to watch for the suspicious *Emma Luychen*. Also, ONI instructed Lieutenant Albert L. Key, the attaché in

Tokyo, to investigate the steamer when it reached Hong Kong. Key's agents discovered that the cargo comprised part of a vigorous Chinese arms trade. "They considered it highly improbable that persons intending to smuggle arms and ammunition into the Philippine Islands would go so far out of their way or would voluntarily run the additional risk of first landing them at Hong Kong or Shanghai," Key cabled. Nevertheless, Beehler continued to fret over sinister cargoes.[15]

Current ONI entanglement in the Philippine question failed to stir the early architects of naval intelligence. The past war had brought them nothing but glory and promotion. Chadwick served as Sampson's chief of staff and commanding officer of the flagship *New York*, duty that advanced him five numbers in rank, thus bringing him up much more rapidly for promotion to the next grade. Rodgers jumped ten numbers for his service as the *Iowa's* executive officer during the Santiago battle in July. Commanding the torpedoboat *Winslow* off Cardenas, Bernadou saw the most bitter combat and suffered a severe leg wound, moving up ten numbers in rank. Ward advanced two numbers for his command of the *Wasp* in Cuban waters. Most others saw war duty. Two pioneers of naval intelligence missed the excitement. Buckingham remained on sick leave, and Mason lay dying at his summer estate on the Hudson River.

Gradually the intelligence officers left their wartime billets and rejoined ONI. Clover returned to Washington in October 1898, replacing Bartlett. By January, Driggs, Peters, and Beehler had reoccupied their desks in the intelligence bureau. These officers manned ONI at a most critical stage in its development. The Spanish-American War had pointed to the necessity of improved intelligence throughout the U.S. government, and both State Department and Secret Service showed some movement toward centralizing such operations. ONI, too, recognized the urgency for consolidation and integration more formally into the naval establishment. Return of the Office to the Bureau of Navigation on 5 December 1898 began this process, but ONI still lacked congressional recognition and official position within the Navy Department. It remained in much the same situation and subject to pressures identical to those confronted almost two decades before by the first chief intelligence officers.[16]

In October 1898, influential Chief of the Bureau of Navigation Crowninshield pressed for formal incorporation of ONI. In recommending such legislation, he noted how the Office had been created in 1882 as an informal bureau to meet specific needs for information to modernize an obsolete fleet. "This necessity is, however, permanent," the senior naval officer argued, "and the duties of the office have become so far-reaching and its operations so extensive that it seems proper that the Office should be authorized and organized by law under the Bureau of Navigation of the Navy Department." [17] Outgoing wartime intelligence chief Bartlett and returning head Clover warmly endorsed this proposal. In the first separate report made by a chief intelligence officer in the secretary of the Navy's annual report, Bartlett warned of grave consequences if the Navy failed to imitate other great navies in organizing an updated intelligence service. "All foreign nations keep fully posted as to our ships and fortifications and improvements in the arts of war," he observed. "For this country to fail to make every effort to do the same is an error." [18]

Recommendations for regular establishment of an intelligence office occurred at an opportune moment. Heady over naval triumphs, the nation appeared receptive to any improvements to its Navy. Moreover, careful observers noted how acquisition of Hawaii, Guam, and the Philippines, combined with increased obligations in the Caribbean, gave the United States a far-flung overseas empire to defend against other imperial powers. A strong, informed navy would be necessary to protect this empire. It was probably more postwar euphoria than careful analysis of future international complications that led to congressional approval in February 1899 of an Office of Naval Intelligence and funds to increase publication of ONI's General Information Series from 1,000 to 5,000 copies. The latter change was a welcome one, since the Office wished to issue extra copies of its popular *War Notes*, which included articles by Spanish Rear Admiral Pascual Cervera Y Topete and German naval observers, commenting about the recent Spanish-American naval operations. [19]

The law of 1899 allowed ONI to hire five civilian clerks, one translator, a draftsman, and one laborer. These civil service openings brought the first permanent women employees into the naval intelligence bureau. Wartime volunteer Nanny E. Kuhlman was retained as a translator at a salary of $1,400 per year, and Clover hired another woman in July 1899. "While the preference is for a male appointee, all things considered, knowledge of languages being of paramount importance, and expert work in typewriting of more importance than stenography, I recommend the transfer of Miss Eva A. Marvin from copyist at $900 in the Department of the Interior to clerk at $1,000 in the Office of Naval Intelligence." [20]

With formalization of the Office and acquisition of a permanent civilian staff, Clover turned next to internal improvements. No naval officer was better equipped to undertake administrative and organizational change. His experience included reforms in the Hydrographic Office and duty on both the Pythian Board on Naval Reorganization in 1894 and the Board to Revise Naval Regulations in 1895. Clover created his own board on reorganization in March 1899 to study revision of ONI classification procedures and administrative structure. The board included veteran intelligence officers Driggs and Peters and recent additions Lieutenants Charles C. Marsh and William L. Howard. The Clover Board approved establishment of six branches or divisions, each focusing on specific subject areas and headed by an intelligence officer. Divisions included ordnance, personnel, communications, steam engineering, ship card indexing, and attaché correspondence. In addition, the board suggested a revision of the old coaling and docking manual and the convening of a monthly conference to discuss Office routine and long-range policy.[21]

Rationalization of both office procedure and policy provided a fitting climax to immediate postwar refurbishment of naval intelligence. It gave ONI a frame of reference to complement the forthcoming establishment of a Naval General Board. It pointed to future intelligence needs on the eve of America's entanglement with the politics of empire and international naval competition. At the turn of the century, with the United States maturing as an expansive world power, ONI emerged finally as an accepted and official part of the naval establishment.

ix

POTENTIAL ENEMY GERMANY

Congressional sanction for the Office of Naval Intelligence coincided with perplexing American entanglement in overseas controversies. The United States fought a colonial war against the Filipino nationalists and joined other imperial powers in crushing the Boxer Rebellion in China. On the other side of the world, Americans became entwined in Caribbean politics, remaining alert to foreign interest in Venezuela and on the Isthmus of Panama. Increased activity propelled the nation into the cauldron of international rivalries and power politics. This process did not occur suddenly as a result of the Spanish-American War, but was rooted instead in the industrial, political, and psychological ferment of the post–Civil War generation. The war with Spain, though, provided a catalyst for world involvement by giving the United States an overseas empire and far-flung naval responsibilities.

Acquisition of insular territory placed new burdens on the U. S. Navy. Possessions in the Pacific Ocean required a two-ocean fleet capable of simultaneously defending both coastlines. It accelerated pressure for control of a canal route through Central America. Empire meant overseas bases, coaling stations, and long-range warships. To some naval officers such developments were welcome. Luce, Wainwright, Mahan, and others had long discussed the economic and defensive dimensions of empire and their interrelationship with sea power. For enthusiastic imperialist Captain Charles H. Stockton, president of the Naval War College, expanding into the other ocean for a country tied so long to the Atlantic shoreline was simply a case of national destiny. "The North Pacific is our sphere of influence by divine right," he wrote Luce in 1898.[1]

More mundane but equally ebullient Captain Henry Clay Taylor discovered in the new naval challenge of empire the opportunity to promote a naval general staff. He presented such a proposal to Secretary Long in early 1900. It was a reasonably moderate plan, taking into consideration traditional American suspicion of such seemingly foreign institutions. Taylor assured Long that "in the development of the Intelligence Office and War College the Navy has been unconsciously forming the elements of a General Staff."[2] New naval obligations, though, required a more formal general staff system to coordinate operations and plan policies, and Taylor advocated formation of a permanent board to meet and discuss overall policy, plan for war, and advise the secretary on all naval questions. Board members would include the chief intelligence officer and his first assistant, the chief of the Bureau of Navigation, and the president of the Naval War College. Perhaps recalling his tiff with ONI several years before, Taylor sought to blend the staffs of the intelligence office and college by recommending that half of each spend four months working for the other.

Secretary Long endorsed Taylor's basic formula, with minor modifications, and on 13 March 1900 issued Order No. 544 creating a General Board of the Navy. This pronouncement avoided mention of the odious term general staff and gave the new board purely advisory power. The civilian secretary had authority to disband the General Board at any time. Nevertheless the organization provided a forum to coordinate planning, organize defenses, and study material and strategic needs of the Navy. Moreover, Admiral George Dewey had been appointed to head the board, and no naval officer dared ignore entirely an organization led by the service's most prestigious war hero. Eleven men sat on the first board in 1900, including Dewey, Taylor, Stockton, and the new Chief Intelligence Officer Captain Charles Dwight Sigsbee.[3]

Sigsbee had devoted most of his early career to coastal surveys and hydrographic projects, heading the Hydrographic Office between 1893 and 1897. He had invented a variety of deep-sea sounding instruments and a nonsliding parallel rule for chart work, and had published the results of his work in books and articles. If his career had ended in the early 1890s, Sigsbee would have been remembered as one of the Navy's brilliant scientists who explored the oceans in the latter half of the nineteenth century. But after years of scholarly endeavor, the officer secured command of a major fighting ship in 1897, the new armored cruiser *Maine*. The tragedy of this command, cut short by the *Maine*'s destruction in Havana harbor, haunted Sigsbee the remainder of his life and brought in its wake a series of professional and personal crises including a sordid divorce affair.[4]

The *Maine*'s sinking had the most direct influence on Sigsbee's judgment and outlook as intelligence chief between 1900 and 1903. He believed that somehow the Navy Department should have provided better intelligence about conditions in Cuba. This feeling helped him focus more critically on the inadequacies of ONI and accounted partly for his crusade to improve naval intelligence. His attack on the current state of the Office began with a captious memorandum to the Chief of the Bureau of Navigation a few weeks after Sigsbee became head of intelligence in February 1900. In it he claimed that ONI lay in near shambles. Civilian clerks handled top secret information without taking secrecy oaths, while cabinets containing confidential data lacked locks. Anyone might wander in off the street and through the intelligence office. "I have been informed that a colored man in Klotz's restaurant on the fifth floor makes use of the watercloset of this office," Sigsbee complained to the superintendent of the State, War, and Navy Department building.[5]

Even the intelligence offices' appearance defied logic. Files were disorganized; charts and blueprints stood stacked to the ceiling; reports on ships, armor, and machinery lay loose on tables. One room contained a dangerous tangle of electrical wires and telephone and telegraph instruments, some left over from the recent war. No area had been set aside for confidential campaign work so that ONI might contribute to operational planning envisaged by formation of the General Board. Amid the bedlam sat the staff, idly clipping out articles from newspapers and journals, work that Sigsbee considered inefficient and often unnecessary.[6]

The new chief found fault with other aspects of naval intelligence. Standard forms sent to officers at sea were so outdated that they served merely to request lists of unrelated details, nowhere seeking to answer larger tactical or strategic questions. "It is submitted that the field of observation of Intelligence Officers of ships," Sigsbee advised in 1900, "is at present too restricted to be of adequate service for war operations."[7] At the same time, the officers, themselves, had received little specific intelligence training. Few had attended the Naval War College to study war gaming, strategy, and naval history.

Sigsbee suggested some immediate reforms. He introduced a new section within ONI to evaluate military, economic, and strategic weaknesses or defects in foreign naval powers. Thus, he forced the staff to relate isolated facts to larger questions. At the same instant, Sigsbee urged the Navy Department to revise training procedures for intelligence officers by requiring them to prepare monographs on theoretical naval operations against one of the leading naval rivals and potential enemies. Such writings, he hoped, would focus the attention of future intelligence officers on larger strategic implications rather than on incidents and technical data. "It is desirable for the Office of Naval Intelligence," the intelligence chief suggested, "especially in its relation to the General Board and the War College, that Officers afloat shall take a broader and more interested view of Intelligence work."[8]

A number of officers on the General Board and at the Naval War College shared Sigsbee's concern. For one, Lieutenant Ellicott blended his experience as an intelligence officer and a member of the college staff in an essay for the Naval Institute *Proceedings* in which he synthesized the various arguments calling for reform of intelligence procedure.[9] Finally, in February 1903 the General Board forwarded to Secretary of the Navy William H. Moody a recommendation for overhaul of intelligence methods. The board called for the distribution of new intelligence questionnaires that outlined the type of information required for war planning. Based upon immediate observations in the field, intelligence officers were expected to prepare a preliminary war plan. "Two plans will be submitted, with sketches explaining same, by the commanding officer and the officer making this report, acting as a Board."[10]

Meanwhile Sigsbee undertook additional steps to improve intelligence. He rushed copies of a new pocket-sized Navy Code to attachés and intelligence operatives so that they might abandon the cumbersome multivolume edition compiled during the Walker years. The intelligence chief also provided his personnel with an improved pocket Kodak camera. Both moves streamlined the intelligence kit and allowed more rapid survey of wider areas of naval interest. In another reform, on 1 January 1901, Sigsbee directed naval attachés to number all correspondence, typewrite letters, and separate professional information from general business. Naval attachés were instructed to sign correspondence with designated code letters, including X for London, Y for Paris, Z for Berlin, T for Rome, W for Tokyo, and other letters as additional attachéships developed. Though they were designed for more efficient communications, at least one attaché found the new directions more confusing than the old. Lieutenant Giles B. Harber, the naval attaché to Paris and St. Petersburg, asked Sigsbee to explain what should be included in the cover letter and in the separate intelligence package.[11]

Each of Sigsbee's measures was aimed at merging ONI more smoothly into a war planning triumvirate with the Naval War College and the General Board. From the outset he plunged eagerly into cooperative efforts with the other two and exhibited an unusual willingness to release information quickly to both college and board. To the Newport school he sent material to assist the war college in its war gaming and operational problems, which between 1900 and 1903 included studies of a theoretical Pacific war between the United States and a Russian-British coalition, and a German-American confrontation in the Caribbean over control of a Panama Canal route. At the same moment he contributed papers and memoranda for almost every meeting of the General Board. Indeed Sigsbee and his assistants became the early board's most vocal members. "The representatives of the Office of Naval Intelligence on the Board have been able to make a pretty good showing," he wrote Clover, now naval attaché in London. "I devised a card catalogue system for the records of the Board, and it was promptly adopted." [12]

Foreign naval developments added to Sigsbee's efforts to modernize ONI and attach it closely to the Naval War College and the General Board. During the past decades naval intelligence had responded to specific crises—Canada in 1886, Chile in 1891, Britain in 1896, and Spain in 1897—but now with rapidly changing diplomatic and military conditions, leavened by increased American stakes in two widely separated maritime regions, ONI could not wait for threats from some power or combination of powers to arise before initiating war planning. ONI needed to estimate future confrontations and complications and determine potential enemies. Such procedure became more urgent to Sigsbee as he watched the growing power of the German Empire.

Emergence of Germany as a major naval rival had long fascinated ONI. Naval attachés who had visited Berlin in the past had been impressed with Kaiser William II's support of the German Navy. "I wish he had control of our service for a while," Buckingham had written Walker in 1888. [13] American naval observers continually extolled the efficiency of the German military machine and the utility of the German general staff system. Half-jokingly, one officer sent the intelligence office a portrait of German war planner Helmuth von Moltke to hang in the chief's private study. Inevitably, German-American rivalry surfaced as both nations built larger navies and coveted overseas possessions in the Pacific Ocean and the Caribbean. Near collision in Samoa and later in Manila harbor comprised only the more notable instances of potential conflict.

The German question confronted Sigsbee as soon as he entered ONI. "At present we are rather concerned with the rapid execution of the German Naval Program," he wrote a friend in 1900. [14] Signals that seemed to point to sinister German activities around the world constantly crossed Sigsbee's desk. Former attaché Nathan Sargent, now commanding the gunboat *Scorpion* in the Caribbean, reported spying a German surveying party near Margarita Island off the Venezuelan coast. To Sigsbee this meant that the European power planned to establish an advanced naval base in the area. Meanwhile, information from China indicated Teutonic interest in leaseholds and bases, while that from Africa showed German agents hoarding supplies of coal at every important port. Finally, by late 1901 the chief intelligence officer had learned enough to dispatch a warning to the department. "This Office believes that Germany in the expansion of her commerce and in the corresponding increase of her Navy, hold [sic] this country in view as her most dangerous competitor for future trade and is directing her energies accordingly."[15]

Recent news on German advances in naval technology augmented Sigsbee's impressions. ONI considered German naval architecture so superior that it encouraged the dispatch of Assistant Naval Constructors Guy A. Bisset, John E. Bailey, and Henry M. Gleason to study at the Berlin Technical School of Naval Architecture. At the same time Sigsbee requested assignment of a full-time clerk to assist the naval attaché in Berlin because "naval matters are of the utmost importance in Germany at the present time."[16]

Beehler's reports of his tour of the Germania Works were the most disturbing. The attaché observed a bronze torpedo equipped with the revolutionary Kaselowsky steering gear and a mighty new torpedoboat destroyer. Both made obsolete torpedoboats of the U. S. Navy, recently emphasized in building programs. Beehler also noted that German experiments with wireless telegraphy were far in advance of similar American progress. After studying the intelligence summaries from Berlin, Sigsbee told the secretary of the Navy that "the Germans are considerably ahead of what the Office had any idea could be accomplished by this time."[17]

Sigsbee resolved to publicize the supposed German menace. He rushed Lieutenant Commander Marbury Johnston to Venezuela in 1902 to watch German efforts to collect debts from a delinquent Venezuelan government. The first naval attaché to any Latin American country, Johnston fulfilled expectations by dispatching several reports covering German bombardment of Fort Cabello and San Carlos by the gunboats *Panther* and *Vineta*. Before the American officer could reveal more evidence of German aggressiveness, however, the Venezuelan crisis faded, and the department recalled Johnston.[18]

Publicizing the German threat through ONI literature offered a better chance of success, since Congress had appropriated funds for 5,000 copies of the annual information series. The edition for 1900 abounded with news designed to stir American concern for German naval development. Lieutenant William L. Howard's essays on naval budgets included comparative diagrams showing how Germany's practice of long-range building programs allowed a steady rate of replacement of older ships by modern construction. Another article, by Lieutenant Orlo S. Knepper, explained how the German Navy League promoted construction of warships and popularized the German fleet. Knepper trusted that the forthcoming U. S. Navy League would likewise benefit the American service.[19]

Sigsbee resorted to direct action, as well. He never tired of telling congressmen and other officials about how German naval construction threatened to catapult Germany ahead of the United States for the dubious distinction of fourth-ranking naval power. ONI prepared elaborate charts and tables to prove this contention. "The excess of the list on one side over the list on the other side in any class shows the preponderance of power of Germany over the United States, or the reverse," Sigsbee wrote Senator Eugene Hale of Maine.[20] The intelligence chief conveyed similar information to Congressman George Edmund Foss, acting chairman of the House Committee on Naval Affairs, and telephoned his fears to influential committee member Henry C. Loudenslager of New Jersey. Sigsbee told these legislators that in order for the U. S. Navy to keep pace with Germany during the next five years, Congress would have to authorize construction of twelve battleships, four armored cruisers, eight protected cruisers, two light cruisers, forty-four destroyers, and seventy-nine torpedoboats.[21]

Though the bogey of German navalism provided convenient arguments for increasing the U. S. Navy, Sigsbee considered Teutonic threats very real. His increasingly obsessive fears came out clearly in efforts to curb the movements of foreign naval attachés in the United States. "The Office begs to submit," he informed the department, "that it is unusual and inadmissible for a Naval Attaché to roam the country without the knowledge of the Navy Department as to his precise whereabouts and operations."[22] The escapades of German attaché Lieutenant H. von Rebeur-Paschwitz and British agent Captain Lewis Bayly stimulated Sigsbee's concern. Both slipped away for weeks at a time to sketch American harbors and coastlines. The inability of an ONI secret agent to locate the wandering naval officers added to Sigsbee's chagrin.[23]

The intelligence chief attempted to control foreign naval attachés by establishing a policy for the reciprocal exchange of information with other governments and by convincing his own department to enforce regulations concerning the movement of visiting attachés. Sigsbee failed in both endeavors. Foreign officials claimed the American's reciprocity plan "savored rather too much of a bargain" and "placed a price on information."[24] At the same time, the Navy Department refused to punish violations of General Order No. 22, Revised, which gave ONI control over all communications between foreign visitors and the department. Bureau chiefs and others ignored this restriction and carried on their own direct conversations and correspondence with alien naval agents. "I regret to state that there is very small evidence that the Bureaus are conforming with this requirement of the order," Sigsbee concluded at last.[25]

Frustrations with the attaché problem spread to other aspects of Sigsbee's work in ONI. Particularly annoying was a departmental decision to replace some staff officers with civilian clerks. The chief lectured the department on why it should maintain a full complement of professional naval officers to keep pace with highly technical data. "It is supposed perhaps even in the Navy Department," Sigsbee explained, "that this Office resorts to various secret methods to obtain this work. This is not true. It is by means of exhaustive study of items, both manuscript and printed, the latter from clippings, that this Office keeps its information up to date."[26] Civilian clerks would be unable to separate useless information from vital changes in technology.

Sigsbee's plea fell on deaf ears, and the department sliced his staff from seven to five naval officers. Somehow this tiny organization published one last edition of the ONI General Information Series. The final volume in the twenty-year-old series boasted 500 pages of text and 105 illustrations of warships, ordnance, and armor trials. The encyclopedic collection derived from the labors of just three intelligence officers—Lieutenant Commander John H. Gibbons, and Lieutenants Louis M. Nulton and Charles L. Poor. Remarkably, their work ranked with the best compiled over the last two decades, forecasting as it did the development of the all-big-gun battleship (Dreadnought), the oceangoing submarine, shipboard adoption of wireless telegraphy, and turbine engines.[27]

Though Sigsbee accomplished some reforms and tied ONI smoothly to the General Board and the Naval War College, his leadership of naval intelligence had been filled with disappointments, particularly in reduction of staff. Nor had he stirred the increasingly confident U. S. Navy to see the dangers from potential enemy Germany. Thus in May 1903 Sigsbee headed anxiously for command of the new Caribbean Squadron, leaving behind to his successor Captain Schroeder a tiny, overworked intelligence bureau.

X

POTENTIAL ENEMY JAPAN

As Captain Seaton Schroeder began his second tour in ONI, he realized that the insurgency which he had encountered while serving in Rodger's Office during the 1880s had long since disappeared. Only memories of those exciting formative years remained, and familiar aspects of intelligence duty such as publication of the annual information series, which he had helped found, now faded into the past. Tired and perhaps expecting shore duty to offer a three-year respite, Schroeder planned to adjust quietly to the new Office routine. An immediate threat to ONI's authority, however, quickly revived his earlier activist spirit.

Shortly after he became chief intelligence officer, Schroeder read Captain Goodrich's recommendations that the head of ONI subserve fleet intelligence officers and their assistants, answering "promptly all questions addressed to him by either of them." Perhaps the former Naval War College president was seeking a measure of revenge for the years when he had less influence than the intelligence chief, but whatever the reason Goodrich advocated making Schroeder a glorified clerk who transmitted information upon command. Schroeder resolved to convince the department that ONI must continue as a vital agency, overseeing the flow of all information to the various parts of the Navy.[1]

Fortunately, the aggressive administration of President Theodore Roosevelt afforded ample opportunities for Schroeder to increase ONI's impact. In January 1904 Acting Secretary of the Navy Charles H. Darling sent the intelligence chief a list of potential international trouble spots that the government wished naval intelligence to study. Darling ordered ONI to collect data on strategic zones such as Panama and East Asia, dividing attention about equally on affairs in both the Atlantic and the Pacific oceans. Once naval intelligence accumulated files on these diverse regions of American naval, diplomatic, and economic interest, Darling suggested, the information would be held in ONI for immediate access by war planners.[2]

Thus assured a continuing dominance of naval intelligence, Schroeder's office focused on the task of accumulating data. ONI looked first to the Caribbean where Sigsbee now warned of increased German machinations. Such information became more important as the Roosevelt administration, through a mixture of threat and diplomacy, acquired control of a canal route through Panama. Thus during Schroeder's leadership of the intelligence office, ONI collected files on both the Caribbean and the Pacific Ocean approaches to the proposed Panama Canal, including material on sites for naval bases and local political conditions, and one ponderous file on the feasibility of the Galapagos Islands off the coast of Ecuador for a coaling station.[3]

Despite initial interest in the Caribbean, ONI soon fixed its attention on the far Pacific Ocean and Eastern Asia. Schroeder lacked Sigsbee's anxiety about the German menace and believed surveillance of Japan's rising naval power more important to the U. S. Navy. Indeed, both the Naval War College and the General Board studied sites for an advanced base in China and evaluated possible Japanese threats to American possessions in the Pacific Ocean. Naturally their concern for Asia diverted naval intelligence away from the Western Hemisphere, while rapidly disintegrating Russo-Japanese relations completed ONI's decision under Schroeder to focus on potential enemy Japan.[4]

On 8 February 1904, Naval Attaché Lieutenant Commander C. C. Marsh cabled from Tokyo that war had broken out between Japan and Russia. The prospect of a confrontation between these two naval powers excited Schroeder and his intelligence staff, since both belligerents possessed substantial battle fleets. The combatants promised to test theories on the impact of big guns against heavy armor, the utility of torpedoes against battleships, fleet tactics in actual combat, and many other speculative questions. Though the Sino-Japanese War had provided some evidence of what might be expected from modern naval warfare, and the Spanish-American conflict had added further enlightenment, heavy warships and modern naval ordnance had evolved considerably since these late-nineteenth-century engagements. Furthermore, the lessons that might be derived from a Russo-Japanese War came at a most opportune time for the U. S. Navy, since it currently was considering the adoption of all-big-gun battleships, new regulations for target firing, construction of torpedoboat destroyers, and improvements in fleet tactics. ONI expected the present fight to provide clues to some of these issues.

Shortly after the outbreak of fighting, Schroeder dispatched a number of assistant naval attachés to the war zone, including Lieutenants Irvin van Gorder Gillis, Newton A. McCully, and Lloyd H. Chandler. They proved of little value. The Japanese denied Gillis permission to accompany their forces or to visit naval bases, although they allowed him access to Imperial Headquarters. Chandler cabled ONI in July 1904 about his inability to obtain news. Meantime, McCully made a remarkable thirteen-month sojourn through Eastern Asia, spending much of his time in besieged Port Arthur; but even though he forwarded several reports on damage to Russian warships and other military matters, the bulk of news consisted of details about the people and places he visited. Apparently the Russians suspected American sympathy for Japan and proved uncooperative with the U. S. Navy's representative in Port Arthur. "There the authorities made decided distinctions between attachés of France and Germany and myself, giving them many privileges denied to me, failing to receive me properly or to recognize official calls and treating me with marked suspicion," McCully wrote.[5]

ONI relied on other sources of information. Marsh remained most useful, forwarding official war reports each day from Tokyo and sending relevant newspaper clippings from the local press. In addition the naval attaché prepared monthly surveys on the location of all foreign men-of-war in Asian waters. These data were transmitted to Washington by special cipher telegraph code arranged especially for the purpose.[6] War correspondent James F. Archibald of *Colliers* operated as a Navy informant, and U. S. Ministers Horace N. Allen in Seoul and William W. Rockhill in Peking sent "noise" to the Navy Department. At times the Navy resorted to subterfuge to gain data. When the Russians refused permission for the *Monadnock*'s intelligence officer to visit the damaged cruiser *Askold* undergoing repair in Shanghai, Captain William L. Redles of the U. S. Marine Corps posed as an English draftsman to gain access to important damage information.[7]

Officials in Washington snatched at each shred of news gathered by naval intelligence, and the General Board demanded a copy of every message received from the war zone. At the same time, President Roosevelt inquired regularly about the fighting. A naval and military enthusiast, TR focused naturally on the bitterly contested campaign. Moreover, he wished to learn something about the capabilities of big foreign warships in order to assist in his own recommendations for increase of the U. S. Navy. Roosevelt's primary concern, though, remained the diplomatic implications of the war in terms of the world balance of power and the Open Door to trade and travel in the Far East. He needed complete information to determine the critical moment for American arbitration to prevent a smashing victory by one side or the other which might upset the equilibrium. ONI provided some assistance in this direction by preparing weekly war bulletins for the president. ONI memoranda were introduced to the cabinet meeting every Friday morning during the Russo-Japanese War, while special papers on battleships and other naval matters went directly to Roosevelt. Staff intelligence officer Whittlesey drew a mammoth map of the war zone for TR with little flags that could be moved to show the positions of opposing forces.[8]

Unquestionably ONI contributed to Roosevelt's growing wariness about Japanese intentions and military potential. One naval intelligence document sent to the president dramatized Japanese efficiency in landing thousands of men, horses, and guns in Korea. "It was deliberate but rapid as the situation required and entirely without noise, fuss or confusion. Every man knew exactly what to do and where to go. The behavior of all the Japanese is excellent and they all seem to be stirred by an all powerful sense of loyalty to their nation."[9] Such reports probably reinforced Roosevelt's determination to get the combatants to the peace table before Japan completely humiliated Russia and destroyed any balance of forces in East Asia.

Japanese success, especially on the sea where Japan crushed the Russian Navy, seemed an ominous portent to U. S. naval observers as well. Beehler, one of ONI's most respected analysts, predicted that Japan had become a direct threat to American security. Not only did Germany contest American interests in the Atlantic, "but there is a distinct peril now menacing us" in the Pacific Ocean as well.[10] Chief Intelligence Officer Schroeder agreed. After gleaning information from his intelligence files, he compiled a prize-winning essay on the Russo-Japanese War for the Naval Institute *Proceedings.* In this essay, he marveled at Japan's adoption of the latest naval technology such as the wireless and noted Japanese superiority in tactics, ship handling, gun crews, and fighting spirit. He called Japan a dynamic sea power untrammeled by obsolete material and obsolescent practices, and dedicated to pursuing an offensive naval doctrine. Schroeder warned Americans to watch out for Japan.[11]

Schroeder's forebodings remained fresh as he left ONI in April 1906 to assume command of the battleship *Virginia.* However, as perennial comrade Raymond Rodgers stepped in as his replacement, Japanese-American relations promised no immediate cause for alarm. Japan's building program called for few new warships, and according to Commander Frank Marble, the naval attaché in Tokyo, Japan expressed friendly attitudes toward Americans.[12] But then relatively harmonious relations disintegrated several months later when the San Francisco school board segregated Japanese-Americans in special public schools for Orientals. This affront shocked sensitive Japan, particularly after its mastery in war over a great Occidental power. It also added to underlying Japanese frustration with American mediation ending the recent conflict and with growing United States influence in the Pacific Ocean. All these factors coincided in the autumn of 1906 to create a war scare.[13]

War planners on the General Board and at the Naval War College clamored for information on Japanese warships and resources. ONI forwarded some numerical information and ship specifications but no other data. Intelligence files appeared thin on other aspects of Far Eastern conditions. Consequently, Captain Rodgers, beginning his second term as intelligence chief, sought to remedy this weakness by dispatching a separate naval attaché to China. Formerly the same officer had represented the department in both Peking and Tokyo, but increased work in Japan prevented the periodic trips to the mainland. Moreover, Rodgers sensed that an independent attaché in China might uncover fresh sources of information. "He might well fulfill the duty for which secret agents have been contemplated," the intelligence chief speculated, "and if deemed necessary, later, establish a system of agents in the principal centers."[14]

Rodgers's superiors concurred, and in May 1907 ordered Lieutenant Gillis to China as naval attaché. A murky character with an unusual grasp of Oriental languages, cultures, and intrigues, Gillis prowled China for months, meeting potential informants and probably personal business contacts as well. He spent freely, joined golf clubs, and attended social events, but he forwarded little naval information. Rodgers remained patient, hoping for organization of a clandestine network that would be available in the event of an Asian crisis. The department failed to share the intelligence leader's estimation, however, and recalled Gillis in June 1908.[15]

Meantime, other American naval attachés bombarded ONI with rumors of Japanese war preparations. Reportedly Japan had ordered 100,000 tons of armored craft from European shipyards, including one 21,000-ton dreadnought from Britain. Confronted with these ominous tidings but skeptical that exhausted Japan could negotiate such extensive purchases, Rodgers ordered his team to discover the validity of the myriad rumors. "The Attaché is in the best position to judge the character and quality of the information received by him," the intelligence chief lectured his agents in Europe.[16]

The attachés tried. Lieutenant Commander Howard hired spies in Hamburg, Hannover, Essen, and Berlin to learn about Japanese activities. The effort was wasted, since Howard's detectives merely unearthed rumors about the "Yellow Peril" so assiduously cultivated in Wilhelmine Germany. One story claimed Admiral Togo, victorious hero of the Russo-Japanese War, toured Germany carrying bags of Chinese gold to buy European weapons. From Rome, Commander Bernadou sent equally fantastic news. Dying from complications brought about by his Spanish-American War wounds, Bernadou hoped to contribute one last service to the Navy. He requested $10,000 from Washington to verify all rumors and to locate any Japanese secret agents in Europe. Rodgers demurred. "Under ordinary conditions,—I mean those in which war is not imminent, it would be of course impracticable to place any considerable sum of money at the disposition of the attaché," he cabled the feverish attaché.[17]

Rodgers discovered one refreshing exception in his batch of nervous overseas contacts. Throughout the school board crisis, Commander John Allen Dougherty in Tokyo counseled moderation and informed Washington about peaceful Japanese intentions. Japan was not rushing work on any new naval construction, the attaché insisted, and in fact delayed shipbuilding because of the serious financial and economic difficulties brought about by the late war. Furthermore, illness raged through the Japanese fleet, laying up the entire Kure Squadron and leaving only three ancient cruisers used to train naval cadets at sea.[18]

As Dougherty and Rodgers suspected, Japan avoided confrontation with the United States over the San Francisco school board affair. Nevertheless, even after tensions eased, naval war planners urged Rodgers to prepare a portfolio on the Japanese and to keep updated on conditions in the Pacific Ocean. In response, the officer sent the General Board a list of persons in East Asian ports who might serve as informants and secret agents for the U. S. Navy in the event of a future Asian war.[19]

Expanded research on Japan forced ONI to seek a full-time translator to survey Japanese language material. Rodgers's staff initiated a year-long search for such an expert, shrouding the recruiting effort in extreme secrecy. "To advertise the fact that ONI requires the services of a translator of Japanese is for diplomatic reasons deemed undesirable," a staff intelligence officer observed in late 1908. The Office rejected one highly qualified prospect because he was a Japanese-American. The translator "must be thoroughly American," ONI insisted. Finally naval intelligence hired a missionary's son then studying in Berkeley, California. Even this choice caused misgivings, since the new recruit changed his name from Hilworth T. B. Jones to Tamura Hilworth before assuming his position. The intelligence bureau's desperate need for an expert on the Japanese language, though, forced acceptance of the eccentric Berkeley student.[20]

Survey of the Japanese press and other documents became more crucial in 1908 as an American battleship fleet prepared to make a good-will visit to Japan as part of President Roosevelt's plan to send the warships on a world cruise. TR's demonstration of the Navy's two-ocean capabilities presented Rodgers's people with the mission to determine Japanese attitudes toward the trip. All information indicated Japan's friendly opinion toward the venture. "The young Japanese girls are learning to dance in order to attend the receptions given by our ships," Dougherty assured Rodgers. Such reports calmed Roosevelt, who, after initial confidence about his decision, had suffered reservations concerning the vulnerability of his ponderous "White Fleet."[21]

The world cruise tested other ONI services. Naval intelligence checked rumors that mysterious foreign agents plotted to sabotage the fleet at some Latin American port as it made its way around South America before crossing the Pacific Ocean. During the cruise, ONI cabled the latest data on harbors, coaling and docking, tides, fishing, athletic clubs, and liberty provisions around the globe. The report on Suez proved especially beneficial: it warned that swimming in local waters was "not practiced on account of sharks." More important, ONI coordinated arrangements with Japanese naval officials for ceremonies, anchorage plans, and entertainment when the U. S. battleships arrived in Japan.[22]

Successful completion of the Navy's visit to Japan marked the culmination of almost four years of intensive ONI concentration on Japanese affairs. The intelligence bureau did not ignore completely events in the Atlantic between 1904 and 1908, helping the Naval War College and the General Board to compile War Portfolio No. 1 for operations on the Atlantic side of the continent. However, this work had been of secondary importance to an Office mesmerized by Asian war, crises, and world cruises.

xi

NAVAL INTELLIGENCE IN TRANSITION

Complications and responsibilities requiring a two-ocean navy were unknown during Rodgers's first term as intelligence chief in the 1880s. In those days the Navy was lucky to maintain a dozen sailable ships on scattered stations, never mind support a battle fleet for each ocean. But the Navy in 1906 contrasted sharply with the squadron of 1886, the year the young lieutenant first entered the old ONI building on Pennsylvania Avenue. Even the offices themselves no longer stood in the familiar place, having been moved to the Mills Building Naval Annex in 1903. The overcrowding that forced relocation symbolized naval expansion in all areas. In 1886 the Navy was an insignificant force with its first steel warships yet to be launched. Design, ordnance, and steel came from abroad, since U. S. naval and industrial technology had failed to keep pace with demands of modern ship construction. The use of electricity was in its infancy, steam engines remained ancient compound plants, and guns used low-efficiency, dirty brown powder.

Now, twenty years later, the U. S. Navy had become a great sea power, possessing one of the world's premier battle fleets. Plans were under way to construct 16,000-ton battleships armed with all-big-gun batteries. In the contemporary Navy, electricity powered most machinery, smokeless powder propelled high-explosive shells, and quiet triple and quadruple expansion engines moved warships through the seas. Experiments were well advanced with oil-fuel turbines, wireless telegraphy, and submarines. Moreover, in addition to technological progress, there had been other changes as well. Through the teachings of Luce, Mahan, and others, the Navy had developed strategic concepts and offensive doctrine to govern its expanding power and global activities, and these theories of sea power had accompanied the tremendous American economic and diplomatic intrusions into the world. Also, the United States had accumulated empire, something remote from the eighties. Since Rodgers's first tour , the U. S. Navy had fought and won a war, had developed a mechanism for war planning, and had developed overseas naval stations. One of the gravest problems in the late 1880s had been reform in personnel promotion and advancement.

Proliferation of ships had remedied this partly, while the Naval Personnel Act of 1899 improved the system through amalgamation of engineers and line officers, increased pay scales, and accelerated promotion rates.

The returning intelligence chief found unfamiliar aspects in ONI as well. In 1886 Rodgers had employed an occasional civilian, but now he relied on nine permanent civilians under Chief Clerk Harry W. Smith. ONI still responded directly to the chief of the Bureau of Navigation but carried on the largest amount of business with the General Board and the Naval War College. No board existed in 1886, and the two-year-old college teetered on the brink of collapse. Not tied to these agencies, Rodgers had directed an almost autonomous organization with undefined responsibilities. There had been a sense of freedom from authority, of missionary zeal to stir modernization, but by 1906 zeal and independence had disappeared. Under the present scheme, the Office simply fed data to others who influenced policy.

As Rodgers settled into his routine in the spring of 1906, other novelties came to mind. The Office lacked the gentlemanly comradeship of the nineteenth-century bureau. At the same time, attachés failed to observe the unwritten rules and felicitous quests for information that had characterized such duty earlier. Foreign attachés now in the United States seemed an unrecognizable, greedy mob. Reportedly they stole secrets from U. S. warships, indiscreetly photographed new naval construction, and ignored correct channels of communications. Japanese agents proved most pestiferous, but Peruvians and other Latin American naval representatives followed closely behind. In fact, suspicious activity by Peru's naval mission finally induced the department to advise: "Should the naval attachés or other foreigners desire to see some special feature for which permission has not been given, he shall be courteously refused and referred to the Chief Intelligence Officer."[1]

Rodgers tried to enforce better security measures. He hired Treasury agents to spy on Japanese at the Fore River Shipbuilding plant at Quincy, Massachusetts. ONI employed another secret service operative to tail Kaneko, an engineer seen photographing the coastal defense batteries at Sandy Hook, New Jersey. Fortunately, the department provided more assistance for Rodgers than it had for Sigsbee several years before by enforcing Order No. 22. Moreover, Secretary of the Navy Victor I. Metcalf cabled officers in February 1907 to prohibit all unauthorized visitors on board U. S. warships. Several days later he issued a directive making gunsights and fire control system off limits to all foreign observers.[2]

Concern for secrecy and security permeated other aspects of Rodgers's labors. His office, troubled over the inadequacies of the Navy Code, demanded creation of a "blind" and updated cipher to include new terms. ONI even rejected its old partner the Naval Institute when the Institute inquired about a cooperative effort to publish ship pictures. Rodgers informed Institute Secretary Professor Philip R. Alger in April 1907 that ONI considered such matters confidential. The department restricted release of information to any naval officer without prior consent from the secretary or his assistant. This sweeping prohibition muzzled Rodgers and prevented participation in a then current debate over the dangers of the Navy's gun turret system, which had caused several accidental deaths. The old insurgent Rodgers was thus prevented from assisting a new generation of modernists such as Bradley Fiske, William Sims, and Albert Key in their crusade between 1906 and 1909 to update the Navy's gunnery system, battleship design, and departmental organization.[3]

Thus frustrated, Rodgers turned to other projects. Careful not to violate the secretary's proscription against unauthorized release of information, the intelligence chief discreetly provided information for Key and Roy C. Smith to prepare a study showing how unfavorably the U. S. Navy's advancement rate to command positions compared to that of other services. At the same time, Rodgers flooded the secretary with memoranda on inadequacies in the Navy's system of coaling warships at sea, submarine development, and constructing battleships. While the U. S. focused on 16,000-ton ships, he warned, "all the great naval powers are now engaged in building, or in preparation for building battleships of 18,000 tons and upward."[4]

The aging intelligence chief felt most comfortable in this world of information about new weapons and technology. He appreciated the routine and certainty engendered by collection and distribution of concrete data. Though a modernist in the late nineteenth century, he never adjusted to demands upon ONI during the subsequent era of transition. In many ways, Rodgers stood closer to the tradition and comradeship of his father's old sailing Navy than to the complexity and secrecy surrounding the twentieth-century service. For the better part of twenty-five years he had served with naval intelligence, and the last three had proved the most trying. He welcomed the opportunity in May 1909 to leave the Office early to one of his former intelligence staffers, Charles E. Vreeland, and to begin a tour of European naval yards for the department. Several months later Rodgers returned quietly and assumed the presidency of the Naval War College, far from departmental tensions and frustrations in Washington.

After Rodgers's departure, Vreeland served as chief intelligence officer for the remainder of 1909, and then handed the Office over to Captain Templin M. Potts, one of Mason's original intelligence crew. Potts was no less perplexed than Rodgers by the transformation of ONI. If anything, he confronted more drastic changes in the intelligence service. ONI was yanked out of the Bureau of Navigation and placed under the Office of the Aid for Operations, one of four aids created by incoming Secretary of the Navy George von Lengerke Meyer to advise the civilian head of the department. Even Potts's official title changed; he became director of naval intelligence rather than chief intelligence officer.

Though the cosmetic changes seemed minor in themselves, they symbolized the larger departmental restructuring made by Secretary Meyer between 1909 and 1913. Meyer's aid system and other administrative reforms marked another phase in years of agitation for a more elaborate operational system to coordinate fleet movements, construction of warships, and general policies. To those intelligence officers who had advanced a naval general staff for the past two decades, the aid system almost fulfilled expectations. Few were bothered by the fact that the four aids headed purely advisory bodies created by executive order, similar indeed to ONI itself in 1882. It mattered most that by placing naval intelligence, war college, and General Board under the Office of Aid for Operations, Meyer had at last formalized ONI's place in the planning organization.[5]

On 1 October 1910 Assistant Secretary of the Navy Beekman Winthrop issued a comprehensive directive, explaining how naval intelligence fit into the scheme of reorganization. For Winthrop, ONI existed largely to complement the Naval War College and the General Board in their war planning. When the board designated a country for which a plan of military action was to be formulated, ONI provided information on every aspect of the potential enemy's resources. Once the General Board approved ONI efforts, the Naval War College employed the information to prepare a strategic war plan. The board reviewed the results, forwarding them to the intelligence office, where plans lay in a "War Portfolio" for continual updating.[6]

The department wasted no time in testing this system. Trouble in Central America in 1910 activated a Naval War Plan for Nicaragua. ONI collated reconnaissance reports from the region made by James H. Oliver, Albert P. Niblack, John H. Shipley, and John C. Breckinridge. Commander of the Nicaraguan Expeditionary Force W. W. Kimball coordinated intelligence gathering and applied it to strategic plans. One of ONI's most capable officers and architect of the early war plan against

Spain, Kimball directed such a thorough collection of information that the State Department borrowed it to formulate policy.[7]

The same year, ONI started to gather data for a war plan against Japan, designated War Plan Orange. Measures against Japan marked culmination of years of suspicion and observation by naval intelligence. Some planning had begun at least as early as 1906, but War Plan Orange was a far more formal exercise. During preliminary stages, ONI contributed data on everything from defensibility of the Philippines to the depth of Kelung harbor in Formosa, from climatic conditions in Korea to the length of Pacific shipping lanes, and from specifications of every Japanese warship to lists of potential secret agents in East Asia. When old files appeared inadequate, ONI increased sources of information by sending Ensigns George E. Lake and Frederick F. Rogers and Marine Corps First Lieutenant W. T. Hoadley to Japan, in 1910, as "language attachés."[8]

Completion of the Orange Plan became more urgent in early 1911 when the U. S. Secret Service claimed Japanese officials had opened secret conversation with the chaotic Mexican government designed to secure a naval base in Magdalena Bay, Lower California. Military Intelligence reacted strongly to the report, and Lieutenant Colonel Hunter Liggett asked Potts to discuss joint intelligence operations in Mexico. The director of naval intelligence showed slight enthusiasm for this cooperation, however, and insisted that ONI had no information and no agents that could be of use to the U. S. Army.[9]

Whether as ignorant of Mexican affairs as Potts pretended, naval intelligence did not long remain idle. In March 1911, Lieutenant Commander Samuel Ira Monger Major and Commander Newton McCully of Russo-Japanese War fame made secret reconnaissances of Vera Cruz, Tampico, and the Gulf of Mexico. McCully reported that if necessary the Navy might seize Vera Cruz without trouble. "Under present conditions, and by a sudden attack, the city might be taken by the fleet and landing force of 5,000 men, vessels steaming directly into the harbor and landing men on the waterfront of the city."[10]

Turmoil in Mexico remained the top priority in 1912. ONI delayed reconnaissance of Pacific islands because of concern for intrigues in Mexico. The possibility of U. S. involvement in Mexican affairs led to preparation of a preliminary War Plan for Mexico, discussing steps for commanders to follow in the event of armed intervention. This ONI memorandum focused on a blockade of Lower California and seizure of Mexican shipping on the Pacific Coast and capture of Vera Cruz on the Caribbean side. Such operations would soon be facilitated by the opening of an American-controlled Panama Canal; but while this waterway offered strategic opportunities, it also required increased intelligence to improve security. Consequently, shortly after preparation of its Mexican study, ONI rushed Major Dion Williams on a secret journey through the Caribbean.[11]

Concern for the Caribbean region reminded naval intelligence that while it concentrated on the Japanese and the Pacific Ocean, potential problems remained with Germany in the Atlantic. Lest ONI forget, Assistant Secretary Winthrop instructed Potts to begin preliminary investigation for a strategic exercise against Germany called War Plan Black. War planning against the European power reached back even further than similar steps against Japan, but once again a coherent plan began with Meyer's secretaryship. ONI collected information for War Plan Black in March 1911, including distance charts and sailing routes to Germany and comparative tables of both fleets. However, serious involvement did not occur until June 1912 when the department informed Potts that Orange Plan was finished.[12]

If formal war planning accelerated ONI 's transition into a twentieth-century organization, the foreign policy of William Howard Taft and Secretary of State Philander Knox offered further avenues of adjustment. Between 1910 and 1913 the two leaders vigorously promoted American business overseas. This "Dollar Diplomacy" touched every aspect of government and seeped into Navy Department and intelligence office. Secretary of State Knox employed ONI agents as salesmen for U. S. manufactures. When he learned that no naval attaché roamed the lucrative Latin American market, Knox informed Meyer that President Taft considered such representation vital in America's struggle with British, German, and Japanese merchants in the Western Hemisphere. In response, the Navy Department ordered veteran attaché Niblack to serve in Rio de Janeiro, Buenos Aires, and Santiago. Knox wanted more naval officers in Latin America, but the Navy refused, finding the expense of supporting attachés prohibitive. Undaunted, the dollar diplomatist agreed to pay $250 per quarter for an additional naval attaché for the Far East. In December 1910, ONI shipped Lieutenant Commanders Gillis and Frank B. Upham to Peking to advance American business in the China market.[13]

The attachés found promotion of Dollar Diplomacy a most difficult undertaking. Niblack sold some manufactures. Argentina ordered two battleships, one each at the Fore River Shipbuilding Company and at the New York Shipbuilding Company in Camden, New Jersey. When Chile advertised contracts for battleships, the department rushed three assistant naval attachés to Santiago to aid Niblack in negotiations. Chile purchased British ships, however, despite efforts by Captain Albert Johnson, Lieutenant Commander Robert W. McNeely, and Assistant Naval Constructor James Reed, Jr. to convince the Latin Americans of superior U. S. products. The Navy's promotional endeavors in Santiago led only to two small contracts, one with Electric Boat of New London for submarines and the other with Bethlehem Steel Company for coast-defense batteries. Reed moved on to Montevideo to evaluate Uruguay's interest in buying from U. S. shipmakers, but once again U. S. efforts fell short.[14]

Dollar Diplomacy perplexed the department in Washington as well. Meyer worried about the legality of his attachés selling goods abroad. Traditionally the Navy had permitted naval attachés and other officers to encourage American business interests overseas. Several had served as representatives for private companies. Barber had worked for Schneider-Creusot, Gillis for Electric Boat, John F. Meigs for Bethlehem Steel, and Edward W. Very for Hotchkiss Ordnance. All had either taken leaves of absence or resigned before assuming private jobs. Finally, in April 1911, Meyer asked Attorney General George W. Wickersham's opinion on the propriety of naval officers on active duty representing business. Taft's appointee suggested that it was illegal for any officer to represent a private company, but that the current administration did not advocate such duty. "If the Navy Department, in order to assist in the extension of United States trade and commerce and to carry out the general purposes indicated in the application by the Department of State thinks fit to send an officer of the Navy, skilled in matters of ordnance, to a South American capital, it is entirely competent for the Secretary of the Navy to direct him to be sent . . . ," Wickersham concluded.[15]

The Taft-Knox program presented other complications. Selling war equipment to foreign powers meant that the Navy had to ease restrictions on visits to shipyards, testing grounds, and factories. By 1911 twenty Argentine naval officers served in U. S. battleships as part of the agreement to purchase two in the United States. Meantime, ONI provided guides to show a Chinese commission around naval facilities. During efforts to sell arms to Chile, one group was given free access to U. S. Navy property. Accompanied by a harassed intelligence officer, the Chilean officers toured the Bethlehem Steel plant, Indian Head Proving Ground, U. S. Naval Academy, Newport Training and Torpedo Station, New York Navy Yard, and the battleships *Utah* and *Delaware*.[16]

Potts encouraged easing restrictions. If foreign customers expected to fabricate battleships in this country, he told the aid for operations, then they must examine secret plans and specifications of latest designs. The DNI recommended extending the "greatest latitude" in allowing the Argentine commission to study blueprints of the new *North Dakota*– class dreadnought. Such revelations prompted one U. S. congressman to push harder for a comprehensive national defense secrets act.[17]

ONI participation in Dollar Diplomacy was diminishing in January 1912 when Meyer transferred Potts to become his aid for personnel. Potts's place was taken by another yachtsman and popular club member, Captain Thomas Slidell Rodgers. Raymond Rodgers's younger brother, T. S. Rodgers had never displayed an unusual aptitude for intelligence work. Indeed, Meyer's selection of the jocular bachelor reinforced impressions that certain shore berths were retreats for a favored clique of officers. Moreover, assignment of Potts to yet another shore billet ruined his chances for promotion to rear admiral.[18]

T. S. Rodgers directed naval intelligence during the last months of the Taft administration and the first part of the incoming Woodrow Wilson regime. Though commanding one of the more capable groups of officers to fill ONI, Rodgers provided indifferent leadership. Moreover, the new president and his idealistic Secretary of State William Jennings Bryan pledged to end the odious promotion of the dollar. Wilson's Secretary of the Navy Josephus Daniels warmly endorsed his chief's avowed intention of reversing Taft's foreign policies, and Rodgers expected Daniels to terminate ONI's uncomfortable cooperation with big business. In any case, the intelligence director believed that ONI could do little in the way of furthering American manufactures. The Chilean Navy had purchased some hardware, one operative informed Rodgers in June 1913, "but I do not believe any attaché here could prevail on the Chilean Navy to buy its battleships in America, unless a very great inducement were offered."[19]

Termination of ONI participation in Taft's program exemplified Rodgers's dilemma in running the Office during a transition from Republican to Democrat administration. His people were expected to continue inherited policies of the outgoing regime while awaiting definition of yet unformed programs of the newly elected government. Since 1897, ONI bureaucracy had not been disturbed by changes from one Republican administration to the next. Wilson and his reformist administrators promised more abrupt changes in policy, and some officers worried that the new president might advocate pacifistic doctrine and oppose war planning.

The question of war planning confronted Wilson as soon as he entered office. Another discriminatory act by California legislators, this time one to prevent Japanese ownership of land, precipitated a war scare in 1913.

The Japanese problem once again drew naval intelligence into revision of War Plan Orange. The General Board demanded fresh data on the Caroline and Marshall islands, Guam, and the Philippines as part of logistical and strategic lines of campaign against an "Asian Power." As ONI funneled information to the board, news of war preparations by the Joint Army and Navy Board leaked to the press. Extremely sensitive to what he believed unwarranted militaristic activity, President Wilson ordered the Joint Board to cease all further meetings. Naval war planners continued to meet, but the president's treatment of the joint body curbed enthusiasm for war preparations.[20]

If the government opposed planning for potential conflicts, there was not much for ONI to do except continue its traditional accumulation of information for future reference. Even this limited objective confronted obstacles. Most data entering the Office came from newspapers and other readily accessible publications. Little original material arrived from the naval attachés, long ONI's primary resource. The attachés' effectiveness had long been diminishing with the concurrent increase in secrecy, and naval intelligence had not done anything to adjust to newer conditions. As former attaché Reginald R. Belknap told the Naval War College in 1913: "Regarding the Office of Naval Intelligence as the body responsible for giving us a correct estimate of possible enemies' forces, I think we need some radical changes in equipping our naval attachés as field agents of the Office."[21]

As Belknap suggested, ONI in 1913 had almost abandoned the attaché system as an important source of data. Instead, the intelligence agency dispatched special agents, traveling incognito or working under cover of other assignments. Thus language attachés Lieutenants Jonathan B. Dowell and Arthur L. Bristol prowled Berlin, while Felix X. Gygax and Chester W. Nimitz quietly observed progress on diesel engines for U-boats at Ghent. "We get much information from the officers sent abroad on special missions and we believe that they can get more information if they are not identified with the Naval Attachés," Rodgers argued in 1913.[22]

The decline of naval attaché duty underscored the dilemma of naval intelligence in transition. Though the condition and mission of the Navy had changed, ONI directors held attitudes of officers trained in the immediate post–Civil War era of limited international involvement, free exchange of information, and outdated equipment. To them intelligence still entailed collection and distribution of information to modernize the fleet. In the end, architects of naval intelligence found it difficult to adjust their Office to war planning, secrecy, departmental restructuring, and the demands of a two-ocean navy. The European war of 1914 would soon force the final transition from an information bureau to an agency for spying, domestic surveillance, and international competition.

xii

THE PREPAREDNESS MOVEMENT

Captain James Harrison Oliver assumed charge of a naval intelligence bureau that in January 1914 had fallen to its lowest point of morale and effectiveness since the gloomy years under Davis in the early 1890s. Oliver welcomed the challenge of reviving ONI. In training and temperament he was suited to adjust naval intelligence to current needs and world crisis. A student of higher strategy and international relations, he had attended one of pioneer military philosopher Emory Upton's first courses at the Artillery School at Fort Monroe and later had lectured at three different terms of the Naval War College. He had performed periodic intelligence duty for the department, particularly in preparation of the War Portfolios. Above all, Oliver liked a good scrap. At the turn of the century, he had blistered foes of gunnery reform. "It seems pretty clear to me," he had written a friend, "that the tender juvenals will eventually succeed in lighting a warm little fire under the tough seniors." [1]

Oliver brought like-minded officers to his staff in 1914. He recalled former war college colleague Major John H. Russell from a reconnaissance mission in Mexico and encouraged him to revive earlier attempts to reform ONI, changes that the previous director had blocked. Oliver also enrolled war planning experts Commander Edward McCauley and Lieutenant Commander John P. Jackson. Retired intelligence sage Whittlesey added his advice. "He is a valuable man to have in this office where continuity is important," a fellow officer observed. [2]

Oliver's most significant addition was Lieutenant Commander Dudley Wright Knox, who came to ONI almost by accident, after failing to find shore duty at the Torpedo Station and on the General Board. Suffering from a stomach ailment and considering retirement, Knox accepted his friend William Sims's advice to try the intelligence office. Attachment to ONI permitted the future naval historian to study the war then raging in Europe. "My new job is almost entirely mechanical," he wrote Sims, "but it involves a great deal of reading, both of foreign and domestic papers and is therefore interesting, particularly at this time." [3]

The novelty of intelligence work soon wore off, and office routine bored Knox. He chafed at the inefficiency and waste of energy that characterized duty in ONI. Several months before entering the Office, he had published an article for the Naval Institute *Proceedings* that called for application of the latest Progressive Era concepts of scientific management to the various parts of the U. S. Navy. Now he determined to apply these theories to ONI.[4]

Fortunately for Knox, Oliver shared his precocious subordinate's progressivism and desire for reform. He encouraged the scholarly officer to join Russell in revamping the entire structure and operation of the intelligence office. By early 1915 the two officers had completed reorganization, dividing ONI into major sections, each with a clearly defined subdivision. Section A focused on general administration, B on incoming information, and C on collating and disseminating intelligence. These and subsequent sections "eliminated duplication of work and the enormous waste of labor occasioned by the reading of all papers and periodicals received in the Office by every officer attached thereto," Russell recalled. In addition to internal structure, Knox and Russell suggested reforms to the system of gathering information, preparing plans for closer cooperation with other intelligence agencies. They also outlined a war information service that would employ businessmen, journalists, and other civilians as naval informers.[5]

Knox wished to move beyond ONI in his application of scientific management to the Navy Department but confronted obstacles. Nothing had ever equaled the present low ebb of the Navy, he complained to Sims. "Utter disorganization, incomprehensible inertia and inefficiency, and rank insubordination and disloyalty permeates the place."[6] Knox and other disheartened activist officers blamed most of the departmental problems on the new Secretary of the Navy Daniels, a North Carolina newspaper editor and virtual unknown. When former intelligence officer Southerland received orders from Daniels to relocate ships of his Pacific Fleet, he responded: "Who is this Daniels giving me orders? I never heard of him."[7]

Soon Daniels's unpopular decisions made every officer in the Navy cogently aware of the tough, plain-speaking Democrat. The secretary pushed improvements in the status of seamen, sent enlisted men and civilian department heads to the Naval Academy, abolished liquor in the officers' shipboard mess, and worked against creation of a naval general staff. The latter issue, which Daniels branded a "plan to Prussianize the American Navy," caused the most animosity and split the service into two competing factions. One group, headed by Aid for Operations Bradley A. Fiske, pressed the secretary to initiate a professional staff to prepare the Navy thoroughly for war emergencies; the other, led by Chief of the Bureau of Navigation Victor Blue, backed Daniels.[8]

A departmental power struggle began almost as soon as Daniels entered office in March 1913. He rejected General Board advice and suggestions by Fiske to pull warships away from Mexican waters and concentrate them in the Atlantic Ocean. The following month, during growing tensions with Japan, Daniels's differences with Fiske and other preparedness advocates grew more pronounced. The rugged newspaperman stubbornly resisted Fiske's entreaties to create a general staff, relocate warships in Manila harbor to protect the Philippines, and take other war measures. The outbreak of the European war in August 1914 intensified departmental schisms. Fiske and his cohorts abhorred the lack of war readiness on the part of the United States. They believed the administration unconcerned about potential threats to American security from Germany and worried that the aging Admiral Dewey no longer provided leadership on the General Board. They became desperate, plotting almost conspiratorially to establish a naval general staff system.[9]

In January 1915 Fiske interested former naval officer and Spanish-American War hero Richmond P. Hobson, now a congressman, in the general staff scheme. As a result, Fiske and six naval officers met secretly with Hobson on the night of 3 January 1915 to discuss legislation for the Navy. The group who gathered in Hobson's drawing room included DNI Oliver and his first assistant Knox. The meeting led ultimately to the passage, in March, of a law to create the Office of the Chief of Naval Operations. The new office was not exactly what Fiske, Oliver, Knox, and the others had in mind, since Daniels cut fifteen assistants out of the package before supporting it. Moreover the secretary selected as his first CNO Captain William Shepard Benson, the patient unassuming commandant of the Philadelphia Navy Yard, not Fiske or some other activist. He selected Benson, Daniels claimed, because of his "freedom from belief in bureaucracy and one-man control."[10]

In some ways the Fiske-Daniels controversy symbolized the larger division between the Wilson government and advocates of military preparedness who bombarded the nation with urgent calls for national defense after Europe exploded into war. Wilson and his peaceful Secretary of State Bryan insisted that the United States remain strictly neutral, avoid belligerent actions, and stay out of the controversy. The president hoped to devote the full energies of his administration to finishing the many domestic reforms spawned by the Progressive Era.

War preparations detracted funds and attention from this primary mission. Ironically, the same Progressive impulses stimulated demands for improvements in the efficiency and war capabilities of the outdated American military establishment.

Progressivism, diverse political forces, and security motives bred accusations that Wilson gravely endangered the country by neglecting the military. If he continued this current policy, critics contended, the United States would be unable to resist German, British, Japanese, or any other encroachment in the Western Hemisphere and would be helpless to protect American neutral rights. This preparedness movement drew a variety of advocates, including former president Roosevelt, Army General Leonard Wood, publisher William Conant Church, and members of assorted national security leagues and clubs. Wilson's own administration featured several concerned proponents of war planning in presidential advisor Edward House, Secretary of War Lindley Garrison, and Assistant Secretaries of War and Navy Henry S. Breckinridge and Franklin Delano Roosevelt.[11]

Oliver shared the deep forebodings of the most vocal preparedness spokesmen. He explained his growing uneasiness with the lack of naval readiness in February 1914, warning that the United States must show "that the ways of peace may be made the very ways of war, thereby never having to rely upon hasty improvisation and having to steer uncharted courses."[12] Several months later Oliver studied an article written by Sims that called for constant vigilance by United States naval forces in order to repulse surprise attacks. "What you are driving at is the thing, to be always and normally ready for anything, normal or abnormal," he told Sims.[13]

Service in ONI only increased Oliver's anxiety. Every day bits of information arrived at his desk forecasting increased dangers to American security in both oceans. He received numerous signals of Japanese threats to the Western Hemisphere, including news of cruisers taking photographs and landing reconnaissance parties in Lower California, rumors of nearly 3,000 Japanese infiltrating Mexico, and a report of the planting of an Asian colony deep in Guatemala. Another intelligence document noted how Japanese agents had acquired all the latest Coast and Geodetic Survey Charts of American harbors, bays, and rivers. Meanwhile ONI heard that the British government planned to sell Japan some super-dreadnoughts in return for assistance against Germany. To the intelligence staff this meant that Japan would now be free to venture against the Philippines, Hawaii, and Lower California without British opposition. Russell concluded simply that Japan would switch sides in the war anyway and join Germany in a coalition against Britain and the United States.[14]

While ONI watched Japan, disturbing intelligence also arrived about German threats to the United States. Reportedly hundreds of Teutonic agents roamed through Latin America, establishing wireless stations, building secret docking facilities for warships and submarines, and mixing in local politics. Naval intelligence investigated many of these allegations but failed to uncover unusual activity. Nevertheless new rumors of a secret German U-boat base on the Yucatan Peninsula revived the intelligence bureau's disquietude. Once again Russell summarized ONI's estimation of the situation. "It has been stated that only the outbreak of war prevented the culmination of the above desires of Germany in defiance of the Monroe Doctrine and that after the European war she will again attempt to establish her supremacy in the Caribbean."[15]

German penetration of the Western Hemisphere did not stop in Latin America and the Caribbean. ONI learned from State Department and other intelligence services about the attempts by German and Austrian officials and agents to sabotage Allied interests in the United States. The machinations of German naval attaché Lieutenant Karl Boy-Ed were of special interest. For its part, ONI collected its own files on German espionage, beginning with a report made by Captain Ridley McLean in 1907 on his observation of alien spies from the *Bremen*, then visiting the United States. At the same time, naval intelligence compiled dossiers on supposed German agents working as cooks at the Indian Head Naval Proving Grounds, the U. S. Navy Aeronautical Base at Pensacola, and American naval facilities in the Panama Canal Zone.[16]

Thus filled with accounts of spies, sinister activities, and dangers to the Navy by potential enemy agents, Oliver agonized over departmental indifference. Secretary Daniels seemed totally unaware of threats to the United States. When the Japanese armored cruiser *Asama* ran aground mysteriously in Turtle Bay, Lower California, Daniels never raised a question about the strange presence of this warship in neighboring waters. To Oliver and other preparedness advocates in the Navy, this response proved their civilian leader's lack of awareness of international naval questions.[17]

Daniels was neither as naive nor as ignorant of naval matters as his critics suspected. In reality he wished to keep advised of overseas developments, whether news of a Japanese cruiser in Mexican waters or European warfare. The secretary understood far better than Oliver and his other detractors that complex political and diplomatic conditions required discretion in the collection of information. Thus on the day Germany declared war on France and invaded Belgium in August of 1914, Daniels quietly directed American naval attachés to apply for service as neutral observers on board belligerent warships. As the fighting progressed, he dispatched a host of assistant naval attachés to Europe. Indeed it was the militant Counselor of the State Department Robert Lansing not cautious Daniels who vetoed in August ONI's plans to send Lieutenant Colonel Thomas C. Treadwell to the Dardanelles to observe the Gallipoli campaign. The State Department, not the Navy Department, forbade applications by naval officers to board belligerent warships. "This Government does not feel justified in insisting further upon permission being given to American Naval Attachés to accompany British fleet," Secretary of State Bryan proclaimed.[18]

Daniels permitted ONI to expand its overseas operations during the first months of the European war of 1914. The secretary informed the State Department that the Navy supported five assistant attachés in London alone, including Naval Constructor Lewis B. McBride, Lieutenant John H. Towers, Lieutenant junior grade Dallas C. Laizure, and Lieutenant Colonels Rufus H. Lane and Thomas Treadwell. Lane, Treadwell, and McBride gathered notes on British mobilization, compiling ONI files on manpower, economic resources, and ships. McBride and Captain Powers Symington, the naval attaché in London, regularly boarded anchored British men-of-war and discussed the war with their officers.[19]

The Navy Department became most anxious to learn about the British Admiralty's wartime employment of the wireless. In response, ONI dispatched Lieutenant Stanford Caldwell Hooper on a special mission to study this question in 1914. As fleet radio officer in the North Atlantic the previous year, Hooper had recommended encoding wireless messages during exercises because the German-owned station at Sayville, Long Island, monitored American war games and manuevers off Block Island. His observations had resulted in preliminary investigation by U. S. naval attachés of foreign practices with the wireless. From London, Symington had reported that the British used four different wavelengths, each with its own code. Naturally, ONI turned to Britain for the latest techniques, sending Hooper to London in 1914. The knowledge acquired laid the groundwork for the U. S. Naval Radio Service.[20]

The French Navy proved less cooperative with ONI. The U. S. Navy attached Major Henry L. Roosevelt and four other officers as assistant naval attachés in Paris, but French officials blocked them from visiting any warships or naval installations. Instead the Americans toured the Western Front. Navy Surgeon A. M. Fauntleroy, Marine Corps First Lieutenant Bernard L. Smith, and others viewed the maze of trenches and bunkers. "The permission they have received from the French Government to visit the front is more general in character and allows them more personal liberty while there than has yet been accorded to any foreign military or naval officer," the naval attaché Commander William Randall Sayles wired Oliver from Paris.[21]

At first the Germans allowed American naval officers to observe their operations. Commanders Walter Gherardi and Reginald Belknap, Lieutenants junior grade Victor D. Herbster and Edward C. Blakeslee, and Surgeon Karl Ohnesorg received permission to inspect German positions in the combat zone. Gherardi, the naval attaché in Berlin, wandered along the trenches and artillery emplacements for five days, accumulating information for ONI. Meanwhile, Herbster gathered data on German aeronautics, slipping quietly down to Vienna to examine a new biplane at the *Flugzeugfabrik Aviatik*. However, this field closed gradually as German-American relations deteriorated during the spring of 1915 following the sinking of the luxury liner *Lusitania* by a German U-boat.[22]

Destruction of the *Lusitania* off the Irish coast in May 1915, with the loss of 128 American lives, comprised only one step in growing tensions between Germany and the United States, but the act provided enough impetus for President Wilson to accept the principles of the preparedness movement. After the incident, Wilson replaced pacifistic Secretary of State Bryan with anti-German Robert Lansing and pursued a more uncompromising policy toward German submarine warfare. Though he consistently resisted pressure to abandon neutrality and join the Allies, in May of 1915 the president gave in to demands for war readiness.

Secretary Daniels adopted Wilson's conversion enthusiastically, despite earlier inclinations toward his close friend Bryan's antiwar philosophy. His department adjusted quickly to the new Wilson. Less than a week after the *Lusitania* sinking, the General Board and the Naval War College rushed completion of a general mobilization plan for war in the Atlantic, including inspection of a number of merchantmen for possible use as auxiliary warships. Departmental war planners also ordered ONI to: "arrange for securing information from abroad as to the strength and movements of enemy's forces. Plan for and prepare now a complete system of secret service, and cipher codes to be used."[23]

Oliver hardly required such encouragement. He welcomed the long-awaited opportunity to complete ONI mobilization plans openly.

Expanding the outline compiled earlier by Knox and Russell, Oliver developed arrangements for an "Information Service in the Naval Defense Districts," which the General Board reviewed and approved in October 1915. Essentially this plan centered on a district information officer called at various times either an aide or an aid for information. After brief training in Washington, the aid would enter his district and with the assistance of the U. S. Secret Service organize an intelligence service, circulating data through the office of the district commandant. The aid for information's primary obligation to ONI was the construction of a secret war portfolio that detailed the district information network of local informants.[24]

In addition to establishment of a system for domestic intelligence, ONI rationalized its overseas organization during 1915 and early 1916. For years naval intelligence had been identifying potential sources of information in foreign lands. In fact ONI already had employed several such secret agents. One, in Fort de France, Martinique, had served naval intelligence in the late 1890s, while another, in Costa Rica, had transmitted secret messages for ONI operatives in Colombia. Oliver hired others. He employed "an information gatherer in South America for the purpose of collecting data of interest and value to this department," paying the informer $50 per month. Designated Agent No. 62, the ONI operative was instructed to provide information on political developments, public opinion, financial conditions, military preparations, and the movement of alien warships in South American waters. Oliver warned No. 62 to observe Japanese and German visitors closely and to communicate with Washington only through the State Department's diplomatic pouch.[25]

Similar directions went to other ONI hirelings. "Your mission is first: To investigate the political situation in Brazil with reference to German colonization and activities," naval intelligence instructed its man in Brazil. The Office required this agent to watch ship movements, visit with officers and passengers, and become acquainted with influential persons. ONI cautioned; "Give your confidence to no one. Acknowledge no connection with ONI to anyone. Make reports only to the persons or addresses specified. Always have in mind that your actions are being observed."[26]

Oliver considered contacts with business firms more important than the individual agents. "It is . . . desirable that, when possible, the foreign plants and agencies of American commercial companies be utilized to further the general plans of this office for the collection of information from abroad," Oliver advised the department.[27] ONI files contained the names of numerous large international concerns that had agreed to collect data for the U. S. Navy. The list included Welles Fargo, Standard Oil, American Tobacco, Pacific Mail Steamship, and the American Trading Companies. In addition, United Fruit, Mc-Connell Fruit and Steamship, Bethlehem Steel, Red D Line, Atlantic Mutual Insurance, Ward Line, Mexican Petroleum, and Vacuum Oil offered their vast communications resources to ONI.[28]

Vacuum Oil, with agents in 260 ports, seemed the perfect vehicle for ONI, since the firm's network was strongest in the strategic South American and Asian regions, and the company agreed to instruct its representatives to cable confidential information regarding ship movements to ONI. Gradually naval intelligence placed its confidence in the big company, extending secret lines of communication and codes to top executives. But then the Office discovered that the oil business had abused its confidential privileges for personal profit. In fact the Vacuum Oil people traded freely with Germany even after American entry into the world war. Fortunately, the others proved more reliable both before and during the war.[29]

Supporting espionage at home and abroad, Oliver realized, required more money. In November he sent a memorandum to Benson explaining the costs of hiring informants and spies. "A person so employed must be well paid for his time and for such risks as are necessary," the DNI observed in 1916. Oliver requested authority to determine how best to spend secret information funds. Secretary Daniels agreed with his intelligence chief that monies must be made available for clandestine operations, but insisted that all funds must be cleared personally either by his office or by Chief of Naval Operations Benson. Such restrictions, Daniels insisted, resulted not from lack of confidence in Oliver but from the desire to coordinate overall intelligence policy.[30]

Despite Daniels's assurance, the intelligence director penciled a vigorous protest to the original memorandum. Oliver resented the secretary's assumption that he lacked sufficient information to make independent decisions on the disbursement of intelligence funds. The directive paralyzed plans for intelligence gathering. "If the Director of Naval Intelligence has not sufficient knowledge of the Department's policy to enable him to utilize the information fund intelligently," Oliver noted sarcastically, "it seems highly improbable that he would be permitted to select the strategic points for placing agents."[31]

Oliver's frustrations increased when he learned that Assistant Secretary of the Navy Roosevelt dabbled in naval intelligence work. In January 1916 the DNI complained that the assistant secretary was attempting to usurp control over such work from ONI. Oliver accused Louis M. Howe, Roosevelt's private secretary, of organizing his own secret information bureau. The intelligence director asked Benson whether the CNO had decided which office held responsibility for coordination of intelligence activities within the Navy Department.[32]

Apparently such controversy had a debilitating affect on ONI in 1916, since during the tiff with Howe, staff officer Knox told Sims that he had "been trying to build a fire under ONI but so far found it incombustible!"[33] Moreover, in preparing a war slate that same month, Oliver predicted that he could run the Office with a few retired naval veterans and volunteers as Bartlett had during the Spanish-American War. "Not many officers would be needed for such duty," he told the Bureau of Navigation in February 1916.[34]

Departmental treatment of ONI during 1916 reflected the larger dilemma of an administration caught between neutrality and preparedness. The secretary confronted tremendous pressures to pursue one course or the other from both within and outside the department. His own proclivities and those of the president prevented precipitate actions or proclamations that might be interpreted as unneutral or warlike. Moreover, Daniels feared creation of either a general staff or an intelligence elite that might bypass civilian control.

The *Lusitania* torpedoeing and steps to arm the United States gradually eroded the government's cautious approach, and Germany's decision to resume unannounced sinkings of all shipping in January 1917 forced Wilson to break diplomatic relations. In March, British naval intelligence conveniently leaked to Washington the contents of the Zimmermann Telegram, which revealed German plots to involve Mexico and Japan in war against the United States. Disintegrating conditions forced the haggard president to appear more often in the offices of the Navy Department to discuss personally the arming of merchantmen, employment of armed guards on ships, and other details to curb the submarine dangers. After receiving a report on the sinking of three American vessels on 19 March 1917, Wilson called on Daniels to discuss methods of protecting U. S. vessels. In turn the secretary at last looked to Oliver and ONI to discover solutions to this problem. Finally declaration of war against Germany on 7 April ended the agony of neutrality, and at the same time brought new opportunities and dilemmas for naval intelligence.[35]

AN INTELLIGENCE ELITE

Oliver's three-year tour as intelligence director ended a few days before the United States entered the European war. As his replacement, the department selected Captain Roger Welles, commandant of the Naval Training Station at Newport. Daniels favored Welles not only because he was a more pliable and obedient subordinate than Oliver but also because he brought fresh enthusiasm to intelligence work. Indeed, such duty had always appealed to Welles. Five years before he had applied unsuccessfully for a naval attachéship and earlier still had gathered information for the Navy in the North Pacific, compiling a most detailed journal of Alaskan resources. In 1892 he had undertaken a special mission to Venezuela for the department in conjunction with the World's Columbian Exposition, trudging through the uncharted Orinoco River region collecting rare monkeys, parrots, and other creatures for display back in the United States.[1]

Welles's Venezuelan jaunt in the 1890s was more than a zoological adventure, however. While in that country he became an intimate friend of U. S. Minister William Lindsay Scruggs, an aristocratic former Atlanta newspaper editor and later notorious promoter of Venezuelan interests in the United States. Scruggs introduced the impressionable officer to wealthy families and the intrigues that characterized this unstable South American land. In the process of collecting specimens for the Navy Department, Welles managed to advise Scruggs of the location of rich mineral deposits in the Orinoco basin. Although return to the United States prevented his further entanglement in the mysterious doings that later forced the government to recall Scruggs, the excitement of this swashbuckling life with the local elite remained with Welles the rest of his career.[2]

In 1917 Welles confidently tackled his new job as intelligence director. He compared himself to Sir William Reginald Hall, the brilliant director of the Intelligence Division in the British Admiralty, who had leaked the infamous Zimmermann Telegram to the Wilson government in March. Welles bragged that soon he would rival the British DID, claiming his ONI team already had developed a "Box Code" more foolproof than those formulated by Hall's people. "I am personally satisfied that our codes are much better than the English codes, and if even one should fall in the hands of the enemy, —which I cannot conceive of, as they are not on board any ships, —I do not believe they could be worked out," Welles bragged. This boast came at a time when Hall's cryptographers solved codes more challenging than those in the U. S. Navy.[3]

The burdens and complexities of wartime intelligence duty soon drained Welles's early enthusiasm. War-induced patriotic hysteria, fear of aliens, and an atmosphere of repression and suspicion which settled over the United States during 1917 filtered down into the Navy Department. Public-spirited informers found enemy aliens and evil spies everywhere. ONI had to investigate each allegation that Teutonic agents or sympathizers were in the sevice. Welles's own office was touched by the security panic when rumors arrived that the German-born wife of one of his most trusted attachés had leaked confidential information to the enemy.[4]

Welles confronted an unprecedented mass of information and directed an unexpected number of operatives both at home and abroad. War mobilization plans and organizational schemes terribly underestimated actual requirements. Oliver's suggestion that a few volunteers and retired officers might run the intelligence office proved illusory. By September 1917 Welles employed seventy people on his Washington staff and hundreds more in the naval districts, but even this expansion of personnel failed to keep pace with increasing demands for intelligence. Already suffering from poor health, which had forced him to take sick leave in 1916, Welles showed signs of strain. He became overtired and irascible. "You can well understand that the organizing of an Office of this size has been a great drudgery," the director observed gloomily in the winter of 1917.[5] Welles's exhausted physical state was given as the reason why the department passed over the intelligence director for promotion to rear admiral in 1917.[6] Surprisingly, the Navy considered his health adequate for him to continue organization of the vital intelligence operations.

The many urgent and unfamiliar assignments for ONI left no time for Welles to recover either health or optimism. The department ordered naval intelligence to protect the Navy's property and secure private factories and shipyards having contracts with the Navy. It also expected Welles to develop details on radio, mail, and cable censorship, passport control, search of merchantmen, and surveillance of aliens. ONI needed to develop policies to collaborate with other branches of the government and with the intelligence networks of the Allied powers. At the same time, traditional naval intelligence services took on novel dimensions. Acting Chief of Naval Operations Volney O. Chase ordered ONI to accelerate the collection and distribution of information to bureaus, stations, district commandants, and naval forces at sea.[7]

Confronted by a multiplicity of tasks and growing concern for security, Welles searched desperately for loyal and reliable assistants to help him organize and carry out his intelligence missions. Fortunately, perennial intelligence staffer Whittlesey agreed to return for one last tour in ONI despite failing eyesight and other ills. The fifty-six-year-old retired lieutenant commander had served in the intelligence office almost continually for various periods during the past twenty years. He had manned the cipher room in April 1898 when Dewey's fateful messages had arrived from the Asiatic Station, and he had offered advice to nearly every intelligence leader since the Spanish-American War. Now, in April 1917, Whittlesey assumed charge of collating and distributing information collected by armed guards on U. S. merchantmen, naval attachés, and other sources. "My idea is to have the reports mimeographed, 200 copies, exactly as they come to us and a copy marked confidential sent every ship big or little for use of commissioned officers," Whittlesey wrote his old friend Admiral Sims, then in London.[8]

Whittlesey's collating section expanded throughout the war. Staff issued biweekly memoranda that summarized the naval situation based on reports from both American and Allied intelligence. They prepared weekly reviews of the enemy press, lists of merchant ships sunk by enemy submarines, and summaries of reports for naval attachés. Concurrently, the section contributed monthly analyses of submarine locations, charted by Colonel Charles C. Carpenter of the Marine Corps. In addition, special memoranda of information appeared from time to time on comparisons of U. S. and Allied forces, tonnage losses to submarines, and lists of ships under construction.[9]

Whittlesey and other retired officers could not run naval intelligence alone; so Welles turned to volunteers and reservists to fill vacancies. The DNI found Assistant Secretary of the Navy Roosevelt anxious to recommend reservists for naval intelligence duty. FDR had organized the Naval Reserve Force in 1916 and in the process had accumulated numerous contacts with eager, patriotic young men willing to serve in the Navy. Though rebuffed earlier by Oliver, Roosevelt consulted gladly with the current head of ONI and undoubtedly dreamed of further involvement in the Navy's spy agency.

Additional help in locating reservists for ONI came from Spencer

Fayette Eddy, an early reservist and the first employed by naval intelligence in 1916. A Harvard graduate, career diplomat, and one-time private secretary to Ambassador John Hay in London, Eddy moved among the highest circles of New York City society, joined the proper clubs, played a strong game of tennis, and raised rare orchids. He knew all the right people to recruit for naval intelligence. In 1916 he had set up a clandestine branch intelligence section in New York City for the department, and with American entry into the war he traveled to Washington to meet Welles to formalize the branch office. Evidently the two men formed an immediate friendship, and throughout the remainder of the war the dapper New Yorker was never far from Welles's side.[10]

The influence of both Eddy and Roosevelt on the selection of reserve intelligence officers was reflected in the backgrounds of the men who formed Welles's inner circle of advisors and operatives. Like FDR and Eddy, they had attended Harvard or other Ivy League colleges and belonged to socially prestigious organizations, especially golf and tennis clubs frequented by Roosevelt and Eddy. The majority came from old Yankee stock, carrying ties to some of New York's oldest and wealthiest families. Although Roosevelt's biographer Frank Freidel claimed later that the Naval Reserve was not simply "college boys, rich young men, well-to-do yachtsmen, etc.,"[11] those who gravitated to naval intelligence leaned in that direction.

Alexander Brown Legare and Lawrence Waterbury were two of FDR's friends and relations who worked for naval intelligence. Founder of the Chevy Chase Hunt Club in Washington and frequent companion of Roosevelt on the links, Legare at least had once attended the Naval Academy for a short time. Waterbury, who married FDR's sister-in-law, belonged to another venerable New York family and ranked internationally as a top polo player. During the war the dashing sportsman also became an expert on mineral resources, helping to revive a declining fortune when he speculated in the U. S. Navy's oil reserves for the Mammoth Oil Company syndicate.[12]

Meantime, Roosevelt's Harvard classmate Steuart Davis applied for intelligence work. Commander of FDR's Volunteer Patrol Squadron, which became the nucleus for the Naval Reserve, Davis wrote his chum Franklin for the job of aid for information in the Second Naval District. The assistant secretary knowingly asked Welles: "I wonder what I can tell him." Two weeks later, Welles appointed Davis as aid for information in the desired district.[13] Other Harvard men appointed to ONI were less intimate with FDR but nevertheless known to the active navalist through their frequency on golf and tennis club circuits. These men included Albert Zabriskie Gray, Herbert G. Pell, and Griswold Lorillard, son of tobacco millionaire Pierre Lorillard.[14]

Additional reserve intelligence officers reflected the New York connection. Indeed, New York lawyers, financiers, and stockbrokers dominated the inner intelligence circle. A Tuxedo Park attorney and owner of one of the largest naval history libraries in the United States, Newbold LeRoy Edgar became Welles's section chief in charge of all correspondence with naval attachés. Edgar selected many assistant attachés, appointed civilian secret agents, and expended secret intelligence funds.[15] Another New York counselor, Warren C. Van Slyke, headed Welles's legal section, coordinated work with the Justice Department, formulated passport regulations, and drew up policy to exclude enemy aliens from within three miles of the coast.[16]

Wall Street banker Lionel A. Stahl, shipping magnates Herman Oelrichs and Philip Albright Small Franklin, and stockbroker William Clarkson Van Antwerp added their diverse talents to naval intelligence. Van Antwerp was most influential. Another Annapolis candidate, forced to resign during the 1880s because of the glut of officers over assignments, Van Antwerp went on to accumulate a fortune in stock speculation and journalism, combining the two in his popular book *The Stock Exchange Within*. Van Antwerp toured the globe for naval intelligence and eventually became Welles's branch intelligence director in San Francisco.[17]

Eddy recruited yet more famous names for ONI. Most active was Ralph Pulitzer, son of Joseph Pulitzer, who had made the *New York World* one of the country's leading newspapers. The younger Pulitzer worked in both Washington and New York as an expert on press censorship and plant protection for Welles's Office. Eddy also enrolled stockbroker William Goadby Loew and banker Reginald C. Vanderbilt as voluntary agents to spy on vacationing naval officers and businessmen at Newport. Prominent New York artist DeWitt Lockman's wartime duties included service as one of Eddy's sleuths and trips to Washington to paint Secretary Daniels's portrait.[18]

Welles personally discovered and enrolled one prominent reservist. At a dinner party, the DNI met Clifford N. Carver and became impressed with the young Princeton graduate's interest in naval intelligence. Son of a Long Island shipping tycoon, Carver had served as personal secretary both to presidential advisor Edward M. House and more recently to Bernard M. Baruch, Wall Street speculator and later chairman of the powerful War Industries Board. Carver's ties with

Baruch most interested Welles. "I asked him to come to my office and he gave me so much information about the location of large amounts of enemy property and the methods used by Germans to smuggle properties out of the country such as ships' stores," Welles noted, "that I urged him to became a voluntary aid."[19]

Carver wanted permanent attachment and enrolled full time, joining Welles's select team. The DNI sent his new recruit as a personal envoy to tour the Naval Districts and organize measures to identify and condemn alien-owned property. Welles claimed his assistant's work convinced President Wilson to create the Office of Alien Property Custodian under A. Mitchell Palmer. "The Office of Naval Intelligence furnished the Alien Property Custodian with information which resulted in the taking over of millions of dollars worth of alien property," the director recalled.[20]

Welles's reliance on Carver increased. He employed the young man, as House and Baruch had before, as private secretary. "When it was necessary for me to have a personal and confidential Aid I detailed Lieutenant Carver for this duty and practically all the correspondence for my signature passed over his desk." Carver provided other amenities. When Welles grew fatigued in the tense Washington atmosphere, he motored out with Colonel House to the Carver estate on Long Island, finding solace in the manicured gardens and rich lawns of his aid's house and the homes of his wealthy neighbors.[21] The DNI enjoyed fraternizing with the rich and powerful and utilized the wartime opportunities to bring such people into his Office. After the war, former ONI members gave Welles a splendid dinner at the New York Yacht Club, and the director expressed his sentiments to the group. "Yes, we certainly were a very happy family at ONI, and I hope that the friendships we all made there will be lasting."[22]

Welles's affinity for and dependence upon these amateur naval officers and sleuths had profound implications for the nature of naval intelligence. The inherent restraint of professional officers had prevented formation of what might be termed an intelligence elite. There were cliques, to be sure, and expressions of autonomy, but national peacetime conditions and strict obligations to duty operated as a brake to such opportunism. The war removed checks, and war-induced hysteria and ultrapatriotism clouded legal boundaries of intelligence work. Moreover, reservists only months out of civilian life often succumbed to the excitement of naval duty and the influence of an outsider's image of intelligence work. To some, service in ONI meant tracking down sinister enemies, spying, and other dangerous duties. In reality, naval intelligence entailed hours of drudgery, paperwork, and routine—not cloak-and-dagger—adventures. Most adjusted to actual conditions. Nevertheless, as in their clubbish atmosphere in civilian lives, the reserve intelligence officers close to Welles formed a clannish group and identified themselves as part of an elite team tied personally to the DNI. "Never have I known a more loyal lot of men, loyal to the service which they had entered and loyal to me personally," Welles remembered.[23]

xiv

DOMESTIC SURVEILLANCE

Welles's intelligence elite provided ONI with a glamorous inner corps of intelligence operatives, administrators, and local directors. Meanwhile hundreds of less well-known personnel carried out daily routine. Nameless volunteers, enlisted men and women, and agents searched passengers on incoming ships, investigated suspects, typed up reports, filed identification cards, and provided security at docks, warehouses, and factories. They located enemy aliens through hours of surveillance, wiretapping, mail opening, and searching bank accounts. They censored cables and wireless messages and prowled through holds of merchantmen in search of bombs. ONI operatives came from every walk of life, from the quiet stenographer to the superpatriot of the American Protective League. These people, rather than the Harvard graduate and society celebrity, held ONI's domestic intelligence operation together.[1]

Most intelligence personnel remained honest representatives of their government. However, the size of wartime organization and hurried screening of candidates for emergency hiring created mistakes. The judge advocate general informed Welles in late 1918 that an assistant aid for information in Philadelphia was the notorious "El Paso Murderer," wanted for blackmail, larceny, and immoral conduct. The local aid admitted that he had not investigated the reservist's background because he looked like a naval officer. "He was a man of very good appearance, had a steady blue eye, strong features, tall, broadshouldered, commanding bearing, good talker and, in fact, had all the attributes that impress one at first sight."[2]

The Philadelphia case was unusual. Welles tried to check many candidates himself or at least let his staff investigate the background of anyone working for ONI. From time to time even harassed Secretary of the Navy Daniels monitored intelligence personnel. Welles "brought in recommendation for enrollment for Navy Leaguer who had been busy with the gang," he observed in 1917. Remembering how the Navy League had opposed moderate Wilsonian policies before the war, Daniels took prompt action on this application for intelligence duty. "I tore it up," he recalled.[3]

Keeping track of nearly 3,000 personnel in the Naval Defense Districts became vexing as the domestic network expanded. Each of the thirteen naval districts on the continental United States had an office for information. On the Atlantic coast, aids for information operated from headquarters in Boston, Newport, New York, Philadelphia, Baltimore, Norfolk, Charleston, and Key West. The aid in New Orleans coordinated work on the Gulf of Mexico and in Texas. The Chicago aid organized intelligence for three districts on the Great Lakes, the Mississippi River, and the Midwest. The aids on the Pacific Coast directed business from San Francisco and Puget Sound. Information officers headed sections in Honolulu and Balboa in the Panama Canal Zone. Moreover, most of these districts had subdivisions with their own tiny staffs.[4]

The Aid for Information Commander H. O. Rittenhouse in New York accumulated the largest organization. Eleven ensigns directed ship inspection, shipboard informants, naval port guards, special investigations, translations, and payroll. Ship inspector Lieutenant Commander Charles J. Gass employed 400 men to examine every ship entering New York harbor. Other major ports rivaled New York. By Armistice Day 1918, Lieutenant R. S. Manley reported that his aid for information office in New Orleans contained an assistant aid, secret service director, legal department chief, heads of filing and suspect divisions, twenty-seven field agents, fifteen vessel inspectors, thirty-three yeomen, 204 port guards, twelve motor dory crewmen, six photographers, and four censors.[5]

Rooted in district intelligence mobilization schemes carried out during Oliver's leadership, the aid for information system soon became an unwieldy giant under Welles. Though the prewar staff had drawn up comprehensive procedures and policies for the system, different conditions at each district created their own sets of problems, often defying rigid direction from Washington. What might succeed in New York, did not apply to New Orleans or Chicago. Oliver's guidelines left unanswered many questions as to method and policy, and Welles's overworked Office often neglected filling the gap. "I have had to feel my way on my own judgment," one aid reported. "No instructions or even suggestions had come until those mentioned."[6]

The aids, themselves, varied in background, training, and competence. Retired officers headed the Third Naval District at New York and the Fourteenth in San Francisco. Coast Guard officers directed Philadelphia and Puget Sound, while reservists headed seven naval district offices of information. All shared Lieutenant William Todd's view of the situation, expressed from his post in Honolulu. "It will be remembered I came into this work absolutely green and the only glimpses I have gotten as to the intentions of the department have been by inference only."[7] When Welles found time to focus on the problems confronted by his aids, he often lectured them on the contradictory presupposition that they were information officers but not intelligence officers.[8]

The establishment of eight Branch Intelligence Offices, which by November 1918 directed over 500 personnel, further complicated the division of authority and definition of duty. Basically, aids for information continued the mission outlined in 1916, while branch officers coordinated factory security, plant protection, and investigation of labor unrest. Welles had direct control of his branch personnel rather than sharing responsibility with district commandants. The DNI selected his branch chiefs, assigning trusted comrades Van Antwerp to San Francisco and Eddy to New York City. Meanwhile, Eddy recommended Clive Runnels to administer the Chicago office, and FDR's yachting acquaintance William Barklie Henry ran the Philadelphia branch. Wealthy Baltimore attorney and ardent golfer James Piper organized ONI branch resources in that port city. Other directors included Edward H. Wales in Washington, D.C., Alfred Winsor in Boston, and George E. Rowe in Pittsburgh. Welles observed that "had it not been for such men who loyally gave time and thought, and in many instances money, to carry on the work of this Office, we should not have arrived at the point of efficiency which I think we had reached at the time the armistice was signed."[9]

Inevitably branch intelligence directors interfered with aids for information. Welles warned Eddy not to duplicate work. "In future no investigation will be instituted by your office on a case which might even remotely be construed to fall within the field of work of the Aid."[10] Van Antwerp, in faraway California, proved equally independent, building his own little intelligence empire, which included a batch of secret agents in Mexico. Rear Admiral William F. Fullam complained that Van Antwerp was usurping intelligence duty from his Pacific Fleet patrols and ignoring regular naval channels of information. In this case, Welles defended his branch director. "While I like to keep the Division Commander informed of everything which may be of interest to him, it is quite out of the question to keep him informed of all your activities," Welles instructed Van Antwerp, "and, therefore, unless of special interest to Admiral Fullam I should say nothing whatever to him about any of your work."[11]

Overlapping missions and rivalries characterized ONI's relations with personnel of other government agencies. Collaboration with the Military Intelligence Division of the War Department was most sensitive. Naval intelligence held traditional disdain for its Army counterpart, and Davis's obvious disgust with the clumsy military intelligence system in the 1890s remained the typical naval attitude. By the world war, however, Military Intelligence under the leadership of Major Ralph H. Van Deman and Brigadier General Marlborough Churchill had grown to rival, and in domestic intelligence to surpass, the size and efficiency of ONI. In fact, the U.S. Navy relied on the Army for information from the Philippines, Hawaii, and the Canal Zone. The Navy's aid in Honolulu worked out of offices in Army headquarters, and Army Intelligence officers carried out all suspect surveillance in Panama for the Navy's aid for information office.[12]

Military Intelligence became one of ONI's most productive sources of information on internal suspects and subversives, Churchill daily sending snippets of news to Welles. But, as might be expected, cooperation between the two military intelligence services was not always harmonious. ONI operatives complained regularly about MID interference in their investigations. Welles's attitude toward the sister service, though, amounted more to embarrassment than hostility or rivalry. In early 1918 he set up a laboratory to study sympathetic ink, invisible writing, and other methods of conveying secret messages. While the Navy lab under chemist Frank Martinek succeeded in locating hidden words, it failed in attempts to decipher them. Thus, Welles had to look to Army Intelligence for assistance.[13]

In July 1918 the DNI ordered Lieutenant William H. Elkins to visit the Army's brilliant and moody cryptographer Herbert Osborne Yardley. The meeting did not go smoothly. "I was not particularly pleased when I was instructed to tell this officer our secrets," Yardley recalled.[14] Nevertheless, ONI turned all deciphering and decoding over to him. Welles refused to suffer humiliation quietly, however, and demanded that MID discontinue the practice of returning all decoded messages to the Navy with Army censorship stamps blotting out ONI references.[15]

ONI relations with the Justice Department proved similarly uncomfortable. Contact betwen the two focused on the surveillance, investigation, and detention of enemy aliens suspected of endangering property of the Navy. That naval intelligence would be dragged into this duty became clear early in the war. In April 1917, Admiral Henry T. Mayo called for investigations of alien activities in the vicinity of naval bases. "Much damage has been done to property during the past two years by aliens of Teutonic sympathies," he warned.[16] At the same time, Assistant Secretary Roosevelt advised ONI to spy on the large German-American colony near the Portsmouth Navy Yard in New Hampshire. FDR suggested somewhat dramatically that these foreign-born people might purchase an aeroplane, fly over the naval yard, and bomb it.[17]

Warnings of real and imagined dangers to naval property forced Welles's office to employ hundreds of civilian and naval detectives to investigate aliens. ONI operatives, often aided by local police and Justice Department officers, quickly learned how to wiretap, use dictagraphs, check personal papers, and eavesdrop. Most often suspects were located for naval intelligence by other agencies. A. Bruce Bielaski, powerful director of the Bureau of Investigation, headed the list of those who sent dossiers on subjects for investigation. Other sources included New York Chief Cable Censor Lieutenant George S. Wheat, Post Office censors, MID, the War Trade Board, the General Black List, the State Department, and Allied intelligence. Members of the ultrapatriotic American Protective League fed ONI data on suspects from its vast network of spies and snoops in shipyards and factories. By November 1918, Welles claimed that his people were working on 15,000 cases a week.[18]

Location and identification of suspects became more urgent as ONI assumed responsibility for plant protection. In November 1917 the Navy Department organized a Naval Contract and Plant Division under Section A of the intelligence office to supervise the manufacture of naval materiel in private factories. Contractors doing business with the Navy sent ONI forms containing an employee census, describing precautions taken to secure plants against fire and sabotage, and noting labor unrest. Over 5,000 such documents arrived in Welles's office during the war. In addition, field agents scoured factories, collecting data on the loyalty of company officials and employees. Naval intelligence exerted direct control over a factory owner's hiring practices. "When required by the Secretary of the Navy, he shall refuse to employ, or if already employed forthwith discharge from employment and exclude from his works, any person or persons designated by the Secretary of the Navy as undesirable for employment on work for the Navy Department."[19]

Most contractors collaborated to keep lucrative naval business. Thus when ONI recommended that the Justice Department arrest ninety-six enemy aliens employed by the Sperry Gyroscope Company of Brooklyn, Elmer A. Sperry agreed to the seizure of his workers and asked for naval supervision of his plant. Others showed less enthusiasm. General Electric officials in Schenectady, New York, tried to prevent ONI agents from snooping about their destroyer turbine shops. Branch Intelligence Director Eddy explained General Electric's reluctance to accept naval inspectors. Not only did the Schenectady plant employ over one hundred known socialists and pacifists, but officials had failed to take proper security precautions. "Anyone bent on destroying the efficiency of the General Electric Company's plant," Eddy observed, "could today walk into the main entrance without being challenged; go directly to the power house; enter it; conceal a considerable quantity of explosive in the vital part of the machinery and leave the plant without being detected."[20]

Though successful in preventing major sabotage, ONI failed to secure every plant. Such was the case at the massive American International Shipbuilding Company on Hog Island in the Delaware River. This hastily constructed facility featured fifty shipways, hundreds of shops and forges, and a sprawling, unattended yard of loose material. Scores of identification badges disappeared on each workshift, while over 1,000 people had access to confidential blueprints. The branch intelligence officer in Philadelphia investigated and discovered too much inefficiency, corruption, graft, and theft to initiate successful protection procedures. Instead, he recommended that the Emergency Fleet Corporation send a team of experts to secure the yard.[21]

Confronted with growing responsibilities under plant-protection duty, ONI tightened methods during the spring of 1918. Naval intelligence began to emphasize plant intelligence rather than protection, a subtle distinction explained by operative Raymond E. Horn: "Plant Intelligence, as distinguished from Plant Protection, . . . meant the procurement and assembling of data relative to anti-American, pacifistic, and radical personages, organizers, agitators, and societies in or out of these plants whose activity threatened to retard the progress of the Naval Establishment."[22] To this end, ONI ordered branch intelligence personnel to root out troublemakers, loafers, and disloyal workers who ignored the Liberty Loan and Red Cross fund drives.[23]

Modification of plant protection policy reflected how indistinct the line had become between legitimate security concerns and suppression of divergent opinions. The efforts of the Wilson administration to stir national pride and loyalty during the war led to less laudable manifestations. "In this Naval District," one aid revealed, "I find much jealousy and suspicion, on the part of some Americans toward naturalized citizens of German birth and ancestry; and that not infrequently such Americans turn in reports founded on nothing except dislike and their own overt jealousy."[24]

Reports arrived in ONI regularly about people who caused suspicion simply because they looked, spoke, or allegedly acted like Germans. Naval intelligence investigated one officer because his long-time housekeeper was very "German-looking," and another because he had married the daughter of a professor of German at the University of Michigan. A Navy chaplain was removed from his post when a vindictive hometown neighbor informed ONI that the Lutheran clergyman once defended Germany's legal right to sink the *Lusitania*.[25]

Anti-German feeling might be expected, while investigation of naval personnel suspected of alien ties conformed to ONI's wartime mission. However, these conditions failed to explain why naval intelligence became obsessed with pursuing American Jews. Perhaps a partial answer lay in a tinge of anti-Semitism in the Navy or in the domination of ONI by Protestant, Ivy League Anglo-Saxons long used to excluding Jews from their clubs and lives. The latter possibility appeared in one case where naval intelligence questioned the loyalty of a Jewish reserve officer simply on the word of "a Christian gentleman, great church worker and leader of boy scouts."[26]

Whatever the reasons, ONI considered Jews prime targets for surveillance, investigation, and often dismissal from naval service. The intelligence office watched one officer because his wife was a "Russian Jewess," and another because he had married a wealthy "Austrian Jewess." In the latter case, however, Welles dropped the investigation of the socially prominent Baltimore family. The director showed no such restraint in hounding a Jewish naval dentist at the Great Lakes Navy Yard. When investigators discovered that the reserve officer came from "an absolutely foreign district of New York," inhabited by "German and Hungarian Jews," Welles secured the dentist's dishonorable discharge from the Navy.[27]

ONI also pursued members of reputedly radical groups during the war. During 1917–18 naval intelligence collected files on Russian revolutionaries, pacifists, socialists, and labor unions. In April 1918 ONI agents followed Socialist author John Reed around New York City, staked out his office, and monitored conversations with Morris Hillquit, member of the Peoples' Council of America for Peace and Democracy and editor of *The Call*. Membership in the Industrial Workers of the World or any other labor organization placed Americans on ONI's suspect cards and often led to investigations. Attempts to organize workers in naval facilities brought instant involvement by naval intelligence. Thus, when a stenographer at the Charlestown Navy Yard organized women for equal pay with yeomen doing identical jobs, ONI launched a vigorous investigation of her private life, sexual activities, and personal finances, eventually forcing her dismissal.[28]

By August 1918, Rear Admiral Leigh C. Palmer, chief of the Bureau of Navigation, suggested that ONI might be pursuing suspects a bit too enthusiastically. He warned Welles to permit people accused of misdeeds to explain their actions before naval intelligence recommended dismissal, arrest, or internment. "In a government of democratic institutions, where we endeavor to keep from so-called 'star-chamber proceedings,' I think in every case we should ask the man for a statement before we fire him summarily from the service," Palmer reminded the intelligence director.[29]

The Justice Department also worried about ONI's exuberance. Special Assistant United States Attorney General John Lord O'Brian wondered why naval intelligence had held one suspect for months without bringing specific charges against him. O'Brian ordered ONI to release the detainee. Welles's office defended its action in this case, explaining that the prisoner belonged to a black-listed chemical dye firm and regularly surveyed the waterfront with marine glasses. Besides, he was a "tall, blond German," ONI declared, and "it seems perfectly clear that on the above facts any reasonable man would be convinced that the subject was aiding or about to aid the enemy."[30]

Such controversy prompted O'Brian to attempt a coordination of all government intelligence agencies. In March 1918, he called representatives of Army and naval intelligence, the State Department, and the Departments of Labor, Justice, and the Treasury to meet and discuss centralization of intelligence. This group vetoed rigid pooling of intelligence resources. They agreed to meet more often to discuss common policy, however. "At these conferences," Welles recalled, "all matters pertaining to the activities of alien enemies, passport regulations, labor troubles caused by aliens, etc., were discussed."[31]

Welles's office defined its own procedures for holding suspects. ONI ordered agents to consult with an attorney before seizing citizens. Grounds for detention included violations of U.S. Statutes, presidential proclamations, and special wartime legislation. "In cases where there is no proof of any violation of a statute, or of the regulations of the Presidential proclamations, and there is mere suspicion and belief that the alien enemy may be dangerous," ONI advised, "a request for internment should be made."[32] In this event, naval investigators without power to arrest suspects would turn them over to the U.S. marshal's office for detention until the Justice Department accepted the case. Despite such clarification, detention of enemy aliens and suspects troubled ONI throughout the remainder of the war.

Arrangements with customs officers of the Treasury Department and immigration officials from the Department of Labor progressed more smoothly than those with Justice. ONI established a coherent and detailed policy with both agencies in order to search ships. Regulations spelled out exactly where agents should look for bombs, contraband, secret messages, and other illegal items. Naval intelligence teams learned to check baggage, frisk passengers, and scrutinize passports for secret marks identifying suspicious bearers.[33]

In addition to extensive duties with established government departments, ONI interacted with the maze of specially created wartime organizations such as the War Industries Board, the War Trade Board, and the Committee on Public Information. Cooperation with the last-named agency was most fruitful. Created on 13 April 1917 by Denver newspaperman George Creel, the Committee on Public Information sought to sell the war to a lukewarm American public and to regulate the flow of news to the press. From the outset, ONI teamed with CPI to determine what naval war information should be released. Secretary Daniels served on Creel's policy board, while Ralph Pulitzer and other newspapermen assisted Welles, assuring intimate cooperation. ONI officers aided CPI in reviewing films for export, studied ship photographs to determine which might be printed, and evaluated news on submarine activity and departure of ships.[34]

Collaboration with the many different agencies pulled ONI further into an interlocking and at times overlapping domestic intelligence network. Tremendous pressure fell on the ailing DNI to determine to whom and where information should go. Perhaps inevitably he began to see enemy agents everywhere. "There is no doubt that even in the departments at Washington," Welles insisted "German agents were at work at all times."[35] Finally, in February 1918, Chief of Naval Operations Benson thought it necessary to redirect Welles's energies. "While I do not desire to limit the scope of activity of the Office of Naval Intelligence in transmitting information to other departments," the CNO suggested, "it must be carefully borne in mind that the primary mission of Naval Intelligence is to furnish information for the use of the Navy."[36]

Benson's note to Welles revealed the dilemma confronting ONI during the first world war. Since the days of Lieutenant Mason, the

Navy's intelligence office had defined its mission in terms of collection, collation, and dissemination of naval information. At times the Office employed the data in war planning and to assist the department in the study of larger strategic questions. Always these tasks had been limited to naval problems. American entry into the European war of 1914 changed many of the well-established traditions, pulling ONI into uncharted regions of domestic surveillance.

XV

THE EUROPEAN WAR

ONI's wartime operations in Europe never approached the size or efficiency of domestic intelligence work. Throughout the first world war Section B, responsible for foreign secret service, contained only one quarter of the personnel employed by Section A's domestic intelligence desks. Allied intelligence already blanketed the European field, and Welles concentrated on strengthening the naval attaché network rather than on inaugurating a tardy espionage system. But even selection of attachés and their assistants confounded the DNI. "My experience in the Office of Naval Intelligence during the war showed one thing very plainly," Welles wrote Captain Ernest J. King, "and that was the difficulty of selecting officers for the duties of Naval Attachés."[1] Despite careful screening, many lacked training in diplomacy, international law, and foreign languages.

Troubles with Captain William Dugald MacDougall, the U.S. naval attaché in London, exemplified Welles's concern. "About all we have received from MacDougall has been stuff about materiel and little or nothing of military value," the director complained.[2] He wanted the attaché to penetrate O.B. 40, the old Admiralty building which housed British naval intelligence headquarters under Admiral Hall. The office contained a most brilliant collection of intelligence experts in every field of espionage and communications. "At the British Admiralty," Sims marveled, "they have a corps of grey-haired Oxford Professors, Egyptologists, Cuneiform Inscription Readers, etc., who break ciphers with great facility, and, I may add, have broken practically every cipher that they have been put up against."[3]

With Britain now an ally, Welles expected to learn everything from Hall's team. "I am particularly anxious to get their lists of enemy suspects in the United States," he wrote Sims, "and I am sure such lists exist in their office."[4] But Hall was not anxious to share his secrets with inexperienced and talkative Americans, and even at this stage probably considered the United States a potential postwar rival. Hall's suspicions affronted Welles. "I think you can assure the Admiralty that they need not fear leaks from this Office," he wired Sims.[5]

Welles dispatched a personal representative, Lieutenant Commander John H. Roys, to London to smooth relations. Roys formed an immediate friendship with Hall, warming him to the thought of closer cooperation with ONI. "It is such a pleasure to have him over here, and to be able to talk over matters first hand," Hall wrote his American counterpart, "and he will, I hope be able to assure you of the close cooperation in Naval Intelligence matters which exists between your people and myself."[6]

Roys had another job as well, to watch Sims. Ever since the veteran naval attaché had arrived in London on 28 April 1917 to coordinate Anglo-American naval operations, Sims had displayed growing frustration with and defiance of control from Washington. He insisted only the force commander could determine the correct situation and make final decisions. Thus began a war-long tussle between Sims and department bureaucracy in Washington for control of tactical and strategic policy in Europe. Welles was caught in the middle but clearly wished all intelligence policy to originate in his office, not with Sims. The DNI considered Sims merely a naval attaché assigned by ONI, but the latter considered himself a second DNI. Neither admitted these views to the other, and they maintained cordial relations throughout the duration, Sims going his own way with a minimum of control from Welles.[7]

Sims grabbed almost complete control over American naval intelligence in wartime Europe, moving too fast for the more methodical and tired DNI back in Washington. Both in intellect and training, Sims towered above Welles. It was no match. Sims pried a commitment from Benson for autonomy in naval intelligence. "Information from military sources will be centralized in the Embassies of the countrys (sic) specified," the chief of naval operations instructed, "and Naval Attachés will be kept informed so as to furnish information immediately and direct to you."[8]

Benson's blank check was not enough. Naval attachés still communicated with Welles, sending news to London too late to be of any use in the fighting. When the CNO visited Sims in November, ostensibly to discuss the proposed North Sea Mine Barrage and other antisubmarine measures, Sims hounded him about coordination of intelligence resources through the force commander. After his meeting with Benson, Sims wrote classmate and longtime friend A. P. Niblack about the results: "I therefore took up the whole subject with Admiral Benson and he entirely agrees with me that all reports made by Naval Attachés should come directly to me so that I can collate them, compare them with the secret information here, and send through what we consider to be the correct dope."[9]

Gradually Sims molded his own office of naval intelligence as a central part of the American Naval Planning Section in London. The organization of the intelligence agency as an integral unit of his general staff reflected Sims's idea of the proper relationship of intelligence to planning. One of his complaints in 1894 as intelligence officer on the *Charleston* had been about the gap between information and analysis. Collecting data only to have somebody file the data without using them negated intelligence duty. The Naval Planning Section in London in 1917 eliminated the intelligence gap. "In the course of solutions or in the preparation for solution of problems," Sims's intelligence instructions directed, "the Intelligence Section assembles whatever data are necessary and presents them in the desired form." [10]

The London intelligence team resembled a second Office of Naval Intelligence. Sims's staff outgrew any previous complement in ONI's Washington offices between 1882 and 1916. If Welles's inner group constituted sort of an elite during the war, so too did the intensely loyal officers who served as Sims's war planners and information gatherers. Commanders John V. Babcock and Dudley Knox, Surgeon Edgar Thompson, and Lieutenant junior grade Tracy B. Kittredge stood closest to the force commander. Knox became Sims's warmest friend and most effective operative, accumulating information on hydrophone experiments, acoustic mines, radio-controlled launches, and the employment of aircraft to spot submarines and mines. [11]

The London staff applied results of their investigations to larger military, political, and economic questions. They consistently addressed themselves to overall strategy and defined doctrine on antisubmarine warfare, minelaying, cooperation with Allied nations, and control of the North Sea. Sims's people sat on the Inter-Allied Naval Council and received full briefings. They composed monographs on the impact of labor, religion, socialism, and propaganda on fighting morale. These model studies proved of such value that the Creel Committee on Public Information adopted them as guidelines for similar CPI work. [12]

Widely regarded as Britain's closest friend in the U. S. Navy, Sims urged candid and thorough collaboration between the two great Atlantic democracies. He encouraged the Navy Department to coordinate its intelligence service with that of the Admiralty. On their part, the British opened resources to Sims and daily briefed him on operations against U-boats. British intelligence supplied Americans with lists of subversives, suspects, aliens, and assorted revolutionaries. ONI files bulged with the names of Irish rebels, Hindu plotters, and Bolshevik terrorists, reflecting British influence on U. S. naval intelligence's selection of dangerous person for its suspect cards. At the same time,

America's ally threw open secrets on cryptography, chemicals, gas warfare, aeronautics, sound detection, wireless telegraphy, and psychological warfare. The opportunities were so rich that special U. S. scientific attachés joined their naval counterparts in London.[13]

Surprisingly, the Navy Department expressed deep reservations about becoming too intimate with the Admiralty. Benson, Welles, and others suspected Britain's postwar intentions. In March 1918 Chairman of the War Trade Board Vance C. McCormick wrote Welles about Allied intelligence spying on Americans. McCormick suggested that any information obtained would be used after the war to gain military and commercial advantages over the United States. Welles agreed, urging his agents to spy on the Allies, especially the British in Latin America. The DNI warned operatives to limit cooperation with foreign agents to the common war effort, and that "in no event should the representatives of any foreign power be given any details in regard to the plan or scope of your organization, the number and location of your agents nor, unless absolutely unavoidable, should the services of any of our agents be shared with any foreign power."[14]

Underlying suspicions failed to detract from Anglo-American naval cooperation during the war, particularly in the exchange of information. ONI enterprises in other European countries never approached the success of Sims's operation in Britain. However, problems in France did not stem from an unwillingness to share data, but from faulty organization, lack of resources, and poorly outlined policy. In May 1917, Commander Sayles, the naval attaché in Paris, admitted sheepishly that he could not give intelligence agents any instructions. As late as the summer of 1918, Welles's assistant Captain Edward McCauley reported that during his visit to France he found "the work coming under the Naval Attaché . . . widely separated and not coordinated." In fact Sayles's successor, Captain Richard H. Jackson, served not only as the naval attaché in Paris but also as staff coordinator for Force Commander Admiral Henry B. Wilson.[15]

During his investigation of U. S. naval intelligence overseas, McCauley learned that counterespionage work along the French coast had collapsed after the death of ONI operative Richard Norton. "It appears that no one else in the office of the Naval Attaché knew the details of the cases that Mr. Norton was working on, nor of the agents he employed."[16] Consequently Welles dispatched Lt. Charles A. Munn as assistant naval attaché to rebuild counterespionage. Stationed at Nantes, Munn and his agents stopped the leak of information about Allied shipping to U-boats waiting off the French coast. In addition, the assistant attaché provided data on enemy submarine movements in local waters. "He was also instrumental in having certain spies executed and interned," Welles recalled.[17]

Munn's arrival remedied only one weakness. McCauley discovered too few crew control guards, nonexistent security at U. S. naval air stations in France, and overlapping functions. Liaison between U. S. and French naval intelligence was haphazard, with French officials often unable to locate their contacts on the American side. "This situation leads to much confusion, as none of the various officers seem to know exactly what their duties are," McCauley reported. "As a result much information is not obtained, or if obtained, is wrongly forwarded."[18]

Naval intelligence in other Allied countries seemed only slightly more efficient. Welles expressed disenchantment with Commander Charles R. Train's enterprise in Italy. "We have now sent an assistant naval attaché to Train," he cabled Sims, "who we think has been tied too closely to his office and has obtained only what was brought to him instead of getting out and looking up information."[19] Soon Train's staff included seven reservists and retired officers. Still the attaché found it difficult to keep abreast of growing enemy activity in Italian waterfront cities. The proliferation of female agents who pumped American sailors for shipping information and then sent the data via pigeon to Austrian U-boats proved particularly troublesome, Train told Welles.[20]

ONI contact with the remaining major Allied power Russia was at best tenuous. When the United States entered the world war in April 1917 Russia verged on complete collapse. Riots, mutinies, and a series of provisional governments plagued the fading ally. Naval Attaché Captain McCully reported from Petrograd that Nicholas II was now just Nicholas Romanoff, private citizen. "One feels quite as if one were taking part in the French Revolution," McCully wrote Welles.[21] McCully's replacement, Commander Walter Selwyn Crosley, sent equally discouraging and useless information: "The Ambassador agrees with me that there is no need here for a Naval Attaché, and nothing for one to do."[22]

If ONI capabilities in Allied nations presented something of an enigma, gathering information from neutral states bordering the war zones and crawling with agents from both belligerent coalitions offered different problems. In the winter of 1917 Navy Department Censorship Intelligence Officer George S. Wheat prepared a memorandum for Welles on Red Flag Stations, danger points from which enemy agents forwarded communications into Germany from the outside after cable connections had been severed: "I would suggest that all Naval Attachés in neutral countries should be asked to submit to the Director of Naval Intelligence a list of the towns in their respective countries which they consider to be dangerous and most likely centers of German activities, and the supposed, or known methods by which German agents communicate with Germany."[23]

Spain, with its many avenues of communication with Latin America, was the most critical area. German agents sent radio messages from Argentina, passing them through Spain and on to Germany. A week after Wheat's memorandum on Red Flag Stations, Welles cabled the naval attaché in Madrid, Captain Benton C. Decker, asking for the names of all towns considered centers of Teutonic activity. A veteran intelligence officer who had drawn up several plans for the General Board's war portfolios, Decker told Welles that Germans transmitted wireless messages from every important Spanish town. "This is the most spy-ridden of all countries," he informed the DNI, and "the very base of the enemy's communication with the world at large."[24]

Decker worried more about enemy submarines in Spanish waters than clandestine transmitters. Early in the war ONI learned that German U-boats replenished supplies in Spain, and Decker struggled to interrupt the flow of fuel oil to the big submarines lurking off local beaches. For months the attaché bombarded Welles's office, the State Department, and the War Trade Board with requests to curb U. S. sales of oil to Spain, much of which found its way to enemy undersea raiders. The dangerous trade continued. Decker grew bitter, attacking American diplomats, war profiteers, and U. S. Ambassador in Madrid Joseph E. Willard for providing Washington with false information and bending to the wiles of Spanish ruling factions.[25]

ONI confronted similar conditions in Holland, another neutral haven for enemy spies and assorted espionage services. German deserters often crossed the border, providing Allied interrogators with fresh information, while German intelligence used Holland as a point of embarkation for its own spies, agents, and smugglers. The Navy Department selected an inexperienced reserve officer, Lieutenant Eugene D. McCormick, to enter this hotbed of intrigue as the naval attaché at The Hague. Sims warned McCormick to contact British intelligence for guidance, but despite the warning the U. S. attaché plunged blindly into the morass of intrigue. Soon he forwarded false intelligence to the force commander in London. "There is no question of McCormick's zeal and energy," Sims cabled Washington, "simply that his agents apparently have been unreliable, and giving him wrong information."[26]

Welles hastily dispatched a special intelligence expert to assist McCormick. The new adviser was Lieutenant Norman B. Coster, a Princeton University graduate and master of several foreign languages. Though another reservist, Coster was a highly trained professional operative, having collected industrial intelligence for British Westinghouse and the India Rubber Company. Now, as an ONI agent, he rushed to Holland where he discovered the Dutch capital crawling with "castoffs of other services." He instructed McCormick to ignore these private spy bureaus which sold fictitious information and consult instead the Allied intelligence.[27]

Wartime activities in Scandinavia took on some of the characteristics of naval intelligence duty at The Hague. Copenhagen, Christiania (Oslo), and Stockholm buzzed with excitement as rival agents struggled for influence and information. At first, ONI relied on news from Lieutenant Colonel James Carson Breckinridge of the Marine Corps. A pompous officer, this naval attaché sent reports which revealed such insights as that German agents drank beer and Russians looked like aborigines. Soon other attachés arrived. John Allyne Gade became attaché in Denmark and his brother Horace the assistant attaché in Norway. A wealthy banker, Harvard graduate, and friend of Assistant Secretary Roosevelt, John Gade established close ties with Allied intelligence and learned their methods of espionage and counterespionage. He picked up guidance wherever he could find it. "Even little neutral countries, in perilous geograhic locations, such as Denmark, had leaves in the books of their secret services which we took and with profit," Gade recalled.[28]

Profit also entered into the work of John's brother, Horace Upton Gade, a noted platinum exporter with international business contacts. Rumors reached ONI that Horace traded with the enemy, and when he tried to explain the circumstances, Welles refused to listen. John rushed to his brother's defense, claiming that some jealous assistant naval attaché had fostered the vindictive allegations. "It was naturally at times extremely hard for him to disregard old obligations," John reported somewhat mysteriously. For some reason, perhaps FDR's influence or the Gade brothers' valuable contributions, Welles dropped the case, and John continued government service after the war as an agent in Belgium and the Baltic.[29]

The naval attaché in Stockholm, Lieutenant E. B. Robinette, caused no such problems and became one of ONI's more pleasant surprises. The reserve officer organized a counterpropaganda agency in Sweden to offset the flood of German press releases, films, and books that circulated through the country. Robinette's schemes for an Allied News Agency impressed British press Lords Northcliffe and Beaverbrook enough for them to send funds to support his enterprise. The American secured $20,000 for film work alone, and so delighted Creel's Committee that it allowed him to direct CPI operations in Sweden.[30]

Though periodically impressive, U. S. naval intelligence in Europe during the world war was for the most part pedestrian. Professional Allied intelligence service overshadowed ONI and seemed more capable and polished than Welles's patchwork crew. Foreign personnel represented a much more daring image and flair for dramatics than their American counterparts. "Our men are like babes of innocence in spite of their drinking and playing and profanity," Welles observed. They were "not up to it in diplomacy and intrigue, nor indeed, in tact and wisdom."[31]

The U. S. service contained one exception: Welles's man in Lisbon, Commander Edward Breck, rivaled the best of the European agents on either side. An adventurer, woodsman, and European fencing champion, Breck had earlier spied for the Navy in Spain during the Spanish-American War. In the months before American entry into the European war of 1914–18 he once again volunteered for a secret mission. Though undoubtedly aware of Breck's earlier indiscretion in publishing an account of his 1898 mission, ONI hired him to infiltrate German communities in Brazil and Argentina. He succeeded spectacularly. "Breck was supposed to be a German and was so successful in covering his identity that he completely deceived the members of the German Embassy in Buenos Ayres," Welles reported after the war. "He joined their clubs and gained the confidence of all Germans in authority to such an extent that at banquets he replied to toasts praising the work of different German officials."[32]

His Latin American adventure recommended Breck for further duty, and when the department decided to cover Portugal, it sent him to Lisbon as naval attaché. In Portugal, Breck assembled a collection of sinister agents including criminals, turncoats, and a former German master spy. But work in this neutral backwater mattered little in the overall war scheme, and Breck spent most of his time tracing rumors that some innocent actress or chanteuse was a dangerous spy. "Having investigated quite a number of these 'terrible' women here," he informed Welles, "I have come to the conclusion that not a single one of them ever did a thing more internationally criminal than possibly to deliver a letter, the nature of which she knew practically nothing about."[33]

Wasting a talent such as Breck's on Lisbon while allowing McCormick to continue at The Hague, defied logic. It reflected the makeshift intelligence service maintained by the U. S. Navy in Europe during the first world war. Officers and staff were a mixture of active duty, reserve, and volunteer agents. Some proved competent; others merely existed or turned the work to their own advantage. ONI provided no overall intelligence policy, methodology, or explanation of goals. Central authority lay divided between Sims in London and Welles in Washington. Theoretically Sims understood the broader implications of strategic doctrine and the part intelligence played in planning, but often he remained too isolated for effective guidance.

The Navy's intelligence mission varied from country to country in Europe. Requirements in Allied nations differed from those in neutral states, while the latter posts each offered their own diversities. When the United States entered the fighting in 1917, Allied intelligence was well developed, and U. S. naval officers looked to it for inspiration. Thus they rarely initiated independent methods or questions, despite lingering doubts about Allied motives. Moreover, the Navy had neither resources nor incentives to develop a superior intelligence system. But Europe was only one field of operation, and ONI agents soon branched out into Latin America and Eastern Asia, forming an international intelligence network.

XVI

AN INTERNATIONAL NETWORK

American naval policies and strategies in Europe in 1917–18 were tied to the aims of the Allied governments, and U. S. naval intelligence reflected this subordination. In other parts of the world, however, ONI developed an independent and highly confidential network of secret agents, spies, and informants. This was the Office's first intensive effort to organize a covert system overseas to supplement the work of the naval attachés; for although there had been earlier plans for such an operation, and periodically ONI had compiled lists of informants, the world war provided opportunity, funds, and justification for the establishment of a formal espionage service with strings of informants throughout Latin America and the Far East.

Mexico continued as the critical region. For the past four years, the Wilson government had mingled in Mexican affairs, resorting to military incursions to promote American interests. Meanwhile British, German, and Japanese businessmen competed with Americans in the Mexican market. Speculation in oil-rich Tampico became particularly intense for these naval powers now undergoing transition from coal to petroleum fuel for their warships. These international rivalries in and around Mexico intensified with the outbreak of world war in Europe. Foreign agents struggled for influence just across the U. S. border, and some of these machinations had been revealed in the Zimmermann Telegram. Additional urgency in Mexican-American relations materialized with reports of Japanese negotiations for a base on Lower California.

As soon as the United States entered the conflict, naval intelligence dispatched Immigration Inspector John E. Woodrome as Agent No. 152 on a secret trip into Mexico. "Your mission is to thoroughly investigate the coast between Tuxpan and Frontera for evidences of enemy bases, and endeavor to organize an information service covering this coast," ONI instructed him.[1] The inconspicuous little immigration official operated under cable cover Gustav Koch and mail cloak Jiro Kimura. Two months later Welles sent a supervisor of Indian Affairs as another secret agent to Vera Cruz. More agents soon followed to man the twelve district stations set up from Rio Grande to British Honduras. "The Mexican coast requires a close watch on the oil supply and basing facilities for submarines," McCauley observed.[2]

In addition to potential U-boat bases, ONI considered Mexico a center for German intrigue. Reports pointed to Mexican territory as sanctuary for slackers, saboteurs, and other undesirables. Wireless and cable messages emanated from Mexico to Havana, Rio de Janeiro, and Buenos Aires, soon finding their way to some neutral haven before retransmission to Germany. Enemy wireless stations allegedly existed throughout Mexico, and in fact naval intelligence located a transmitter at Ixtapalpa. Increasingly worried about growing Japanese power in the Pacific Ocean, ONI monitored communications between Japan and Mexico, some discussing military collusion and arms deals.[3]

Concern for threats to the United States from just south of the Rio Grande prompted naval intelligence to interfere in internal Mexican politics. Branch Intelligence Director Van Antwerp ordered a secret expedition into Mexico to locate transmitters and make contacts with reputedly pro-American cliques, offering aid in overthrowing rival provincial governments who supposedly sympathized with Japan or Germany. Van Antwerp asked Welles to inquire about whether the American government would free one sympathetic Mexican leader, serving time in a U. S. jail for arms smuggling. Welles's staff discussed the question with State Department intelligence experts Frank Polk and Leland Harrison. Perhaps jealous of ONI's intrusion on the State Department's dominant intelligence position, Polk and Harrison advised against Van Antwerp's proposals.[4]

ONI pursued questionable activities in Mexico anyway. Welles informed Joseph K. Hutchinson, the intelligence officer in San Diego, that even though the State Department opposed ONI's Mexican adventures "you must not become in the least discouraged and make any suggestions to this office abandoning any plans." Then Welles revealed how far he had wandered from traditional ONI concepts of intelligence duty. "You are suffering in a very small degree, comparatively, the same difficulty that this Office experiences constantly in a large degree," he told his Pacific Coast agents, "and that is the legal restrictions placed upon the carrying out of all matters of the kind in which you are engaged."[5] This suggestion that naval intelligence was above the law was stimulated by the war situation, but it also underscored the increasingly complex, secretive, and competitive aspects of intelligence work.

ONI's Mexican sojourn produced other complications. Once again Admiral Fullam tried to find out what Van Antwerp and ONI were doing. Welles told Van Antwerp to ignore the aging commander of the Pacific Fleet's reserve force. Fullam persisted, and the branch intelligence director asked Welles to get the old man off his back. "This Office frequently finds it necessary to send men to and across the border," Van Antwerp explained. "It is of the utmost importance that their work should be kept secret."[6] Still Fullam refused to leave the local intelligence director alone, complaining to Washington about Van Antwerp's ostentatious lifestyle of lavish dinners and extravagant parties. Finally, to avoid further controversy, Welles told his wealthy friend to share information with Fullam.[7]

Though not nearly so troublesome, operations in other Central American regions caused minor difficulties. Naval Intelligence hired a substantial number of agents and informants in the region, who accumulated information on possible plots against the Panama Canal and on revolutionary disturbances. ONI instructed its Central American people to collect data on local businesses trading with the Germans and companies serving as fronts for foreign interests. Once an operative had gathered sufficient material, he prepared a collated folder for ONI with a provocative title such as "The Honduras Story, Nicaragua Story, (or) Mexican Revolutionary Stuff."[8]

Welles dispatched his own special observers to tour the entire region. One such, Agent No. 219, journeyed through Mexico and Guatemala City, and on down the Pacific coast of South America to the Chilean nitrate fields. Before service with naval intelligence this wandering spy had received a graduate degree in botany and had worked for the U. S. Department of Agriculture. With this background, ONI conveniently placed the cloak agricultural explorer on his passport and gave him the cover of a scientific mission to study tropical plants. Other disguises for the Central American station proved less creative. "There are three 'cloaks' which are worn threadbare," Aid for Information Henneberger warned from Balboa, "i.e., mining-man, cattle-man, and timber-man. The only possible way for any of these to really serve their purpose is for the Agent employing the 'cloak' to actually have one of the above professions—on top of which he should be connected with some house in the United States to lend color to his story." Henneberger suggested a possible new cloak in the form of a merchandiser of "cheap jewelry, cutlery, paper novelties, and notions" for sale to local natives.[9]

In early 1917 ONI sent Agent No. 94 to Guatemala to reconnoiter for clandestine wireless stations and U-boat bases. He established close connections with Guatemalan authorities, receiving ample funds to collect information through the United Fruit Company intermediary. In testimony made later to the Justice Department, Agent No. 94 insisted that "while at Guatemala the Navy Dept. was assisting him in every way and they were working in conjunction with the Govt. of Guatemala."[10]

Apparently the naval intelligence agent revealed his cover or started private contract work for the Guatemalan president to purchase arms and radios in the United States. In any case, when he returned to his country on an arms shopping trip, ONI asked the Justice Department to detain him, whereupon naval intelligence questioned him, claimed "he is not all there," and placed him in St. Elizabeth's Asylum for the Insane.

Twice Agent No. 94 escaped from the mental hospital, once to his family in Massachusetts, and twice armed ONI guards hunted him down and returned him to St. Elizabeth's. Whether the Navy's spy was disturbed or put away for other reasons was never determined in the official dossier on the case. However, Agent No. 94's letters in this file were lucid explanations of his predicament. Moreover, as soon as the war ended, he was promptly released from the asylum.[11]

ONI routine in neighboring Caribbean regions was less hectic. Major Jay M. Salladay quietly organized an information service in the Virgin and Windward islands, mostly with local consular officials, but he welcomed any source. "Business firms and other reliable persons having interests in the island should co-operate and could render valuable service by making reports," Salladay observed.[12] At the same time, special agent Carlos J. Rohde prowled revolution-torn towns in the Dominican Republic, while others visited strife-plagued Venezuela to watch for foreign influence.[13]

Revolutionary unrest in Cuba in early 1917 prompted Welles's office to order Commander Carleton R. Kear in Havana to develop local intelligence. Concurrently, the intelligence officer at Santiago de Cuba, Lieutenant Roger W. Peard of the Marine Corps, organized a spy network that included employees of the leading sugar companies. However, despite such work, naval intelligence in Cuba faltered. ONI suspected that several of their informants worked for the Germans. Meanwhile, Kear struggled with his assignment. The base commandant at Guantanamo lectured him on his proper duty: "An efficient intelligence service must do more than merely furnish specific information on request." Several months later, Commander of the American Patrol Detachment in Cuban Waters Rear Admiral Edwin A. Anderson added his complaints. "Kear, who was Liaison Officer at HAVANA, was of absolutely no use to me in this respect. I could get no information of value whatsoever from him and I felt very much handicapped on this account," he informed Welles.[14]

Confronted with declining intelligence services in Cuba, Welles dispatched Carlos V. Cusachs to Havana as U.S. naval attaché. A language instructor at the U. S. Naval Academy for almost seventeen years, Cusachs had served most recently as assistant naval attaché to Madrid under Benton Decker. While in Spain, Cusachs had pushed American influence in Spanish political and business circles, becoming so effective that Ambassador Willard had demanded his recall for interfering in diplomatic questions. Though the Navy Department had recalled Cusachs, Daniels and Welles had considered him a victim of interdepartmental rivalry over the control of U. S. policy in Spain.[15]

No sooner had Cusachs returned from Madrid, than Welles hustled him off to Havana. Arriving in early May 1918, Cusachs discovered a remarkably pro-German attitude for a country long dominated by American influences. "I feel the enemy's forces all around me and I have never felt so absolutely helpless to combat them," he wrote Washington.[16] Moreover, Cusachs found U. S. intelligence on the island in disarray. Kear's office was disorganized, with authority split between Guantanamo and Peard's service in Santiago de Cuba. Everywhere Cusachs turned he found rivalry. Army Intelligence, the State Department, and other services investigated naval matters. "The War Trade Board seem to have taken thorough control of the shipping and this Office is being pushed aside and given to understand that the War Trade Board is responsible for all shipments."[17]

Cusachs recommended a complete reorganization of intelligence operations in Cuba, and he received a sympathetic hearing in Washington, where his old friend Decker presently served as assistant DNI. Meanwhile, the attaché pursued his own reorganization, sending field agents new instructions for data on labor conditions in the sugar cane fields, location of wireless station, and submarine bases. At the same time he launched an attack on a German espionage group in Havana headed by Herman and Albert Upmann. A wealthy banker and president of the German Club of Cuba, Herman led a spy ring that included the former Austrian consul and other German-born businessmen on the Caribbean island. Not only did this syndicate dominate many Cuban establishments, but it had financial control as well over a bank in New Orleans, a chemical company in St. Louis, and a steel firm in Pennsylvania. Through these contacts, the Upmanns collected industrial information about the United States. Though naval intelligence had learned earlier about the ring, Kear had failed to curb its activities. Cusachs wasted little time in breaking Upmann's syndicate.[18]

ONI poured most of its resources in the Western Hemisphere into the Caribbean zone, but also attempted to cover South America. Several experienced intelligence officers ran this network, including retired Captain John H. Gibbons in Buenos Aires, retired Rear Admiral Reginald F. Nicholson in Santiago, and Captain Frank K. Hill in Rio de Janeiro. Several unusually competent assistant naval attachés supported them. Connecticut lawyer Charles Bates Dana covered Montevideo and added judicious advice in Argentina, while Lieutenants F. E. Hufnagel and C. Moran checked Lima and Quito, and one agent reportedly infiltrated the Chilean foreign office.[19]

Hill recruited the most elaborate intelligence system in Brazil, including a mail censor, an assistant at the port of Pernambuco, two civilian clerks, three field agents, and a liaison officer with the Brazilian Navy. He employed the American representatives in Brazil of the Baldwin Locomotive, Borden Milk, and Bethlehem Steel companies, the last serving as the naval attaché's private secretary. Hill's best informant was an agent of the Central and South American Cable Company, who "had wide knowledge and connections in Brazil; thorough knowledge of all code system and language qualifications."[20]

Hill's diverse staff confronted a variety of tasks: The attaché's office investigated rumors of nearby enemy submarines and monitored attempts to purchase ships in Brazil. It prepared files on Brazil's Navy, foreign policies, and economic situation, paying close attention to labor conditions in the manganese mines of Minas Gerais. Hill's people surveyed the local press, interviewed informants, and studied rumors of internal unrest. Apparently, much of their intelligence work went toward counteracting British influence, including outbidding Vickers and Armstrong to win a lucrative contract for Bethlehem Steel to repair Brazilian battleships.[21]

Hill and his ONI colleagues in the Western Hemisphere collected data on wartime associate Japan as well as on Britain and the enemy. As the war progressed, naval intelligence became increasingly fascinated by Japanese policies and military potential. Suspect files often lumped Japanese spies on the list of America's enemies along with German and Austrian operatives, and ONI spent nearly as much time gathering data on Japanese pearl fishermen in Panama as on German wireless stations in Mexico. Wartime dossiers documented Japanese interest in Magdalena Bay, real estate transactions in Central America, and business ventures in South America.[22]

U. S. Naval Attaché Lieutenant Commander Frederick Joseph Horne in Tokyo hoped to establish a secret information service in Japan. Assisted by Lieutenant Colonel William L. Redles, Horne proceeded cautiously. Japanese language expert Ensign Robert G. Payne arrived under the cover of a clerk assigned to count merchantships in Japanese waters. However, growing Japanese suspicions limited Horne's effectiveness, and many wartime reports dealt in vague generalities.[23]

Information from Gillis in China was more provocative. The experienced agent bombarded ONI with ominous reports of Japanese plots to conquer China, Manchuria, and Siberia. "Unless checked, Japan's aggressive policy in the Far East will bring war either with us or the British (or perhaps both) sooner or later," he warned, "and it is with the object of doing all in our power to prevent this deplorable event that I suggest our using every effort to obtain publicity."[24] His sense of urgency increased with each new request for money. Gillis asked for $10,000 to cover investigations in the East Indies and another $5,000 to check Japanese intrigue in Siberia. But apparently the latter sum was not well spent, since the U. S. naval attaché in Peking claimed his sources reported that the Bolsheviks were mere terrorist bands run by "Jews and former convicts."[25]

Gillis demanded the dispatch of more agents to East Asia, including code experts and operatives to tap cables and intercept Japanese messages. "I am even not so sure but what it might be well for you to be in a position to lay your hands on a skilled 'cracksman' so that he could be available at short notice if it ever became desirable or necessary to resort to such extreme measures as breaking into a safe to get information of an incriminating character," Gillis wrote ONI.[26]

Naval intelligence did not rush a safecracker to Peking but displayed unusual ingenuity in covering its Far Eastern agents with clever cloaks. A female employee of Bonwit Teller & Company toured Asia on a clothes-buying trip while collecting information for ONI. At the same time, Welles hired the curator of mammals at the American Museum of Natural History as an operative for China. The Office supplied him with $4.00 a day and instructions to transmit messages to Gillis in invisible ink. "It is hoped good use can be made of his abilities and cover," Welles cabled his attaché in Peking. Another traveler used by the director worked as a salesman for the Nicholson File Company of Rhode Island, and mailed information to ONI from the Orient through his home office. For Southeast Asia, the intelligence agency came up with a forestry adviser to visit the area under the pretense of studying local supplies of timber.[27]

Providing agents to follow Japanese activities in the Pacific islands seized from Germany during the war proved far more difficult than finding good operatives for China. Welles informed the U. S. naval governor on Guam that he urgently required intelligence from the Marshalls, Carolines, and Marianas. Several missionaries reported observing Japanese fortifications on Truk and a wireless station and military garrison on Yap. Welles wanted verification and suggested that the Navy Department send a private schooner filled with ONI undercover personnel to the Marshalls and the Carolines; but Admiral Benson vetoed the plan, warning the DNI never again to raise this sensitive question.[28]

Information about Japanese escapades closer to the United States became more voluminous. Indeed Van Antwerp uncovered what he believed was a major Japanese plan to take over Lower California. He discovered that a mysterious Japanese agent named Kondo owned the Mexican Industrial Development Company and the Lower California Fisheries Company, and held concessions for coastal fishing off the Pacific coast of Mexico. The local intelligence director learned further that Kondo's firm planned to construct a chain of packing houses and wharves from Guaymas to Turtle Bay. "This will give this Japanese Company stations at practically every big point on the Lower California peninsula, as well as the West Coast, and will keep them in close touch with conditions at Magdalena Harbor," he complained.[29]

Whether Van Antwerp's concern for Kondo stemmed from military or commercial reasons remained unclear. Were Kondo's packing houses potential sites for naval bases or noisome competition for entrepreneur Van Antwerp? Many civilian operatives and businessmen-reservists freely mixed private business with intelligence work, using informants, cable censorship, mail opening, and the Blacklist to destroy rival firms and foreign competitors. Access to the Navy Department's communication system helped. The international intelligence network of reservists and their business allies pursued a coherent policy to promote American interests in world markets, though they never formed a tightly coordinated organization. "This office, from the start . . . took the position that, not only were our investigations of cable users to be conducted with a view to stopping possible enemy activities," Spencer Eddy concluded, "but that every effort should be made to *assist* legitimate American business in its use of the cables."[30]

If ONI envisioned the establishment of a permanent international system to aid U. S. business enterprises after the war, the Armistice ending the European conflict delayed such plans. Conclusion of fighting meant hasty demobilization of U. S. forces overseas. Naval intelligence dismantled its organization with embarrassing rapidity, reservists returning promptly to civilian life as lawyers, bankers, or businessmen. In late 1918 ONI headquarters had employed over 300 reserve officers, but by 1 July 1920 only 24 remained. Branch offices closed in December

1918, and personnel went home. Boxes of suspect files, lists of potential agents, and administrative records lay disorganized in some unused storage room.

Recently promoted to rear admiral, Roger Welles assumed command of the 1st Division of the Atlantic Fleet, with veteran attaché Albert P. Niblack replacing him as director of naval intelligence on 1 May 1919. Niblack approached this duty with the same traditional view of ONI methods, goals, and definition of intelligence that had governed his outlook since the late nineteenth century. He abhorred interference in domestic affairs and resisted departmental pressure to investigate wartime scandals at Newport. He distrusted espionage and extralegal operations. "It has been the aim of the office to use only reputable business methods and avoid anything savoring of 'gumshoe' methods," Niblack wrote in 1920. "This point can not be too strongly emphasized."[31]

Though Niblack wished to return to intelligence concepts of earlier years, the world war had altered the character of such endeavors. ONI might shrink in size after the war, but an increasingly complex postwar world of ideological, economic, and political struggle prevented resurrection of a simple mission to collect information. Secret negotiations at Versailles to thrash out a peace gave some indication of the problems. Bitter Japan, paranoid France, vengeful Germany, and Bolshevik Russia all created almost irreconcilable international situations. Terrible economic dislocation and destruction of material and human resources plagued Allied victors as well as defeated nations. Even postwar America failed to escape the new environment, plunging into Red Scares, isolationism, and political corruption.

The next decades of disarmament, depression, and another world war promised to modify ONI further. DNIs would discover as their predecessors had earlier that their work reflected and responded to the total naval, political, and international environment. No intelligence chief between 1882 and 1918 had been able significantly to affect larger national or naval events. Those men remained second-level bureaucrats within the Navy Department. Moreover, as professional officers, they followed the official service attitude toward the limited overall value of intelligence, rather than formulating their own broader conception of a national intelligence policy. No matter how persuasive intelligence obligations might be in fostering an independent and critical attitude, their three-year billet was soon over, and they returned to sea duty, far from the attractions and frustrations present in ONI. Nevertheless, some were more successful than others in harnessing their agency to immediate trends and requirements. Thus Mason and Rodgers undoubtedly influenced opinion in favor of the New Navy. Sigsbee stimulated centralization and coordination of departmental planning and policy. Oliver and his progressive comrades found ONI a useful vehicle to air their reformist impulses, while Welles and his civilian cohorts adjusted the Office to larger missions.

ONI never became an important part of the professional lives of most other naval officers. At first naval engineers and constructors borrowed extensively from intelligence files, but advances in American naval technology and restrictions on easy access to information overseas curtailed cooperation. Luce, Mahan, and other naval theorists consulted ONI from time to time for information and encouragement, although these exchanges were more of a routine than a motivational nature. Still, there were always a few officers who considered the intelligence bureau an important instrument to prod a conservative naval bureaucracy to adopt modern technology, tactics, and organization. Walker, Sims, Fiske, Knox, and other insurgents hoped to advance reform through ONI. These impatient reformers stood outside the mainstream of the naval establishment, however, similar indeed to ONI itself.

Naval intelligence's relationship to the civilian bureaucracy manifested identical inconsistencies. Several late-nineteenth-century secretaries of the Navy turned to their intelligence branch for vital data with which to build a modern fleet. Two decades later the war emergency forced Daniels to consult more often with his intelligence agency, while the assistant secretary of the Navy developed an unusual affinity for ONI. In between, few departmental executives bothered much with the intelligence office, although President Theodore Roosevelt, often acting as his own secretary of the Navy, conferred regularly with ONI. So too did Taft and his Secretary of State Knox, both of whom employed the naval intelligence bureau to advance American business in overseas markets.

Between 1882 and 1918, then, the Office of Naval Intelligence had an occasional effect on the course of naval and national policy. But while policymakers periodically consulted the Office, most refused to recognize the importance of intelligence or to employ it in decision making, planning, and operations. Gradually ONI became insulated from the public, the government, and the rest of the Navy, and began to develop its own inner dynamism and organic coherence. Regardless of changes in intelligence personnel and policies, ONI preserved an institutional continuity and exhibited a remarkable resiliency in recovering from periods of neglect. Convinced of its own importance as an interpreter and defender of American interests and confronted with a seemingly endless disregard by the bureaucratic establishment, ONI moved toward covert conduct such as spying, counterespionage, domestic snooping, and other natural outgrowths of intelligence work. Thus when World War I removed early restraints, ONI displayed extralegal tendencies, endangered civil liberty, and threatened the democratic process.

In conclusion, this study has suggested that even in its earliest and most basic stage, ONI set precedents, evinced disturbing proclivities, and raised fascinating questions about the subsequent history of organized intelligence in America.

NOTES

1. ROOTS OF NAVAL INTELLIGENCE

1. James Robert Green, "The First Sixty Years of the Office of Naval Intelligence," 7; Lewis R. Hamersly, ed., *A Naval Encyclopaedia* (Philadelphia: Hamersly, 1881), 849; Richard Deacon, *The Silent War*, 13ff.

2. Frances Leigh Williams, *Matthew Fontaine Maury*, 396–417; also, see Vincent Ponko, Jr., *Ships, Seas, and Scientists: U. S. Naval Exploration and Discovery in the Nineteenth Century* (Annapolis: Naval Institute Press, 1974).

3. Charles Oscar Paullin, *Paullin's History of Naval Administration, 1775–1911*, 263–64; Rear Admiral Albert S. Barker, *Everyday Life in the Navy*, 32.

4. Robert E. Johnson, *Thence Round Cape Horn*, 131–33; Kenneth J. Hagan, *American Gunboat Diplomacy and the Old Navy, 1877–1889*, 38, 144, 149; Gustavus A. Weber, *The Hydrographic Office*, 31–33.

5. Radford to Robeson, 9 Aug. 1869, enclosed in 27 Aug. 1869, Letters to Officers Commanding Squadrons or Vessels, National Archives, Record Group 45, microfilm roll 230, hereafter cited as Squadron Letters; Radford to Capt. Wm. H. Macomb, 26 Aug. 1869, Area File of the Naval Records Collection, 1775–1910: Area 4, NA, RG 45, microfilm roll 21, hereafter Area 4 File.

6. Radford to Robeson, 31 Aug. and 12 Nov. 1869, roll 230, Squadron Letters.

7. Marvin to Radford, 9 Nov. 1869, ibid.

8. Marvin to Radford, 4 Aug. 1870, roll 232; Luce to Robeson, 12 Sept. 1870, Luce to Glisson, 22 Sept. 1870, roll 231; Breese to Glisson, 16 Oct. 1870, roll 231, all in ibid.

9. Robeson to Rodgers, 8 Nov. 1870, Appointments, Orders, and Resignations, No. 42, Records of the Bureau of Naval Personnel, National Archives, Record Group 24, hereafter cited as Appointments.

10. Robeson to Wilson, 12 May 1870, Reed to Supts. of Dockyards, 15 June 1870, in *Report of Assistant Naval Constructor Theodore D. Wilson on the Dock Yards of Europe, 1870*, National Archives, Record Group 45.

11. Robeson to Simpson, 30 June 1870, Letters to Naval Academy, Commanding, and Other Officers, No. 1, NA, RG 45, hereafter cited as Officers Letters; Cdr. Edward Simpson, *Report on a Naval Mission to Europe Especially Devoted to the Material and Construction of Artillery*, 2 vols. (Washington, D.C.: Government Printing Office, 1873).

12. Hamersly, ed., *Naval Encyclopaedia*, 326–32, 999–1000.

13. Chief Engineer J. W. King, *Report of Chief Engineer J. W. King, United States Navy, on European Ships of War and their Armament, Naval Administration and Economy, Marine Constructions, Torpedo-Warfare, Dock-Yards, Etc.* (Washington, D.C., 1878).

14. King, *Report*, 19.

15. Paullin, *Naval Administration*, 326–32; Walter LaFeber, *The New American Empire*, 39–46.

16. T. B. M. Mason, "The United States Naval Institute," *The United Service*, I (1879): 295.

17. For personnel on station, see Squadron Letters, roll 66.

18. Rodgers to the Secretary of the Navy, 5 June and 17 July 1879, Rodgers to Board on Injuries received by the *Huascar* in the Action of Oct. 8, 1879, Squadron Letters.

19. Rodgers to Board on Injuries, ibid.
20. Rodgers to Secretary of the Navy, 4 and 11 Nov. 1879, ibid.
21. Stevens to Hunt, 4 May 1881, ibid.

2. AN INTELLIGENCE OFFICE

1. James D. Richardson, *A Compilation of the Messages and Papers of the Presidents*, X: 4638; Paullin, *Naval Administration*, 370, 388.
2. Thomas Hunt, *The Life of William H. Hunt;* Paullin, *Naval Administration*, 370, 388.
3. Mason, "Naval Institute," 295.
4. Mason, "Naval Institute," 295.
5. Captain J. M. Ellicott, "Theodorus Bailey Meyers (sic) Mason, Founder of the Office of Naval Intelligence," 266; Mason, "The Necessity for Divers in Our Navy," *The United Service*, 5 (Oct. 1881): 400–1; other Mason essays in, Hamersly, ed., *Naval Encyclopaedia*, 217–18, 423–24, 510–11, 514, 627–28.
6. Walker to Mason, 7 June 1882, Appointments, No. 53; Ellicott, "Mason"; Frances P. Thomas, *Career of John Grimes Walker;* T. B. Mason Papers, Naval History Division, Smithsonian Institution, Washington, D.C.
7. Chandler to Mason, 25 July 1882, Officers Letters, vol. 12.
8. Mason, "A Medal of Honor for Officers," *The United Service*, IV (Jan., 1881), 10.
9. *Annual Report of the Board of Regents of the Smithsonian Institution* for the years 1882 and 1883 (Washington, D.C., 1884); Walker to Baird, 16 Nov. 1883, The Papers of Rear Admiral John G. Walker, Naval Historical Foundation Collection, Library of Congress, hereafter cited as NHFC.
10. Register of Personnel of the Office of Naval Intelligence, 1882–1918, Records of the Office of the Chief of Naval Operations, National Archives, Record Group 38, hereafter cited as ONI Register; Rear Admiral A. G. Berry, "The Beginning of the Office of Naval Intelligence," *United States Naval Institute Proceedings*, 63 (Jan. 1937): 102, hereafter cited as *USNIP*.
11. C. C. Rogers, "Naval Intelligence," *USNIP*, 9 (1883): 660.
12. Ronald Spector, *Professors of War*, 16–17; Rogers, "Naval Intelligence," 659ff.
13. Rogers, "Naval Intelligence," 678–79, 683.
14. Berry, "Office of Naval Intelligence," 102; Miers Fisher Wright, *Operations of the French Navy in War with Tunis*, ONI War Series No. 1 (Washington, D.C., GPO, 1883); Davis to consular officers, 20 Nov. 1883, General Correspondence of the Office of Naval Intelligence, 1882–1899, National Archives, Record Group 38, hereafter cited as ONIGC.
15. Skerrett to Walker, 6 Oct. 1882, Terry to Walker, 8 Aug. 1882, Grant to Walker, 13 Sept. 1882, Rodgers to ONI, 12 Aug. 1882, Barker to Walker, 19 May 1883, ONIGC.
16. Walker to Allison, 27 Oct. 1883, Walker Papers.
17. Quoted in Walker to Capt. Albert Kautz, 16 Feb. 1883, also, see Walker to Chandler and to the President, 27 Oct. 1883, Walker to Cooper, 31 Aug. 1882, Walker to Crosby, 27 Feb. and 19 Mar. 1883, Walker to Chandler, 7 Aug. 1883, Walker Papers.
18. Luce to Mason, 24 Nov. 1883, ONIGC.
19. Sigsbee to Mason, 18 Mar. 1883, ibid.
20. Francis T. Bowles, "Our New Cruisers," *USNIP*, 9 (1883): 622; also, see Bowles to Mason, 9 Nov. 1881, Mason Papers.
21. Miscellanies Written by or Relating to Mason, Mason Papers.

3. THE NEW NAVY

1. William (Sims) to his mother, 9 Mar. 1897, The Papers of Admiral William S. Sims, NHFC.

2. Colwell, "Discussion," *USNIP,* 16 (Mar. 1890): 509; Colwell in *Naval Reserves, Training and Materiel,* ONI General Information Series No. VII (Washington, D.C., 1888), 5; Buckingham to Walker, 14 Sept. 1888, Letters Sent by Naval Attachés, 1885–1905, National Archives, Record Group 38; Seaton Schroeder, *A Half Century of Naval Service.*

3. Schroeder, "The Preservation of Iron Ships' Bottoms," in *Naval Reserves,* 263–87.

4. Chambers to Sicard, 14 Sept. 1881, 27 June 1882, The Papers of Captain Washington Irving Chambers, NHFC; Chambers, "A Modified Monitor, with a New Method of Mounting and Working the Guns," *USNIP,* 7 (1881), 437–46.

5. Chambers, "The Best Method for Reconstruction and Increase of the Navy," *USNIP,* 11 (1885): 3–83; Thomas to Chambers, 3 Apr. 1884, Chandler to Chambers, 15 Dec. 1884, Chambers Papers.

6. Smithsonian Institution, *Annual Report* for the Year 1883, 26; John B. Bernadou, "Korea and the Koreans," *National Geographic Magazine,* 2 (1890): 233–40.

7. ONI Register.

8. Richardson, *Messages and Papers,* X: 4923, 4936.

9. See, Mark D. Hirsch, *William C. Whitney;* Leonard Alexander Swann, Jr., *John Roach, Maritime Entrepreneur.*

10. Overseas purchases discussed in, Buckingham to Walker, 17 Dec. 1885, Chadwick to Whitney, 4 Dec. 1885, 20 Feb. 1886, Naval Attaché Letters, National Archives, Record Group 38, hereafter cited as NAL; Walker to Whitney, 8, 12, and 15 Sept. 1887, Walker Papers.

11. Jones to Porter, 20 Apr. 1885, Ingraham to Assistant Secretary of State Rives, 6 Feb. 1889, McCalla to Chief Bureau of Navigation, 21 Dec. 1888, forwarded by Bayard to Whitney between 1885 and 1889, ONIGC.

12. Bayard to Whitney, 14 Jan. 1887, ibid.

13. Walker to Ramsay, 10 June 1886, ibid.

14. Hugh B. Hammett, *Hilary Abner Herbert,* 109–45; Herbert to Rodgers, 8 Feb., 13 June, 18 July 1886, 23 Jan. 1887, 22 Aug. 1888, ONIGC.

15. Walker to Rodgers, 30 July 1885, Hichborn to Rodgers, 25 Apr. 1889, Scott to Rodgers, 16 Mar. 1888, ONIGC; Bradford to Sargent, 20 June 1889, Correspondence of Lieutenant Nathan Sargent, National Archives, Record Group 45.

16. Spector, *Professors of War,* 50ff; Walker to Luce, 30 Sept. 1887, The Papers of Rear Admiral Stephen Bleecker Luce, NHFC.

17. Robert Seager II and Doris D. Maguire, eds., *Letters and Papers of Alfred Thayer Mahan,* 3 vols., I: 627, 630, 640, 649–50, 656, 659, 664, 689; Mahan to Rodgers, 1 Nov. 1888, ONIGC.

18. Humphreys to Rodgers, 18 May 1885, Luce to Rodgers, 22 Dec. 1887, Vreeland to ONI, Apr. 1886, Thomas to Raymond (Rodgers), 8 Jan. 1889, Thomas to Chief Bureau of Navigation, 3 Apr. 1886, Snowden to Chief Intelligence Officer, 19 Dec. 1888, ONIGC.

19. Walker to Chadwick, 22 May 1887, Walker Papers.

20. Walker to Ramsay, 26 Sept. 1888, ONIGC.

21. Tyler to Whitney, 23 Feb. 1888, Thompson to Rodgers, 25 Jan. 1889, ibid.

22. Miller to Walker, 4 Jan. 1886, Moore to Miller, 29 Dec. 1885, Hogg to Dyer, 3 Sept. 1888, Dyer to Bureau of Navigation, 4 Sept. 1888, 22 Nov. 1888, Leary to Kempff, 5 Nov. 1888, ONIGC.

23. Walker to Franklin, 15 July 1885, Area 4 File, microfilm roll 21. Walker also criticized Mahan in 1884 when as commanding officer of the *Wachusett* on the Pacific Station, he ignored all intelligence work, Seager and Maguire, *Mahan Letters,* I: 563–64.

24. S. A. Staunton, "Naval Training and the Changes Induced by Recent Progress in the Implements of Naval Warfare," in *Naval Reserves,* 66.

25. Walker to McCalla, 6 Apr. 1885, Walker Papers. Also, see C. C. Rogers, *Intelligence Report of the Panama Canal* (Washington, D.C., 1888); Walker to Luce, 24 Nov. 1886, Luce Papers; W. W. Kimball and W. L. Capps, *Special Intelligence Report on the Progress of the Work on the Panama Canal During the Year 1885* (Washington, D.C., 1886).

26. Walker to Gridley, 25 July 1886, Walker Papers; also, see John A. S. Grenville and George Berkeley Young, *Politics, Strategy, and American Diplomacy*, 63–71.

27. Walker to Fourth Auditor Shelley, 13 Sept. 1887, Walker Papers; ONI compiled an "Intelligence Report on War Resources of Canada," which Mahan borrowed for his "Contingency Plan of Operations in Case of War with Great Britain, 1890," Seager and Maguire, *Mahan Letters*, I: 656, III: 559–76.

4. THE FIRST ATTACHÉS

1. Alfred Vagts, *The Military Attaché*, 6–8, 27–29.

2. Lt. William L. Sachse, "Our Naval Attaché System," 663; Hunt to Shufeldt, 18 Mar. 1881, Appointments, vol. 52.

3. Chadwick, *Report on the Training System for the Navy and Mercantile Marine of England and on the Naval Training System of France, Made to the Bureau of Equipment and Recruiting, U.S.N. Department, Sept. 1879* (Washington, D.C., 1880).

4. Walker to Chadwick, 22 Aug. 1882, Chandler to Chadwick, 12 July 1882, Officers Letters, vol. 12; Walker to Chadwick, 28 Oct. 1882, Appointments, vol. 53.

5. Acting Secretary Nichols to Chadwick, 5 Aug. 1884, Chandler to Chadwick, 1 Feb. 1884, Officers Letters, vol. 14.

6. Chandler to Secretary of War Lincoln and to Chadwick, 29 Mar. 1884, ibid.

7. Chadwick to Walker, 13 June 1885, Chadwick to Whitney, 13 Nov. 1887, 7 Oct. 1887, NAL; an inventory of Chadwick's earliest dispatches can be found in, Bureau of Navigation Letterbooks, 1882, National Archives, Record Group 24.

8. Nichols to Foulk, 13 Nov. 1883, Chandler to Foulk, 3 Nov. 1883, Officers Letters, vol. 14.

9. Frelinghuysen to Foulk, 12 Nov. 1883, Diplomatic Instructions from Department of State, Korea, National Archives, Record Group 59; Tyler Dennett, "Early American Policy in Korea, 1883–87: The Services of Lieutenant George C. Foulk," *Political Science Quarterly*, 37 (1923): 82–103.

10. Buckingham, Foulk, and McLean, *Observations upon the Korean Coast, Japanese-Korean Ports, and Siberia, Made During a Journey from the Asiatic Station to the United States through Siberia and Europe, June 3 to Sept. 8, 1882*, ONI General Information Series No. 1 (Washington, D.C., 1883); Buckingham to Rodgers, 23 Apr. 1885, ONIGC.

11. Harmony to Buckingham, 11 Nov. 1885, Appointments, vol. 56; Buckingham to Rodgers, 15 Mar. 1889, Letters Sent by Naval Attachés, National Archives, Record Group 38.

12. Buckingham to Rodgers, 6 May 1887, LSNA.

13. Buckingham to Chief Bureau of Navigation, 3 Sept. 1886, Buckingham to McCalla, 28 July 1886, ibid.

14. Buckingham to Fried. Krupp, Esq., 30 Oct. 1888, Buckingham to Chadwick, 24 Oct. 1888, ibid.

15. Whitney to Sargent, 20 Nov. 1888, Appointments, vol. 58; Luce to Sargent, 10 July 1881, Sargent Papers, NHFC; Sargent, "Suggestions in Favor of More Practical and Efficient Service Exercises," *USNIP*, 10 (1884): 233–40.

16. Sargent to Walker, 17 June 1889, Sargent Correspondence.

17. Rodgers to Sargent, 10 Apr. 1889, ibid.

18. Ibid., 30 Mar. 1889.

19. Sicard to Sargent, 23 Jan. 1889, Bradford to Sargent, 20 June 1889, Rodgers to Sargent, 11 Feb. 1889, ibid.

20. Buckingham to Chadwick, 28 June 1886, LSNA.

21. Rodgers to Sargent, 30 Nov. 1888, Sargent Corres.

22. Sargent, "Diary," entry 16 Dec. 1891, Sargent Papers.

23. Buckingham to Barber, 22 June 1886, LSNA.

24. Buckingham to Shelley, 4th Auditor, Treasury Department, 25 June 1886, Buckingham to Walker, 20 Sept. 1887, Buckingham to Fieldmarshal (McCalla), 28 June 1886, ibid.

25. Buckingham to McCalla, 8 Mar. 1886, ibid.; for a complete collection of naval attaché visiting and calling cards see, Sargent "Scrapbooks," Sargent Papers.

5. AN UNDESIRABLE BILLET

1. Walker to Chandler, 9 Sept. 1887, Walker Papers.

2. "Report of Navy Policy Board," in *USNIP*, 16 (1890): 202–11; B. Franklin Cooling, *Benjamin Franklin Tracy*; Walter R. Herrick Jr., *The American Naval Revolution*.

3. Lt. Mentz, "The Ministries of Marine and Personnel of Several European Navies," in *A Year's Naval Progress, June 1890*, ONI General Information Series No. IX (Washington, D.C., 1890), 226.

4. Tracy to Ramsay, 3 Oct. 1890, ONIGC; Paullin, *Naval Administration*, 243ff; Charles H. Davis, *Life of Charles Henry Davis, Rear Admiral, 1807–1877*.

5. Tracy to Alusna London (cable address for U. S. Naval Attaché), 31 July 1889, Emory to Bureau of Navigation, 16 and 18 June 1890, Ramsay to Alusna, 19 June 1890, Translation of Cipher Messages Sent, NA, RG 45, hereafter cited as Ciphers Sent; Edward W. Very, "The Annapolis Armor Test," *USNIP*, 16 (1890): 645; Dean C. Allard, Jr., "The Influence of the United States Navy upon the American Steel Industry, 1880–1900"; Cooling, *Tracy*, 90ff; Herrick, *Naval Revolution*, 79.

6. Ramsay to Sargent, 31 Jan. and 15 Apr. 1890, Davis to Sargent, 15 and 19 Oct. 1889, 17 Dec. 1889, Singer to Sargent, 28 Apr. 1890, Sargent Corres.

7. Folger to Sargent, 5 Jan. and 21 July 1891, Folger to Fletcher, 18 Feb. 1891; Singer to Sargent, 18 Oct. 1889, Sargent Corres.

8. W. H. H. Southerland, "Notes on Ordnance and Gunnery," 97–101, 113, and "The Development of the Rapid-Fire Guns for Naval Use," 325–26, both in, *A Year's Naval Progress, June 1890;* Singer to Sargent, 1 July 1890, Sargent Corres.

9. Grenville and Young, *Politics, Strategy*, 95–101; LaFeber, *New Empire*, 130–36.

10. Cooling, *Tracy*, 118–19.

11. Cooling, *Tracy*, 120; Johnson, *Cape Horn*, 146; Seager and Maguire, *Mahan Letters*, II: 59, 734; Tracy to Remey, 17 May 1891, Tracy to Brown, 1 Sept. 1891, Ciphers Sent.

12. Folger to Soley, 2 Jan. and 15 Feb. 1892, Holmes Steamship Co. to Secretary of the Navy, 23 Dec. 1891, Cooke to Secretary of the Navy, 17 Nov. 1891, ONIGC; Tracy to Walker, 25 Jan. 1892, Tracy to Brown, 9 Dec. 1891, 17 Jan. 1892, Ciphers Sent; also, "The Dairy of Charles O'Neil," 3 Jan. 1892, The Papers of Rear Admiral Charles F. O'Neil, NHFC.

13. Evans to Secretary of the Navy, 17 Jan. 1892, Translations of Cipher Messages Received, NA, RG 45, hereafter cited as Ciphers Received; Sears to Davis, 15 and 22 Jan., 10 July 1892, ONIGC.

14. Rear Admiral Albert Gleaves, *William Hemsley Emory*, 134–36; Emory to Soley, 2, 25, 26, and 28 Jan. 1892, Emory to Consuls, 26 Jan. 1892, NAL; Sargent to Soley, 3 and 18 Jan. 1892, NAL; Sargent to U. S. Consuls, 23 Dec. 1891, Sargent Corres.

15. Davis to Mentz, Peters, and Simpson, 23 Dec. 1891, to Davis, 24 Dec. 1891, ONIGC; Mahan to Luce, 10 Jan. 1892, Luce Papers.

16. Walker to Soley, 20 Jan. 1892, ONI to Walker, 18 Jan. 1892, ONIGC; C. C. Rogers, *Confidential Notes on the Defenses and Military Resources of the Republic of Chile* (Washington, D.C., 1892), 16.

17. Davis to Sargent, 17 Mar. 1892, Sargent Corres.

18. Walker to Chandler, 22 Dec. 1887, Walker Papers; Singer to Sargent, 24 Dec. 1889, Sargent Corres.; Davis, *Davis*, 9, 336.

19. Singer to Sargent, 13 and 29 Jan. 1890, 6 Jan. 1891, Davis to Sargent, 12 Nov. 1889, 9 May 1890, 6 Jan. 1891, Sargent Corres.

20. J. R. Soley, *Report on Foreign Systems of Naval Education* (Washington, D.C., 1880); *Dictionary of American Biography*, vol. 17: 392; Spector, *Professors of War*, 27ff.

21. Singer to Sargent, 23 Oct. 1892, Sargent Corres.

22. Singer to Sargent, 9 Dec. 1889, ibid.

23. Pickering to Secretary of the Navy, 14 Mar. 1892, ONIGC; Sims to People (his family), 25 Nov. 1894, Sims Papers: Sargent "Diary," 16 Dec. 1891, Sargent Papers.

24. Davis to Sargent, 29 Sept. 1891, Sargent Corres.

25. Singer to Sargent, 31 Aug. and 6 Nov. 1892, ibid.

6. THE WIDENING INTELLIGENCE FIELD

1. Singer to Sargent, 24 Feb. 1893, Sargent Corres.

2. Ibid.

3. Singer to Sargent, 6 Nov. 1892, Sargent Corres.; *The International Columbian Naval Rendezvous and Review of 1893 and Naval Manoeuvres of 1892*, ONI General Information Series No. XII (Washington, D.C., 1893), 15–16.

4. Bradley Fiske, *From Midshipman*, 163; Damon E. Cummings, *Richard Wainwright*, 191–93; Singer to Sargent, 6 Nov. 1892, Sargent Corres.

5. Singer to Sargent, 27 Sept. 1892, Chadwick to Sargent, 7 Oct. 1892, 22 Mar. 1893, Sargent Corres.; Rodgers to Chadwick, 19 Oct. and 19 Dec. 1892, LSNA.

6. Emory to Soley, 27 Jan. 1892, NAL.

7. Vagts, *Military Attaché*, 222–24; Rodgers to Assistant Secretary, 12 Oct. 1892, LSNA.

8. Rodgers to Chadwick, 2 Dec. 1892, LSNA.

9. Rodgers to Chadwick, 11 Mar. 1893, ibid.

10. Rodgers to Sargent, 8 June 1893, Rodgers to Nordenfeldt, 22 May 1893, Rodgers to Simpson, 23 Oct. 1892, ibid.

11. Rodgers to Singer, 7 July 1893, ibid.

12. Richardson, *Messages and Papers*, XIII: 5883.

13. Herbert to Rodgers, 18 June 1896, Confidential Letters Sent; Herbert to Cowles, 12 Dec. 1896, Cowles to Secretary of the Navy, 9 Dec. 1896, NAL. Also, see Hammett, *Herbert*, 177–79; Herrick, *Naval Revolution*, 181–83.

14. Karmany, "Notes on Small Arms," in *Notes of the Year's Naval Progress, July 1894*, ONI General Information Series No. XVI (Washington, D.C., 1897), 73–140.

15. LaFeber, *New Empire*, 210–18; Hammett, *Herbert*, 199–202; Yates Stirling, *Sea Duty*, 22–23; Grant, "Events in Harbor of Rio de Janeiro, Brazil," VI File, Subject File, 1776–1911, NA, RG 45, hereafter cited as Subject File; Rogers, "The Revolt in Brazil," *Notes 1894*, 374–415.

16. John L. Rawlinson, *China's Struggle for Naval Development, 1839–1895* (Cambridge, Mass.: Harvard University Press, 1967), 168–96; Jeffery M. Dorwart, *The Pigtail War: American Involvement in the Sino-Japanese War of 1894–1895* (Amherst: University of Massachusetts Press, 1975), 101–6.

17. Herbert to Carpenter, 24 Sept. 1894, 9 Oct. 1894, 18 Feb. 1895, Ciphers Sent.

18. Folger to Carpenter, 14 Jan. 1895, Area 10 File, microfilm roll 357; "General Notes on Ships of the Japanese Navy after Battle of Yalu," 00 File, Subject File; Sims to his family, Dec. 1894, Sims Papers.

19. Herbert to CO *Petrel* (Emory), 30 Mar. 1895, Ramsay to CO *Petrel*, 8 Apr. 1895, Herbert to CinC Asiatic Station, 30 Mar. 1895, Herbert to Emory, 27 Mar. 1895, The Papers of Rear Admiral William Hemsley Emory, NHFC.

20. Cowles to Assistant Secretary, 22 Sept., 13, 24 Oct. 1894, NAL; Rodgers to Assistant Secretary, 4 Jan., 4, 12, Mar. 1895, LSNA.

21. Barber to Bureau of Navigation, 18 July 1898, LSNA; Barber to Assistant Secretary, 26 Sept., 30 Dec. 1895, NAL: Tokyo, Madrid, etc.

22. Cowles to Assistant Secretary, 22 Apr. 1896, NAL.

23. Hammett, *Herbert*, 202–6; Grenville and Young, *Politics, Strategy*, 120–69; Cowles to McAdoo, 21 Mar. 1896, Cowles to Herbert, 12 Feb. 1896, NAL.

24. Taylor to Luce, 22 Jan. 1896, Luce Papers.

25. Ira Harris, "Naval Conditions of the Great Lakes, 6 Mar. 1896," Lt. John Quimby, "Fleet Action Near Florida Keys, 1896," Lt. Hunker, "Attack on Halifax and Adjacent Waters," Capt. H. C. Taylor, "Outline of Plan for Construction of Vessels after Outbreak of War, March 1896," in UNOpP File, Intelligence and Technological Archives, Record Group 8, Naval War College Historical Collection, Naval War College, Newport, Rhode Island, hereafter cited as NWCA; Herbert to Taylor, 21 Mar. 1895, Naval War College Papers, Miscellany, NHFC.

26. Herbert to Gridley, 23 Jan. 1896, Venezuela Incident, 1896, OL File, Subject File.

27. Taylor to Luce, 2 Dec. 1895, Luce Papers.

28. Spector, *Professors of War*, 97–98.

7. PLANNING FOR WAR

1. Cummings, *Wainwright*, 23–66.

2. Ibid., 73–74.

3. Roosevelt to Wainwright, 4 Nov. 1915, quoted in, Cummings, *Wainwright*, 256.

4. Wainwright, "Our Naval Power," *USNIP*, 24 (1898): 43.

5. Cummings, *Wainwright*, 68–78 passim; Roosevelt to Chief Intelligence Officer, 4 Mar. 1898, ONIGC; Roosevelt to Long, 22 Jan. 1898, in Gardner Weld Allen, ed., *Papers of John Davis Long*, 41.

6. Grenville and Young, *Politics, Strategy*, 270–71; Long to CinC Pacific Station, 20 July 1897, Confidential Letters Sent; Cummings, *Wainwright*, 74; Wainwright, "Our Naval Power," 65.

7. W. W. Kimball, "War with Spain—General Scheme," Records of Naval Operating Forces, NA, RG 313; Kimball, "War with Spain, 1896," box 11, Basic Joint, Combined and Navy War Plans and Related Documents, 1905–41, Naval War Plans in the General Board Papers, Operational Archives, Naval History Division, U. S. Navy, Washington Navy Yard, hereafter cited as, OpA; "Solution to Problem, 1897," Student Problems and Solutions, Record Group 12, NWCA; Cummings, *Wainwright*, 79; Grenville and Young, *Politics, Strategy*, 272–76.

8. Roosevelt to Long, 16 Dec. 1899, quoted in, Allen, ed., *Long Papers*, 287–88.

9. Niblack to Wainwright, 18 June 1897, Albert P. Niblack Letterbook, National Archives, Record Group 45.

10. Driggs, "The Increase in Naval Strength," in *Notes on Naval Progress, 1898*, ONI General Information Series No. XVII, Part I (Washington, D.C., 1898), 72.

11. Cummings, *Wainwright*, 83ff; Herrick, *Naval Revolution*, 210ff; LaFeber, *New Empire*, 347–49; J. E. Wisan, *The Cuban Crisis Reflected in the New York Press* (New York: Columbia University Press, 1934).

12. Roosevelt to Alusna London, 26 Feb., 3, 9 and 17 Mar. 1898, Cables from Naval Attaché, London, Spanish-American War Correspondence, NA, RG 38, hereafter cited as Spanish-American War Cables.

13. Colwell to Assistant Secretary, 2 Mar. 1898, ibid.

14. White to Roosevelt, 18 Mar. 1898, The Papers of Theodore Roosevelt, Library of Congress, microfilm series 1, roll 1.

15. Colwell to Secretary of the Navy, 11, 14, 19, 26 Mar. 1898, Spanish-American War Cables; White to Roosevelt, 18 Mar. 1898, Roosevelt Papers.

16. Long to Alusna London, 4 Apr. 1898, Colwell to Secretary of the Navy, 2 Apr. 1898, Hay to Secretary of the Navy, 5 Apr. 1898, Spanish-American War Cables.

17. Sims to Macora Bros., 26 Apr. 1898, John C. Colwell Letterbooks, NA, RG 45; Sims to his mother, 8 May 1898, Sims Papers.

18. Sims to Assistant Secretary, 23 Apr. 1898, Spanish-American War Cables; Assistant Secretary, 19 Apr. 1898, Colwell Letterbooks; Sims to his mother, 8 May 1898, Sims Papers.

19. Colwell to Secretary of the Navy, 29 Apr. 1898, Records of the Naval War Board, General Records of the Department of the Navy, NA, RG 80, hereafter cited as Naval War Board Records; Colwell to Bureau of Navigation, 10, 23, 24, and 29 June 1898, Colwell Letterbooks; Colwell to Chief Bureau of Navigation, 14 May 1898, Spanish-American War Cables.

20. Niblack to Assistant Secretary, 6, 9, and 24 Apr. 1898, Niblack Letterbooks.

21. Roosevelt to Clover, 4 Mar. 1898, Records of the Assistant Secretary of the Navy, Letterbooks, vol. 3, NA, RG 80.

22. Roosevelt to Clover, 15 Mar. 1898, Assistant Secretary Letterbooks, vol. 3; O'Neil to Chief Intelligence Officer, 23 Mar. 1898, ONIGC; Crowninshield requested intelligence about the Philippines as early as 10 Mar. 1898, Area 10 File, roll 362.

23. Barker, *Everyday Life*, 276–79.

24. Niblack to Wainwright, 4 Jan. 1897, Niblack Letterbook; Roosevelt to Long, 22 Jan. 1898, in Allen, ed., *Long Papers*, 41; Dyer to Chief Intelligence Officer, 24 Mar. 1898, NAL.

25. Dyer to Chief Intelligence Officer, 16 Apr. 1898, NAL; Sims to his mother, 6 Feb. 1898, Sims Papers; Sims to Assistant Secretary, 20 Apr. 1898, Colwell Letterbook.

8. WAR WITH SPAIN

1. *Appendix to Annual Report of the Secretary of the Navy, 1898*, 374.

2. For memories of a clerk in the Bureau of Navigation during 1898, see Hudnell to Baldridge, 22 Aug. 1940, Whittlesey to Long, 22 Aug. 1901, Area 10 File, roll 363; Memorandum for Disbursing Officer, 15 Nov. 1901, case 3750, ONIGC Cases 1899-1912.

3. Sicard to Long, 19 May 1898, Naval War Board Records.

4. *Appendix to Annual Report, 1898*, 33; Crowninshield Memorandum for the Board of Promotions, 19 Nov. 1898, Confidential Letters Sent; John D. Long, *The New American Navy*, II: 80–82.

5. Sicard to Secretary of the Navy, 19 May 1898, Naval War Board Records.

6. Elting E. Morison, *Admiral Sims*, 54; Barber to Bureau of Navigation, 9, 13, and 14 June 1898, Letters Sent by Naval Attachés; Long to Alusna, 25 Apr. 1898, Letters Sent to Naval Attachés, NA, RG 38; Colwell to Secretary of the Navy, 7 Sept. 1898, Special Letters Sent from Naval Attaché, London, 1898–99, NA, RG 45.

7. Sicard to ONI, 14 July 1898, Naval War Board Records.

8. Rhodri Jeffreys-Jones, *American Espionage: From Secret Service to CIA*, 29–41; Sicard to War Board, 31 May 1898, in Long to Alusna, Paris, 31 May 1898, Allen to Alusna, 1, 11, June 1898, Long to Alusna Paris, 18 June 1898, Sims to Chief BuNav, 24 May 1898, Long to Alusna, 31 May 1898, in Spanish-American War Cables; Mahan to Long, 28 July 1898, in Allen, ed., *Long Papers*, 166–67; Seager and Maguire, *Mahan Letters*, III: 627–43; Long to Rogers, 11 May 1898, Naval War Board Records.

9. Long to Sampson, 18 Apr. 1898, Spanish-American War Cables; Memorandum of Information for *Oregon* by ONI, NA, RG 45.

10. Colwell, "Influence of the Spanish-American War on Naval Practice Abroad, 16 Sept. 1899," VN File, Subject File.

11. William R. Braisted, *The United States Navy in the Pacific, 1897–1909*, 33–37; Long to Barber, 22 July 1898, Spanish-American War Cables; Barber to Bureau of Navigation, 2 Sept. 1898, 14 July 1898, Letters Sent by Naval Attachés; Sicard to Secretary of the Navy, 20 May 1898, Area 10 File, roll 363.

12. Sims to Chief Bureau of Navigation, 12 Feb. 1899, Massios to Secretary of the Navy, 31 Jan. 1899 in Clover to Bureau of Navigation, 7 Feb. 1899, ONIGC; Sims to Bureau of Navigation, 20 Aug. 1899, Spanish-American War Cables; Gibbins to Colwell, 22 Feb. 1899, Gibbins to Long, 31 Mar. 1899, Clover to London Attaché, 20 Apr. 1899, NAL; (Edward Breck), "A Dangerous Mission to Spain," *Cosmpolitan,* XXVI (Nov. – Dec. 1898): 3–4, 113–19; Barber to Bureau of Navigation, 8 Dec. 1898, LSNA.

13. Niblack's Extract Log of *Oregon,* 13 June 1899, roll 369, Pigman to CinC Asiatic Station, 28 July 1899, roll 370, Ellicott to ?, 30 Aug. 1898, roll 364, Area 10 File.

14. Beehler to Secretary of the Navy, 22 Dec. 1899, Clover to Beehler, 23 Dec. 1899, Clover to Secretary of the Navy, 16 Jan. 1900, Long to Beehler, 16 Jan. 1900, ONIGC; Colwell to Chief Bureau of Navigation, 17 Mar. 1899, NAL.

15. Key to Chief Bureau of Navigation, 1 Sept. 1899, ONIGC; Key to Chief Bureau of Navigation, 7 Mar. 1900, A. L. Key Letterbook, NAL.

16. Clover to Chief Bureau of Navigation, 19 May 1900, NAL.

17. Report of the Chief of Bureau of Navigation, *Appendix to Annual Report, 1898,* 322.

18. Ibid., 379, 449.

19. Paullin, *Naval Administration,* 441; *Spanish-American War Notes,* ONI War Series Nos. I–VI (Washington, D.C., 1898).

20. Clover Memorandum, 12 July 1899, ONIGC.

21. Driggs, Peters, Marsh, Howard to Chief Intelligence Officer, 21 Mar. 1899, Clover to Bureau of Navigation, 30 June 1899, ibid.

9. POTENTIAL ENEMY GERMANY

1. Stockton to Luce, 5 June 1898, quoted in Rear Admiral Albert Gleaves, *Life and Letters of Rear Admiral Stephen B. Luce,* 280–81.

2. Capt. H. C. Taylor, "Memorandum on General Staff for the U. S. Navy," *USNIP,* 26 (Sept. 1900): 445–46.

3. Cdr. Daniel Joseph Costello, "Planning for War: A History of the General Board of the Navy, 1900–1914"; Henry P. Beers, *The Bureau of Navigation,* 233; Proceedings of the General Board, No. 1, General Board Records, OpA.

4. Memorandum of the Service of Captain C. D. Sigsbee, U. S. Navy, The Papers of Charles D. Sigsbee, New York State Library, Albany; Sigsbee, *Deep Sea Soundings and Dredging* (Washington, D.C., 1880); Sigsbee, "Graphical Method for Navigators," *USNIP,* 11 (1885): 241–63.

5. Beehler to Baird, 7 Oct. 1899, Alger to Secretary of the Navy, 25 Jan. 1899, Sigsbee to Chief Bureau of Navigation, 12 Mar. 1900, ONIGC; Sigsbee to Baird, 26 Apr. 1901, Sigsbee to Clover, 5 Nov. 1900, Sigsbee Papers.

6. Sigsbee to Chief Bureau of Navigation, 6 Aug. 1901, case 3376, ONIGC; Sigsbee to Bingham, 28 Nov. 1900, Sigsbee Papers.

7. Sigsbee to Chief Bureau of Navigation, 3 Aug. 1900, ONIGC.

8. Sigsbee to Taylor, 10 July 1902, General Board File 421, General Board Records, OpA.

9. Ellicott, "Naval Reconnaissance in Time of Peace," *USNIP,* 17 (Sept. 1901): 562.

10. "Confidential Memorandum of Questions to be Answered by Officers Making Examinations for the General Board," 16, in Dewey to Secretary for the Navy, 26 Feb. 1903, General Board File 409, OpA.

11. "Confidential Memorandum of Instructions Governing Official Correspondence of the U. S. Naval Attachés, 1900," Breck to Chief Intelligence Officer, 5 Sept. 1901, case 3576, ONIGC; Harber to Sigsbee, Jan. 1901, Letters Sent by Naval Attachés.

12. "Sigsbee Memorandum," 21 May 1900, Proceedings General Board, No. 1, OpA; Sigsbee to Clover, 12 June 1900, Sigsbee Papers.

13. Buckingham to Walker, 14 Sept. 1888, Letters Sent by Naval Attachés.

14. Sigsbee to Mulligan, 13 Jan. 1900, Sigsbee Papers.

15. Sigsbee to Secretary of the Navy, etc., 22 Oct. 1901, case 3648, ONIGC.

16. Sigsbee to Bureau of Navigation, 10 May 1900, ONIGC.

17. Sigsbee to Secretary of the Navy, 11 Nov. 1901, case 3689, ONIGC.

18. Intelligence Report on Bombardment of Fort San Carlos, Venezuela, 21 Apr. 1903, VI File, Subject File; Johnston to ONI, 21 Apr. and 6 June 1903, Communications with Naval Attachés, 1882–1934, NA, RG 38.

19. Lt. W. L. Howard, "Increase in Naval Strength as Shown by Naval Budgets," 13–15, Lt. Knepper, "Some Navy Leagues—What They Are and What They Are Doing," 347, in Notes on Naval Progress, July 1, 1900, ONI General Information Series No. XIX (Washington, D.C., 1900).

20. Sigsbee to Hale, 9 Dec. 1902, ONIGC.

21. Memorandum for Foss, 17 Feb. 1900, ibid.

22. Sigsbee to Chief Bureau of Navigation, 4 June 1902, case 3363, ONIGC Cases.

23. Holger H. Herwig, Politics of Frustration, 52–53; Sigsbee to Chief Bureau of Navigation, 5 Aug. 1901, 11, 15, and 29 Apr., 4 June 1902, Long to Secretary of State, 30 Apr. 1902, ONIGC.

24. Harber to Bureau of Navigation, 24 Feb. 1903, case 3363, ONIGC Cases.

25. Sigsbee to Taylor, 2 May 1902, Sigsbee Papers.

26. Sigsbee to Taylor, 9 June 1902, ibid.

27. "Notes on Ships and Torpedo Boats," in Notes on Naval Progress, ONI General Information Series No. XXI (Washington, D.C., 1902), 9–83.

10. POTENTIAL ENEMY JAPAN

1. Capt. C. F. Goodrich, "Naval Intelligence During War," USNIP, 29 (June 1903): 359; Green, "Office of Naval Intelligence," 44.

2. Darling to President of General Board, 4 Jan. 1904, Confidential Letters Sent, NA, RG 45. ONI held information in three War Portfolios. Portfolio I covered the Atlantic, II included Asia, and III treated the Pacific Ocean, Naval War Plans in the General Board Papers, OpA.

3. Taylor to CinC Caribbean Squadron, 17 Feb., 18 Apr. 1904, Confidential Letters Sent; Taylor to Moody, 26 and 28 Dec. 1903, Marble to Intelligence Officer Olympia, 19 Jan. 1904, Marble Memo., 26 Jan. 1904, Converse to CinC Pacific Squadron, 21 Dec. 1904, General Board File 409, OpA.

4. S. A. Staunton, "Plan for the Occupation and Use of San Mun Bay, China, as a Temporary Advanced Base, Oct. 1905," UNOpP file, NWCA; advanced Asian base discussed in General Board on 26, 28, and 29 June 1900, Proceedings General Board No. 1, OpA; Braisted, U. S. Navy 1897–1909, 137–43.

5. McCully, The McCully Report, ed. by Richard von Doenhoff, 255; also, see "Diary and Related Records of Lt. N. A. McCully while Covering the Russian-Japanese War, Feb. 1904–Nov. 1905," NA, RG 38.

6. Marsh to ONI, 4 Mar. 1904, case 5509, Marble to Chief Bureau of Navigation, 13 Nov. 1906, case 8339, ONIGC.

7. Archibald to Navy Dept., n.d., General Board File 429-1, General Board Records; Marsh to Bureau of Navigation, 28 Apr. 1904, case 5447, ONIGC; Capt. W. L. Redles, "Tactical Question IV," XING File, Record Group 8, NWCA.

8. HHW (Whittlesey) Memorandum to Roosevelt, 22 July 1904, roll 46, Converse to Loeb (Roosevelt's secretary), 27 Oct. 1904, roll 48, Appendix to Memorandum "Battleships in the Russo-Japanese War," roll 49, Roosevelt Papers.

9. ONI to Roosevelt, 18 May 1904, roll 44, ibid.

10. Beehler, "Comments on Prize Essay for 1905," USNIP, 31 (Mar., 1905): 187.

11. Schroeder, "Gleanings from the Sea of Japan," *USNIP*, 32 (Mar., 1906): 79, 47–93.

12. Marble to ONI, 31 Mar. 1906, cited in Braisted, *U. S. Navy, 1897–1909*, 185.

13. Ibid., 191ff.

14. Rodgers to Bureau of Navigation, 19 Jan. 1907, case 7911, ONIGC.

15. Secretary of the Navy to Secretary of State, 23 May 1907, case 7911, Rodgers to Gillis, 30 Dec. 1907, case 8846, Rodgers to Gillis, 18 Nov. 1907, Gillis to Rodgers, 8 Jan. 1908, case 8731, Secretary of the Navy to Secretary of State, 17 June 1908, case 9348, ONIGC.

16. Gibbons to Rodgers, 15 Mar. 1907, case 8030, Gibbons to ONI, 6 Apr. 1907, case 8162, Howard to Rodgers, 16 May 1907, case 8139, Bernadou to ONI, 2 and 7 Mar. 1907, case 8032, Rodgers to Bernadou, 13 Apr. 1907, case 8038, ibid.

17. Howard to Rodgers, 1 July 1907, case 8444, Bernadou to Rodgers, 25 Aug. 1907, case 8139, Rodgers to Bernadou, 10 Nov. 1907, ibid.

18. Dougherty to Rodgers, 25 Nov. 1907, Rodgers to Secretary of the Navy, 29 May 1908, case 8139, Dougherty to Rodgers, 2 Sept. 1907, case 8474, Dougherty to Rodgers, 2 Feb. 1908, case 8897, ibid.

19. ONI Memorandum for General Board, 24 Sept., 7 Oct. 1907, case 8588, Whittlesey to Dougherty, 5 Aug. 1907, case 8487, ibid.; Braisted, *U. S. Navy, 1897–1909*, 203–15.

20. Whittlesey to Eberle, 30 Sept. 1908, case 9120, ONIGC.

21. Dougherty to Rodgers, 27 Mar., 2 Oct. 1908, case 8705 and case 9484, ONIGC; Robert Hart, *The Great White Fleet* (Boston: Little, Brown, 1956).

22. Rodgers to Chief Bureau of Navigation, 16 May 1908, Sperry to Bureau of Navigation, 2 Apr. 1908, Rodgers to L. S. Adams, 20 June 1908, Dougherty to Rodgers, 12 Aug., 7 Sept. 1909, case 9181, ONIGC.

11. NAVAL INTELLIGENCE IN TRANSITION

1. Dewey to Secretary of the Navy, 18 Apr. 1906, Newberry to President General Board, 23 Mar. 1906, General Board Records.

2. Rodgers to Welles, 8 Nov. 1907, Rodgers to Wilkie, 23 Oct. 1907, Metcalf to CinCs, 8 Feb. 1907, case 8570, ONIGC.

3. Departmental prohibition in Secretary of the Navy to Chief Intelligence Officer, 18 Mar. 1908, file 26150, General File; Metcalf to Rodgers, 18 Mar. 1908, case 9065, ONIGC; code revision in Whittlesey and Logan to Rodgers, 28 Mar. 1907, Rodgers to Chief Bureau of Navigation, 12 June 1907, case 8339, ONIGC; General Board meeting of 25 Oct. 1905, Proceedings, No. 2, General Board Records; relations with Institute in Rodgers to Alger, 30 Apr. 1907, case 7999, ONIGC; Morison, *Sims*, 178ff.

4. Rodgers Memorandum to Secretary of the Navy, 4 Jan. 1907, case 7830, Memorandum to General Board, 8 Dec. 1908, case 9668, ONI Memoranduum for Chief Bureau of Navigation, 6 Apr. 1907, case 8139, ONIGC; Rodgers Memorandum for the General Board, 6 Apr. 1907, General Board File 429, General Board Records.

5. M. A. DeWolfe Howe, *George von Lengerke Meyer,* 418ff; Cummings, *Wainwright,* 205ff.

6. Winthrop to Chief Intelligence Officer, 1 Oct. 1910, case 10799, ONIGC.

7. Naval War Plan for Nicaragua, 22 June 1910, War Portfolio No. 1, folder no. 2, Naval War Plans in the General Board Papers, box 1, OpA; Richard Challener, *Admirals, Generals, and American Foreign Policy,* 314.

8. Michael Vlahos, "Orange Special Situation"; "ONI, Data for the Preparation of Strategic Plans for the Possible Hostile Operations Against Japan, November 1910," UNOpP file, NWCA; Instruction to Language Attachés, 24 Feb. 1910, case 10390, Winthrop to Chief Intelligence Officer, 6 Oct. 1910, case 10799, ONIGC.

9. Challener, *Admirals,* 273–77; Potts to Liggett, 9 Feb. 1911, case 10788, ONIGC.

10. McCully to Secretary of the Navy, 3 Apr. 1911, General Board File 409; also see "McCully Plan on Vera Cruz," UNOpP File, NWCA.

11. ONI Memorandum for Commander Blue, 1 May 1912, Portfolio 1, folder no. 8, Southerland to Secretary of the Navy, 4 Dec. 1912, General Board File 409, General Board Records; Memorandum for Aide for Operations, 18 Nov. 1911, case 11503, ONIGC.

12. Potts to Secretary of the Navy, 2 May 1911, case 11207; Memorandum for DNI, 24 June 1912, case 10799; also, see Herwig, *Politics of Frustration.*

13. Knox to Secretary of the Navy, 5 May 1910, Potts to Knox, Meyer to Secretary of State, 9 Dec. 1910, case 10601, ONIGC; Winthrop to Knox, 10 Nov. 1910, file 121.55/113, State Department Decimal File, National Archives, Record Group 59, hereafter cited as Decimal File.

14. Niblack to ONI, 1 Oct. 1910, case 10782, Johnson to Potts, 3 Sept. 1912, case 11765, Whittlesey to Reed, 14 Aug. 1911, case 11201, ONIGC; Reed and McNeely in 121.55/125, Decimal File.

15. Wickersham to Secretary of the Navy, 18 Apr. 1911, case 11201, ONIGC.

16. Potts to Naval Attaché, Buenos Aires, 27 Oct. 1911, ibid.

17. Potts Memorandum for Aid for Operations, 5 Apr. 1910, Memorandum for Secretary of the Navy, 1 Mar. 1911, case 10509, Hobson's House Bill 25292, case 10525, ONIGC.

18. Josephus Daniels, *The Wilson Era,* 280–83; Fiske, *From Midshipman,* 531.

19. Daniels, *Wilson Era,* 157–60; T. S. Rodgers Memorandum for the Navy Department, 18 June 1913, Johnson to Rodgers, 31 Dec. 1912, 5 Aug. 1913, case 11575, ONIGC.

20. President General Board to Secretary of the Navy, 10, 14 May, 25 June 1913, General Board File 409, General Board Records; E. David Cronon, ed., *The Cabinet Diaries of Josephus Daniels,* 64–68.

21. R. R. Belknap, "Naval Attachés," 6, copies of this Dec. 1913 paper in General Board File 429, OpA, and XINA File, NWCA.

22. Roosevelt to Secretary of State, 5 May 1913, Moore to Bureau of Intelligence, 15 May 1913, file 121.55/99, Winthrop to Secretary of State, 12 Dec. 1911, file 121.55/158, Decimal File; Roosevelt to Nimitz, 29 July 1913, Gherardi to DNI, 4 and 13 Aug. 1913, case 20985-135, Rodgers to Symington, 8 Jan. 1913, case 21036-3195, ONI Confidential General Correspondence, 1913–24, NA, RG 38, hereafter cited as ONI Confidential Corres.

12. THE PREPAREDNESS MOVEMENT

1. Service of Rear Admiral James Harrison Oliver, Biographical File, OpA; Oliver to Sims, 15 Oct. 1904, Sims Papers.

2. Knox to Sims, 23 Sept. 1915, Sims Papers.

3. Knox to Sims, 5 Dec. 1914, also 25 Aug., 31 Oct. 1914, ibid.

4. Lt. Cdr. Dudley W. Knox, "Trained Initiative and Unity of Action: The True Bases of Military Efficiency," *USNIP,* 39 (Mar. 1913): 41–62.

5. Russell to DNI, 7 Aug. 1919, ZU File, Subject File, 1911–27.

6. Knox to Sims, 5 Dec. 1914, Sims Papers.

7. Quoted in Daniels, *Wilson Era,* 246.

8. Ibid., 243; Cronon, ed., *Daniels Diaries,* 6, 14, 537.

9. Bradley Fiske "Diary," 3 Jan. 1915, also 4, 9, 15 Jan. 1915, vol. 1, Library of Congress Manuscript Division. Growing concern for military unpreparedness can be seen in Proceedings General Board, vol. 6, late 1914 meetings, General Board Records.

10. Knox to Sims, 10 Mar. 1915, Sims Papers; Daniels, *Wilson Era,* 244.

11. See John Patrick Finnegan, *Against the Specter of a Dragon.*

12. Oliver to Sims, 10 Feb. 1914, Sims Papers.

13. Oliver to Sims, 23 Mar. 1914, ibid.

14. CinC Pacific to DNI, 5 June 1914, Oliver to General Board, 22 June 1916, General Board File 429, General Board Records; Braisted, *U. S. Navy, 1909–1922:* 205–6; JHR (Russell), "Foreign Policies and Relations Affecting the United States, 20 Jan. 1916," ONI Register 6151, WX-8 File, Subject File, 1911–27.

15. Intelligence Officer to Nugent, 6 Nov. 1916, Oliver to Kennedy, 19 Dec. 1916, *Sacremento* to DNI, 21 Jan. 1917, case 20961-583, ONI Confidential Corres.; JHR, "Foreign Policies."

16. JHR, "Foreign Policies."

17. Cronon, ed., *Daniels Diaries,* 98.

18. Daniels to Naval Attachés, 3 Aug. 1914, case 21066-6-A, Lansing to Secretary of the Navy, 6 Aug. 1915, case 21035-487, ONI Confidential Corres.; Bryan to Ambassador, London, 25 Aug. 1914, File 121-55/257a, Decimal File. Daniels actually took measures two days before the General Board recommendation to send officers overseas; see General Board File 425-A.

19. Daniels to Bryan, 18 Aug. 1914, file 121.55/270, Decimal File; Symington to McCrary, 21 Sept. 1914, file 21066-6-A, ONI Confidential Corres.; Treadwell to Naval Attaché, London, 26 Oct. 1914, Treadwell to NI, 17 Nov. 1916, 10 Aug. 1917, McBride to Naval Attaché, London, 3 Oct. 1914, WA-2 File, Subject File, 1911–27; "Notes from Fleet Diary," The Papers of Powers Symington, NHFC, Library of Congress.

20. Typescript "Psychological Warfare Broadcasting," Hooper to CinC Atlantic Fleet, 15 May 1913, DNI to Naval Attaché, London, 21 June 1913, Symington to Secretary of Navy, 12 Sept. 1913, The Papers of Stanford Caldwell Hooper, NHFC, Library of Congress; Daniels to Secretary of State, 27 Aug. 1914, file 121.55/259, Decimal File.

21. Sayles to DNI, 26 July 1915, file 21066-6-A, ONI Confidential Corres.; also file 121.55/270, Decimal File.

22. Gherardi to Oliver, 24 Oct. 1914, Graham to Gherardi, 10 Jan. 1916, file 21036-2247, ONI Confidential Corres.

23. Capt. J. S. McKean, "Mobilization Plan, U. S. Fleet," "Procedures to be Followed in Inspection of Merchant Vessels, 15 May 1915," UNOpP File, NWCA; Finnegan, *Specter of a Dragon,* 115–17; Cronon, ed., *Daniels Diaries,* 100–2; Daniels, *Wilson Era,* 491–93.

24. "Naval Defense Districts, Instructions for Information Service, Aid for Information," in Dewey to Secretary of the Navy, 5 Oct. 1916, Chief of Naval Operations to Secretary of the Navy, 29 Jan. 1916, Daniels to ONI, 18 Apr. 1916, Oliver to CNO, 27 July 1916, Instructional Material Sent to Intelligence Officers and Naval Attachés, NA, RG 38, hereafter cited as Instructional Material; Meeting of 19 Feb. 1915, General Board Proceedings, General Board Records; U. S. Navy, Naval History Division, *Fifty Years of Naval District Development, 1903–1953* (Washington, D.C., 1956).

25. Orders to "No. 62," 12 Feb. 1917, WX File, Subject File, 1911–27; "General Considerations," War Portfolio I, OpA.

26. Orders to "No. 6," 2 Mar. 1917, ibid.

27. DNI to CNO, 12 Feb. 1916, file 28642-8, General File.

28. "General Considerations and Data," folder 1, War Portfolio I, OpA.

29. Daniels to Whaley, 24 June 1916, Whaley to McCauley, 11 Apr. 1917, Daniels to Vacuum Oil, 21 Apr. 1917, Hoff to Director of Naval Communications, 5 May 1917, file 20951-40, also see files 21115-2, 21127-2, ONI Confidential Corres.

30. Oliver to CNO, 14 Nov. 1916, Daniels to DNI, 20 Nov. 1916, file 20961-616, ONI Confidential Corres.

31. Oliver to CNO, n.d., penciled attachment to Daniels to DNI, 20 Nov. 1916, ibid.

32. Oliver Memorandum for CNO, 26 Jan. 1916, ibid.

33. Knox to Sims, 16 Feb. 1916, Sims Papers.
34. Oliver to Bureau of Navigation, 26 Feb. 1916, file 21036-3241, ONI Confidential Corres.
35. Cronon, ed., *Daniels Diaries*, 109, 116, 122; Barbara Tuchman, *The Zimmermann Telegram*.

13. AN INTELLIGENCE ELITE

1. Welles "Journal," Curtis to Welles, 23 Apr. 1892, The Papers of Roger Welles, NHFC, Library of Congress.
2. Scruggs to Welles, 7 June 1892, Welles Papers.
3. Welles to Sims, 15 Sept., 9 Nov. 1917, Sims Papers; David Kahn, *The Code Breakers: The Story of Secret Writing* (New York: New American Library, Signet Books, 1973), 133ff.
4. Kerin to Daniels, 5 June 1917, Unarranged Correspondence and Material on Subversive Activities, 1917–27, NA, RG 38.
5. Welles to Sims, 9 Nov. 1917, Sims Papers.
6. Cronon, ed., *Daniels Diaries*, 256.
7. Chase to ONI, 10 Apr. 1917, file 28640-42, General File.
8. Allen, ed., *Long Papers*, 380; Whittlesey to Sims, 9 Aug. 1917, Sims Papers.
9. Bi-Monthly General Information Reports, Historical Section, Secret and Confidential Publications Received, 1917–1919, NA, RG 38; Welles to Chief Bureau of Navigation, 31 Dec. 1919. Whittlesey to Welles, 29 Aug. 1919, Welles Papers; Prospectus of Work Done in Intelligence Section, 15 Jan. 1919, WX-1 File, Subject File, 1911–27; Welles to General Board, 13 June 1917, Whittlesey to DNI, 9 May 1917, General Board File 429, General Board Records.
10. *Cyclopeadia of American Biography*, III: 401; *New York Times*, 8 Oct. 1939: 49; Eddy to Director of Naval Intelligence, 16 Aug. 1917, file 21116-2, ONI Confidential Corres.
11. Frank Freidel, *Franklin D. Roosevelt: The Apprenticeship*, I: 257.
12. Elliott Roosevelt, ed., *F.D.R., His Personal Letters, 1905–1928* (New York: Duell, Sloan & Pearce, 1948), 5–6, 306–7; *New York Times*, 24 Oct. 1943: 44, 27 May 1943: 28.
13. Davis to Franklin (Roosevelt), 5 Feb. 1918, Roosevelt to Welles, 21 Feb. 1918, Welles to Davis, 8 Mar. 1918, file 20944-942, ONI Confidential Corres.; *F.D.R Letters*, 5–6.
14. Welles's personal list of agents, Welles Papers; *New York Times*, 30 Aug. 1964: 93, 19 July 1961: 29, 7 Sept. 1942: 19.
15. Welles to Chief Bureau of Navigation, 31 Dec. 1919, Welles Papers; *New York Times*, 7 Jan. 1924: 9.
16. Welles to Chief, 31 Dec. 1919, Welles Papers; *New York Times*, 8 Apr. 1925: 21.
17. *New York Times*, 18 Feb. 1938: 19; Welles's personal list, Welles Papers.
18. Cronon, ed., *Daniels Diaries*, 173, 272, 280, 375, 422; Eddy to Welles, 16 Feb. 1918, file 21116-3-A, Eddy to DNI, 5 Aug. 1918, Memorandum for Capt. Decker, 31 July 1918, file 21116-2, ONI Confidential File.
19. *New York Times*, 8 Mar. 1965: 29; Welles to Sir John Maxwell, 12 Feb. 1919, Welles Papers.
20. Welles to Maxwell, 12 Feb. 1919, Welles Papers.
21. Ibid.
22. Welles to Stewart, 4 July 1919, ibid.
23. Welles to John A. Gade, 31 Jan. 1919, ibid.

1. Eddy to Branch Intelligence Officers, 26 Oct. 1917, file 20957, Branch ONI to Edie, 29 Nov. 1917, file 21116-2, Irvin to DNI, 1 Sept. 1918, file 21116-3-A, ONI Confidential Corres.; Welles's personal list of agents, Welles Papers; "The Organization of the Aids for Information," ZU File, Subject File, 1911–27.

2. Judge Advocate General to DNI, 2 Dec. 1918, Aid for Information, Phila. to ONI, 21 Dec. 1918, file 20954-823, ONI Confidential Corres.

3. Cronon, ed., *Daniels Diaries*, 180.

4. Aid for Information organizations in, boxes 78–86, ONI Confidential Corres.

5. "The Organization of the Aids for Information and Branch Intelligence Offices," ZU File, Subject File 1911–27; Welles to Chief Bureau of Navigation, 31 Dec. 1919; Report from the 8th Naval District, New Orleans, file 211108-3-A, ONI Confidential Corres.

6. William Todd to Fowler, 23 Apr. 1918, file 21114-2, ONI Confidential Corres.

7. Ibid.

8. DNI to Aid 13th Naval District, 14 June 1918, file 21113-5, ibid.

9. Eddy to DNI, 16 Aug. 1917, file 21116-2, Piper to DNI, file 21137-10, Welles to Piper, 11 Jan. 1919, file 20944-112, ibid.

10. Welles to Officer in Charge New York Branch, 23 May 1918, New York Branch Office files, NA, RG 38.

11. Welles to Van Antwerp, 2 Apr. 1918, file 20961-710, ONI Confidential Corres.

12. Commandant to DNI, 18 Sept. 1917, file 21115-1, Henneberger to DNI, 3 June 1918, file 21115-1, ONI Confidential Corres.; Walter C. Sweeney, *Military Intelligence*, 86–87.

13. Van Antwerp to DNI, 13 May 1918, file 20961-710, DNI Memorandum, 6 June 1918, Fowler to Wales, 4 June 1918, file 20961, ONI Confidential Corres.

14. H. O. Yardley, *The American Black Chamber*, 137.

15. Welles to Churchill, 25 Sept. 1918, file 20961-766, ONI Confidential Corres.

16. Mayo to Meyers, 7 Apr. 1917, WX-1 File, Subject File.

17. F. D. Roosevelt to McCauley, 17 Apr. 1917, file 20995-38, ONI Confidential Corres.

18. Welles to Sims, 9 Nov. 1917, Sims Papers; Eddy to Branch Intelligence Officer, 26 Oct. 1917, file 20957, Chief of Bureau of Investigation to McCauley, 5 May 1918, file 21113-2, McCauley to Bielaski, 18 Feb. 1918, Van Deman to ONI, 9 May 1918, file 20979-256, also file 20952-455, ONI Confidential Corres.; see Joan M. Jensen, *The Price of Vigilance*, for American Protective League.

19. *Congressional Naval Investigation*, 2713, scattered pages relating to ONI in ZU File, Subject File.

20. Cronon, ed., *Daniels Diaries*, 209–12; Branch ONI, New York, to ?, 29 Nov. 1917, file 21116-2, Inspector of Engineering Material to ONI, 5 Apr. 1918, ONI to Branch Office, 28 Feb. 1918, Eddy to ONI, 12 Apr. 1918, file 21037-98, ONI Confidential Corres.

21. Branch ONI Phila. to DNI, 15 Feb., 29 Apr. 1918, file 20945-32, ONI Confidential Corres.

22. DNI to Branch Intelligence Officers, 5, 6 June 1918, McCauley to Branch Intelligence Officer, 27 Mar. 1918, "Address by Commander Raymond E. Horn, USNR, 28 Jan. 1931 to Naval Intelligence Officers of the Ninth Naval District." Instructional Material.

23. Decker to Branch Officers, 21 Aug. 1918, ibid.

24. Aid for Information 13th Naval District to DNI, 12 Dec. 1917, file 20952-37, ONI Confidential Corres.

25. Military Intelligence to McCauley, 2 Feb. 1918, file 20952-102, Welles to Commandant, USMC, 8 Dec. 1917, file 20952-42, Clinton to ONI, 21 May 1918, file 20952-14, ibid.

26. Bielaski to McCauley, 31 May 1917, file 20952-289, ibid.

27. Van Deman to McCauley, 3 Nov. 1917, file 20952-42, DNI to Bureau of Navigation, 12 Jan., 2 Mar. 1918, file 20952-54, ibid.

28. Reed in file 21036-29, revolutionary groups in file 21116-2, yeowoman in file 20940-946, seamen's union in file 20952-219, IWW in file 21112-2 and 20957-218, ibid.

29. Palmer to Welles, 28 Aug. 1918, file 20952-404, ibid.

30. O'Brian to McCauley, 29 Jan. 1918, Latham to Melville, J. France, 16 Nov. 1917, ONI Memo, 31 Jan. 1918, McCauley to O'Brian, 4 Feb. 1918, file 20953-84, ibid.

31. "Minutes of Conference Heads, March 1918," New York Branch Corres., NA, RG 38; Jensen, *Price of Vigilance,* 85, 102–4; Welles in *Congressional Naval Investigation,* 2715, ZU File, Subject File.

32. McCauley to Officer in Charge Branch Intelligence Office, 20 Apr. 1918, New York Branch Corres.

33. Assistant Secretary of the Treasury to Secretary of the Navy, 17 Aug. 1917, WX-1 File, Subject File; Confidential Memorandum Regarding Secret Marks on Passports in DNI to Kear, 28 Mar. 1918, Classified Correspondence for U.S. Naval Attaché in Havana, RG 38, NA, hereafter Havana Classified Corres.; "Regulation for the Men Attached to the Ship Searching Detail," file 21036-2497, ONI Confidential Corres.

34. James R. Mock and Cedric Larson, *Words that Won the War,* 72, 82, 154; Cronon, ed., *Daniels Diaries,* 280.

35. Welles quoted in Rear Admiral A. P. Niblack, *The History and Aims of the Office of Naval Intelligence* (Washington, D.C., 1920), 16.

36. Benson to Welles, 7 Feb. 1918, file 28640-42, General File.

15. THE EUROPEAN WAR

1. Welles to King, 17 Dec. 1919, Welles Papers.

2. Welles to Sims, 19 Sept. 1917, Sims Papers.

3. Sims to Welles, 10 Oct. 1917, file 21500-610, ONI Confidential Corres.

4. Welles to Sims, 15 Sept. 1917, Sims Papers.

5. Welles to Sims, 9 Nov. 1917, ibid.

6. Roys to Welles, 2 Oct. 1917, Hall to Welles, 6 Apr. 1918, file 21500-610, ONI Confidential Corres.

7. Welles to Sims, 16 Sept. 1917, Sims Papers.

8. Benson to Sims, 29 Aug. 1917, WX-6 File, Subject File.

9. Sims to Niblack, 10 Dec. 1917, Sims Papers.

10. *American Naval Planning Section, London* (Washington, D.C., 1923), 312.

11. Ibid., 197–201, 230–3.

12. Ibid., 84–91.

13. Sims to Secretary of Navy, 1 June 1917, WX-1 File, Subject File; Admiral Sir William James, *The Eyes of the Navy: A Biographical Study of Admiral Sir Reginald Hall,* xx, 44; Robert M. Grant, *U-Boat Intelligence, 1914–1918* (London: Putnam, 1969), 19; Office of Scientific Attaché, London, records in NA, RG 38; Reports from Dr. H. A. Bumstead, Scientific Attaché, London, file 21036-300A, ONI Confidential Corres.

14. Welles to McCormick, n.d., Gibbons to DNI, 13 May 1918, McCormick to Welles, 20 Mar. 1918, DNI Memo for Naval Attachés, 14 Mar. 1918, file 21036-244, ONI Confidential Corres.

15. Sayles to Edie, 10 May 1917, WX-1 File, Subject File; Naval Attaché Paris to Naval Intelligence, 28 Mar. 1918, Confidential Dispatches, 1918, NA, RG 38; McCauley to DNI, 30 Sept. 1918, ZWE-3 File, Subject File.

16. McCauley to DNI, 30 Sept. 1918, ZWE-3 File, Subject File.

17. Welles to Chief Bureau of Navigation, Dec. 1919, Welles Papers.

18. McCauley to DNI, 30 Sept. 1918, ZWE-3 File, Subject File.

19. Welles to Sims, 7 Nov. 1917, Sims Papers.

20. Train, "Historical Memorandum of the Intelligence Section, Office of Naval Attaché, Rome," ZK File, Subject File; Train to DNI, 29 Jan. 1918, file 20961-369, ONI Confidential Corres.

21. McCully to DNI, 20 Mar. 1917, file 21036-2254C, ONI Confidential Corres.

22. Crosley to Navintel, 26 Feb. 1918, Confidential Dispatches, 1918.

23. Wheat Memorandum for DNI, 21 Dec. 1917, File 20961-369, ONI Confidential Corres.

24. Decker to DNI, 28 Jan. 1918, file 20961-369, ibid.

25. Decker to DNI, 28 Jan. 1918, file 20961-369, also files 20951-40, 20952-47, Callahan to Welles, 16 Nov. 1917, file 20944-8, White to McCauley, 15 Feb. 1918, file 20951-40, ONI Confidential Corres.; ONI to Naval War College, 11 June 1917, WX-1 File, Subject File.

26. Sims to OpNav, 18 Oct. 1917, WX-5 File, Subject File; Sims to Secretary of the Navy, 21 Dec. 1917, file 20944-855, ONI Confidential Corres.

27. Coster to Naval Attaché London (Sims), 20 Dec. 1917, WX-5 File, Subject File; Force Commander (Sims) to Acting Naval Attaché, The Hague, 28 Dec. 1917, file 20944-855, ONI Confidential Corres.; "Work Done During the War by Office of Naval Attaché, The Hague, Holland," WX-6 File, Subject File.

28. Breckenridge to ONI, 5 Dec. 1916, 28 Dec. 1917, files 21036-2254D, 20961-369, Breckenridge to Oliver, 19 and 24 March 1917, file 21036-2254C, ONI Confidential Corres.; Vagts, *Military Attaché*, 75 note 6; Gade to DNI, 5 Aug. 1926, Plans for Intelligence Through Commercial Firms, NA, RG 38.

29. H. Gade to DNI, 2 Jan. 1918, Acting DNI to Bureau of Navigation, 18 Feb. 1919., file 21500-498, ONI Confidential Corres.; J. Gade to Welles, 20 Jan. 1919, Welles Papers.

30. Sims to Welles, 26 Mar. 1918, Sims Papers; Mock and Larson, *Words that Won the War*, 279–80.

31. Welles to Chief Bureau of Medicine, 27 Feb. 1918, file 20944-744, ONI Confidential Corres.

32. Welles to Knight, 12 Jan. 1920, Welles Papers.

33. Breck to Director of Naval Intelligence, 20 Feb. 1919, also 23, 27 Aug. 1918, WX-6 File, Subject File.

16. AN INTERNATIONAL NETWORK

1. Fowler to No. 152, 16 Apr. 1917, file 21500-507, 20944-918, ONI Confidential Corres.

2. McCauley to Polk, 24 Jan. 1918, file 20944-531, ibid.

3. Germans in Mexico, files 20980-4, 20948-109, Japanese in Mexico, files 20980-4, 20948-109, ONI Confidential Corres.; James, *Eyes of the Navy*, 163.

4. Van Antwerp to DNI, 24 Jan. 1918, Welles to Polk, 6 Feb. 1918, McCauley to Harrison, 27 Feb. 1918. Van Antwerp to Welles, 19 Feb. 1918, file 20961-748, ONI Confidential Corres.

5. Welles to Van Antwerp, 2 Apr. 1918, file 20961-748, ibid.

6. Van Antwerp to Welles, 25 Mar. 1918, ibid.

7. Fullam to Welles, 6, 14 June, 2 July 1918. Navintel to Hutchinson, 10 Sept. 1918, ibid.

8. Aid for Information New Orleans to DNI, 30 Nov. 1918, files 20963-1341, also 20963-1340C, 20963-1734, Sargent to DNI, n.d., file 21115-2, ONI Confidential Corres.; Wedgewood to DNI, 17 Dec. 1918, Welles to Commandant 15th Naval District, 30 Dec. 1918, 14 Jan. 1919, Havana Classified Corres.

9. ONI to Agent No. 219, file 20944-362, Henneberger to Commandant 15th Naval District, 14 Mar. 1918, file 21115-3, ONI Confidential Corres.

10. Memorandum for DNI, 22 July 1919, file 20944-976, ibid.

11. Niblack to Chief Bureau of Navigation, 28 May 1919, Asst. DNI to Chief of Police, Fall River, 22 July 1919, ibid.

12. Salladay to Gov. Virgin Islands, 16 Nov. 1917, Havana Classified Corres.

13. Rohde to DNI, 26 Nov. 1918, Welles to Commandant 15th Naval District, 4 Jan. 1919, Wedgewood to DNI, 17 Dec. 1918, Havana Classified Corres.; Caribbean file 20968-129, ONI Confidential Corres.

14. Welles to Kear, 27 Sept. 1917, Peard to Kelley, 2 Nov. 1917, Peard to Knox, 24 Nov. 1917, Peard to Kelley, 1 Apr. 1918, Commandant Guantanamo to Kear, 8 Feb. 1918, Havana Classified Corres.; Anderson to Welles, 2 May 1918, file 21500-547-A, ONI Confidential Corres.

15. Cusachs file 20996-1884, ONI Confidential Corres.; Cronon, ed., *Daniels Diaries*, 270.

16. Cusachs to McCauley, 14 June 1918, Havana Classified Corres.

17. Cusachs to Decker, 22 July 1918, ibid.

18. Decker to Cusachs, 24 Oct. 1918, Postal Censor Key West to Cusachs, 21 Oct. 1918, Van Natta to Menocal, 8 Oct. 1918, Naval Attaché Havana to DNI, 1 July 1918, Cusachs to McCauley, 14 June 1918, Cusachs to Decker, 22 July 1918, Memorandum, Office of the Counselor, 20 Aug. 1918, ibid.

19. Naval Attaché Chile to Navintel, 14 May 1918, Confidential Dispatches, 1918; *New York Times*, 3 Dec. 1948: 25.

20. Naval Attaché Brazil to ONI, 13 Feb. 1919, "U. S. Naval Intelligence Service in Brazil During the World War," WX-6 File, Subject File; Hill to Navintel, 5 Apr. 1918, 18 Feb. 1918, 16 Mar. 1918, Confidential Dispatches, 1918.

21. Naval Attaché Rio (Hill) to ONI, 13 Feb. 1919, WX-6 File, Subject File; Naval Attaché to Navintel, 30 May 1918, Confidential Dispatches, 1918; Cronon, ed., *Daniels Diaries*, 550.

22. Japanese activity in files 21067-34, 21067-26, 21067-14, 21067-13, ONI Confidential Corres.

23. Payne, in file 20942-76, ONI Confidential Corres.; W (Horne) to ONI, 5 Nov. 1917, WX-6 File, Subject File.

24. Gillis to DNI, 19 Nov. 1917, file 21127-2, ONI Confidential Corres.

25. Gillis to Navintel, 8 Apr., 11 May 1918, Confidential Dispatches, 1918.

26. Gillis to McCauley, 19 Oct. 1917, file 21127-2, ONI Confidential Corres.

27. Welles to Gillis, 10 June 1918, file 21012-93, also files 20953-23, 20964-183, ONI Confidential Corres.; Gillis to Navintel, 11 May 1918, Confidential Dispatches, 1918.

28. Gillis to Navintel, 11 Nov. 1918, Todd to DNI, 27 May 1918, Benson Memorandum for ONI, 29 July 1918, file 21067-3, ONI Confidential Corres.

29. Van Antwerp to Cable Censor San Francisco, 27 Nov. 1918, file 20955-636, ibid.

30. Eddy to King, 22 Nov. 1918, file 21116-3-A, ibid.

31. Green, "First Sixty Years," 77–78; Niblack, *Office of Naval Intelligence*, 6.

BIBLIOGRAPHY

MANUSCRIPT COLLECTIONS

Personal Papers

Library of Congress, Naval Historical Foundation Collection
  Belknap, Reginald Rowan
  Chambers, Washington Irving
  Emory, William Hemsley
  Gleaves, Albert
  Hooper, Stanford Caldwell
  Knox, Dudley Wright
  Luce, Stephen Bleecker
  O'Neil, Charles Francis
  Rodgers, William L.
  Sargent, Nathan
  Sims, William S.
  Symington, Powers
  Taylor, Henry Clay
  Walker, John G.
  Welles, Roger
Library of Congress, Manuscript Division
  Daniels, Josephus
  Fiske, Bradley
  Roosevelt, Theodore
New York State Library, Manuscripts and Special Collection
  Sigsbee, Charles Dwight
Smithsonian Institution, Naval History Division
  Mason, Theodorus B. M.

Manuscript Collections—Official Records

National Archives, Record Group 24. Records of the Bureau of Naval Personnel.
  Appointments, Orders, and Resignations.
  Registers of Letters Sent and Received, 1882–1890.
National Archives, Record Group 38. Records of the Office of the Chief of Naval Operations, Office of Naval Intelligence.
  Branch Naval Intelligence Office, New York, Administrative Files, 1917–1918.
  Cable Correspondence with U. S. Naval Attachés during the Spanish-American War, 1898–1900.
  Communications with Naval Attachés, 1882–1918.
  Confidential Dispatches Received from Naval Attachés and Others, 1918.
  Diary and Related Records of Lt. N. A. McCully, 1904–05.

General Correspondence, Cases, 1899–1912.
General Correspondence, Letters Received, 1882–83, 1886–99.
General Records of the Naval Contract and Plant Division.
Instructional Material Sent to Intelligence Officers and Naval Attachés.
Letters from U. S. Naval Attachés, 1882–1900.
Letters Sent by Naval Attachés, 1885–1905.
Letters Sent to U. S. Naval Attachés, 1899–1905.
List of Persons Suspected of Being Foreign Agents, 1917–18.
Memoranda of Information, 1899–1900, 1901–03.
Registers of Naval Attachés, 1886–1922.
Register of Personnel, 1882–1918.
Secret and Confidential Publications Received, 1917–19.
Security Classified General Correspondence of the U. S.
    Naval Attaché, Havana, Cuba, 1917–19.
Security Classified Publications, 1882–1954.
Unarranged Correspondence and Material on Subversive Activities, 1917–27.
National Archives, Record Group 45. Naval Records Collection of the Office of Naval
Records and Library.
    Area Files of the Naval Records Collection, 1775–1910.
    Confidential Letters Sent, 1893–1908.
    Confidential Memorandum from ONI to *Oregon*.
    Correspondence of Lt. Nathan Sargent, 1888–93.
    Letters from Lt. John C. Colwell, 1897–98.
    Letters from Officers Commanding Squadrons, 1841–86.
    Letters Sent by Lt. Albert P. Niblack, 1896–98.
    Letters and Records Sent by Naval Attachés of the United States in London,
        1889–1914.
    Letters to Naval Academy, Commanding, and Other Officers, 1869–1884.
    Letters to Officers Commanding Squadrons or Vessels, 1861–86.
    Report on British Dockyards, Theodore D. Wilson, 1870.
    Subject Files, 1776–1911, 1911–27.
    Translations of Messages Received in Cipher, 1888–1910.
    Translations of Messages Sent in Cipher, 1888–1910.
National Archives, Record Group 59. General Records of the Department of State.
    Decimal File, 121.55 (Naval Attachés).
National Archives, Record Group 80. General Records of the Department of the Navy.
    General File, 1897–1926.
    Naval War Board Records, 1898.
    Records of the Office of the Assistant Secretary of the Navy, 1894–98.
Naval War College Archives, Naval War College Historical Collection, Newport, Rhode
Island.
    Intelligence and Technological Archives, 1894–1945.
    Student Problems and Solutions, 1894–1916.
Operational Archives, Naval History Division, Washington Navy Yard.
    Biography (ZB) File.
    Records of the General Board of the Navy, 1900–17.

BOOKS AND ARTICLES

Alden, Commander John D. *The American Steel Navy: A Photographic History of the
    U. S. Navy from the Introduction of the Steel Hull in 1883 to the Cruise of the Great
    White Fleet, 1907–1909.* Annapolis: Naval Institute Press, 1972.
Allard, Dean C., Jr. "The Influence of the United States Navy upon the American Steel
    Industry, 1880–1900." M. A. Thesis, Georgetown University, 1959.

Allen, Gardner Weld, ed. *Papers of John Davis Long, 1897–1904.* Boston: Massachusetts Historical Society, 1939.

The Annual Reports of the Secretary of the Navy, 1882–1917. Washington, D.C.: Government Printing Office, 1882–1917.

Barker, Read Admiral Albert S. *Everyday Life in the Navy: Autobiography of Rear Admiral Albert S. Barker.* Boston: Richard G. Badger, 1928.

Beers, Henry P. *The Bureau of Navigation, 1862–1942.* Washington, D.C.: The National Archives, 1942.

Berry, Rear Admiral A. G. "The Beginning of the Office of Naval Intelligence." *U. S. Naval Institute Proceedings,* 63 (Jan. 1937): 102–3.

Braisted, William R. "China, the United States Navy, and the Bethlehem Steel Company, 1909–1920." *Business History Review,* XLII (Spring 1968): 50–66.

Braisted, William R. *The United States Navy in the Pacific 1897–1909.* Austin: University of Texas Press, 1958.

Braisted, William R. *The United States Navy in the Pacific, 1909–1922.* Austin: University of Texas Press, 1971.

Brodie, Bernard. *Sea Power in the Machine Age.* Princeton: Princeton University Press, 1943.

Challener, Richard D. *Admirals, Generals and American Foreign Policy, 1898–1914.* Princeton: Princeton University Press, 1973.

Cooling, B. Franklin. *Benjamin Franklin Tracy: Father of the Modern American Fighting Navy.* Hamden, Conn.: Archon Books, 1973.

Costello, Cdr. Daniel Joseph. "Planning for War: A History of the General Board of the Navy, 1900–1914." Ph.D. Dissertation, Fletcher School of Law and Diplomacy, Tufts University, 1968.

Cronon, E. David, ed. *The Cabinet Diaries of Josephus Daniels, 1913–1921.* Lincoln: University of Nebraska Press, 1963.

Crosley, Commander Walter S. "The Naval War College, the General Board, and the Office of Naval Intelligence." *U. S. Naval Institute Proceedings,* 39 (Sept. 1913): 965–74.

Cummings, Captain Damon E. *Admiral Richard Wainwright and the United States Fleet.* Washington, D.C.: Government Printing Office, 1962.

Daniels, Josephus. *The Wilson Era: Years of Peace, 1910–1917.* Chapel Hill: University of North Carolina Press, 1946.

Davis, Charles H. *Life of Charles Henry Davis, Rear Admiral, 1807–1877.* Boston: Houghton Mifflin, 1899.

Deacon, Richard. *The Silent War: A History of Western Naval Intelligence.* New York: Hippocrene, 1978.

Ellicott, Captain J. M. "Theodorus Bailey Meyers (sic) Mason: Founder of the Office of Naval Intelligence." *U. S. Naval Institute Proceedings,* 78 (March 1952): 265–67, 1025–26.

Finnegan, John Patrick. *Against the Specter of a Dragon: The Campaign for American Military Preparedness, 1914–1917.* Westport, Conn.: Greenwood Press, 1974.

Fiske, Rear Admiral Bradley A. *From Midshipman to Rear Admiral.* New York: Century, 1919.

Franklin, Samuel R. *Memories of a Rear-Admiral.* New York: Harper & Bros., 1898.

Freidel, Frank. *Franklin D. Roosevelt,* 3 vols. Boston: Little Brown, 1952.

Gleaves, Rear Admiral Albert. *The Life of An American Sailor: Rear Admiral William Hemsley Emory, United States Navy, From His Letters and Memoirs.* New York: George H. Doran, 1923.

Gleaves, Rear Admiral Albert. *Life and Letters of Rear Admiral Stephen B. Luce, U. S. Navy.* New York: Putnam, 1925.

Goodrich, Caspar F. *Rope Yarns from the Old Navy.* New York: The Naval History Society, 1931.

Green, James Robert. "The First Sixty Years of the Office of Naval Intelligence." M.A. Thesis, The American University, 1963.

Grenville, John A. S. and Young, George Berkeley. *Politics, Strategy, and American Diplomacy: Studies in Foreign Policy, 1873–1917.* New Haven and London: Yale University Press, 1966.

Hagan, Kenneth J. *American Gunboat Diplomacy and the Old Navy, 1877–1889.* Westport, Conn.: Greenwood Press, 1973.

Hamersly, Lewis Randolph. *The Records of Living Officers of the U. S. Navy and Marine Corps.* New York: Hamersly, 1902.

Hammett, Hugh B. *Hilary Abner Herbert: A Southerner Returns to the Union.* Philadelphia: The American Philosophical Society, 1976.

Herrick, Walter R., Jr. *The American Naval Revolution.* Baton Rouge: Louisiana State University Press, 1966.

Herwig, Holger H. *Politics of Frustration: The United States in German Naval Planning, 1889–1941.* Boston: Little, Brown, 1976.

Hirsch, Mark D. *William C. Whitney: Modern Warwick.* New York: Dodd, Mead, 1948.

Howe, M. A. DeWolfe. *George von Lengerke Meyer: His Life and Public Services.* New York: Dodd, Mead, 1920.

Hunt, Thomas. *The Life of William H. Hunt.* Brattleboro: Hildreth, 1922.

Huntington, Samuel P. *The Soldier and the State: The Theory and Politics of Civil-Military Relations.* Cambridge, Mass.: Harvard University Press, 1957.

Ind, Colonel Allison. *A Short History of Espionage.* New York: David McKay, 1963.

James, Admiral Sir William. *The Eyes of the Navy: A Biographical Study of Admiral Sir Reginald Hall.* London: Methuen, 1955.

Jeffreys-Jones, Rhodri. *American Espionage: From Secret Service to CIA.* New York: The Free Press, 1977.

Jensen, Joan M. *The Price of Vigilance.* Chicago: Rand McNally, 1968.

Johnson, Robert E. *Thence Round Cape Horn: The Story of United States Naval Forces on Pacific Station, 1818–1923.* Annapolis: Naval Institute Press, 1963.

Karsten, Peter. *The Naval Aristocracy: The Golden Age of Annapolis and the Emergence of Modern American Navalism.* New York: Free Press, 1972.

LaFeber, Walter. *The New American Empire: An Interpretation of American Expansion, 1860–1898.* Ithaca: Cornell University Press, 1968.

Long, John D. *The New American Navy,* 2 vols. New York: Outlook, 1903.

McCully, Lt. Cdr. Newton A. *The McCully Report: The Russo-Japanese War, 1904–05,* edited by Richard von Doenhoff. Annapolis: Naval Institute Press, 1977.

Mock, James R. and Larson, Cedric. *Words that Won the War: The Story of the Committee on Public Information, 1917–1919.* New York: Russell & Russell, 1968 (reissue of Princeton University Press, 1939).

Morison, Elting E. *Admiral Sims and the Modern American Navy.* Boston: Houghton Mifflin, 1942.

Paullin, Charles Oscar. *Paullin's History of Naval Administration, 1775–1911: A Collection of Articles from the U. S. Naval Institute "Proceedings."* Annapolis: Naval Institute Press, 1968.

Richardson, James D. *A Compilation of the Messages and Papers of the Presidents,* 20 vols. New York: Bureau of National Literature, 1917.

Sachse, Lt. William L. "Our Naval Attaché System: Its Origins and Developments to 1917." *U. S. Naval Institute Proceedings,* 72 (May 1946): 661–72.

Schley, Winfield S. *Forty-Five Years Under the Flag.* New York: Appleton, 1904.

Schroeder, Seaton. *A Half Century of Naval Service.* New York: D. Appleton, 1922.

Seager, Robert, II and Maguire, Doris D., eds. *Letters and Papers of Alfred Thayer Mahan,* 3 vols. Annapolis: Naval Institute Press, 1976.

Shields, Capt. Henry Seward. "A Historical Survey of U. S. Naval Attachés in Russia: 1904–1941." Defense Intelligence School, Mar. 1970.

Spector, Ronald. *Admiral of the New Empire: The Life and Career of George Dewey.* Baton Rouge: Louisiana State University Press, 1974.

Spector, Ronald. *Professors of War: The Naval War College and the Development of the Naval Profession.* Newport, Rhode Island: Naval War College Press, 1977.

Sprout, Harold and Sprout, Margaret. *The Rise of American Naval Power, 1776–1918.* Princeton: Princeton University Press, 1944.

Stirling, Yates. *Sea Duty.* New York: Putnam, 1940.

Swann, Leonard Alexander, Jr. *John Roach, Maritime Entrepreneur, The Years as Naval Contractor, 1862–1886.* Annapolis: Naval Institute Press, 1965.

Sweeney, Lt. Colonel Walter C. *Military Intelligence: A New Weapon in War.* New York: Frederick A. Stokes, 1924.

Thomas, Frances. *The Career of Rear Admiral John G. Walker.* Boston: private printing, 1959.

Trask, David F. *Captains and Cabinets: Anglo-American Naval Relations, 1917–1918.* Columbia: University of Missouri Press, 1972.

Tuchman, Barbara W. *The Zimmermann Telegram.* New York: Viking, 1958.

Vagts, Alfred. *The Military Attaché.* Princeton University Press, 1967.

Vlahos, Michael. "Orange Special Situation: The Naval War College and the Creation of the Inevitable Enemy. M.A. Thesis, Fletcher School of Law and Diplomacy, Tufts University, 1978.

Weber, Gustavus A. *The Hydrographic Office: Its History, Activities, and Organization.* Baltimore: The Johns Hopkins Press, 1926.

West, Richard S., Jr. *Admirals of American Empire: The Combined Story of George Dewey, Alfred Thayer Mahan, Winfield Scott Schley, and William Thomas Sampson.* Indianapolis and New York: Bobbs-Merrill, 1948.

Williams, Frances Leigh. *Matthew Fontaine Maury, Scientist of the Sea.* New Brunswick: Rutgers University Press, 1963.

Yardley, H. O. *The American Black Chamber.* London: Faber & Faber, 1931.

165

INDEX

167

168

171

172

173